Toward an Alternative Culture
of Work

Toward an Alternative Culture of Work

Political Idealism and Economic Practices in West Berlin Collective Enterprises

Birgit Müller

Westview Press
BOULDER • SAN FRANCISCO • OXFORD

To my father

Copyright © 1991 by Westview Press, Inc.

Published in 1991 in the United States of America by Westview Press, Inc., 5500 Central Avenue, Boulder, Colorado 80301, and in the United Kingdom by Westview Press, 36 Lonsdale Road, Summertown, Oxford OX2 7EW

Library of Congress Cataloging-in-Publication Data
Müller, Birgit.
   Toward an alternative culture of work : political idealism and economic practices in West Berlin collective enterprises / Birgit Müller.
      p. cm.
   Includes bibliographical references and index.
   ISBN 0-8133-8079-0
   1. Producer cooperatives—Berlin (Germany). 2. Corporate culture—Berlin (Germany). I. Title.
HD3190.B47S67   1991
306.3'6'0943155—dc20   90-48294
                                                                           CIP

Printed and bound in the United States of America

(∞) The paper used in this publication meets the requirements
      of the American National Standard for Permanence of Paper
      for Printed Library Materials Z39.48-1984.

10   9   8   7   6   5   4   3   2   1

Contents

Preface

After five years of study abroad and intensive research into precolonial Nigerian society, I felt in the autumn of 1981 that I was missing out on one of the most interesting developments in my own West German society. Friends in Berlin were talking constantly, and with admiration, about alternative projects that had been recently set up and the alternative funds to which they were contributing. During a visit to Berlin in 1980, they had proudly shown me the *Mehringhof* and convinced me to take out a subscription to *die tageszeitung*. Other friends, however, were less enthusiastic and severely criticised "these individualistic solutions to the problems of society," explaining to me why small alternative workshops set up by "freaks" had to be a failure and a political mistake. Their insistence did not discourage my curiosity and, in September of 1982, I was able to set out to find out about these "alternative movements," thanks to a generous three-year scholarship from St John's College, Cambridge.

For my first period of fieldwork, I stayed in Berlin for almost two years, from September 1982 to September 1984 (with an interruption of one term in Cambridge). I soon decided to concentrate my research on collectives and chose four for closer analysis. Two — *FahrradBüro*, a bicycle shop, and *Wuseltronick*, a group of electronic engineers — were in the service sector, whereas *Oktoberdruck*, a printing shop, and *KoMet*, a toolmaking enterprise, were involved in production.

I visited collectives of other trades, participated in innumerable meetings and discussions, and was drawn into the regular meetings of the *Lundkreis*, which prepared a congress of alternative enterprises in Berlin in January of 1984 and the first issues of the collective bulletin *contraste*. Since completing the first stage of my fieldwork in 1984, I have continued to keep in close touch with the collectives I had studied most intensively, culminating in a follow-up study in the summer of 1988.

In the course of my research, I was always aware of the typical contradiction inherent in the role of the anthropologist as participant observer: I was at times treated like a member because I shared the collectivists' activities, but at other moments, I felt very clearly the distance that the role of an observer implied. Most members were interested in a systematic study of their collectives, and they collaborated by giving me access to the minutes of their meetings, their internal statutes, charts, and even legal correspondence. But I do not think they expected my work to be of any help in elucidating their own problems and contradictions. They may hope, however, that the book might give a clearer insight into collective organisation and its problems to people who are now vaguely sympathetic toward it.

If my readers don't mind me waving the flag, I was myself fascinated by the collectives I was studying. Their importance is certainly not in the economic impact they make. It is not clear how an economy would look that was entirely composed of collectives of the Berlin type. What lends them a significance that goes far beyond their number and size are the explosive ideas that they not only express but put into practice. They indicate that democracy has to start at the basic level, with the right of self-determination of the producing individual, to whom skills and information have to be returned. Or to say it with Bravermann (1974: 445): "Without the return of requisite technical knowledge to the mass of the workers and the reshaping of the organisation of labour — without, in a word, a new and truly collective mode of production — balloting within factories and offices does not alter the fact that the workers remain as dependent as before upon 'experts,' and can only choose among them. "

Handing over property to the state while maintaining the old hierarchies and division of labour does not necessarily change the conditions of the workers either. The organisation of work in a Hungarian factory, as described by Haraszti (1976), resembles the capitalist version in its basic principles. The workers do unskilled tasks at a piece rate, concentrating only on squeezing as much money as possible out of their badly paid tasks, while administrators try to invent still new methods to make them work harder. "It is a well known secret, that Soviet administrators largely prefer to exchange ideas with an experienced Western manager, than with any 'communist' or liberal sociologist," wrote Heinrich Böll in the preface to Haraszti's book (1976:8).

Numerous communes and communities, from Oneida to the Kibbutz, have tried to create alternative structures to those of the dominant capitalist and industrialist society, but they have done this by demanding asceticism and the strict subordination of the individual to the community. The difference in the Berlin experiment is the strong emphasis on individual differences and their realisation in a collective context.

Note: I did not alter the names of members nor of collectives although, following their own usage, I have only used first names. Surnames of members only appear if they have published under their full names. The capitalization and use of lower-case letters in the spelling of the names of collectives and alternative institutions follow the collectivists' practice. I have translated all German terms, sometimes leaving the German expression in brackets.

Birgit Müller

Acknowledgments

The research on which this book is based was supported financially by a St. John's College scholarship. Jack Goody was indefatigable in his help and encouragement all through the fieldwork and writing. I wish to thank Keith Hart for the interest he took in my work and for the sharp and valuable comments he made.

I am grateful to Lothar Lappe of the *Max Planck Institut* in Berlin for giving me an insight into working conditions in the modern machine-building industry and for letting me use his own research material at will. My friend Michal Bodemann of the University of Toronto contributed valuable ideas to the manuscript. I also wish to thank Georg Elwert of the Institute of Ethnology at the Free University of Berlin for his comments. This work was stimulated by numerous controversial — and as time goes by, less controversial — discussions with my father on business politics and by constant disagreements with my friend Arno Hager of the Institute of Sociology at the Free University of Berlin. Heated discussions with Constantin Bartning, as well as access to his unpublished manuscripts, have helped me shape my view of collectives. My talks with Tonio Milone have helped me to understand the ideals that underlie them.

Of course, my greatest debt is to Ulrike, Veronika, Marita, Jürgen, Gisela, Fritz, Noppe, Günther, Arthur, Ebi, Julius, Marlene, Michael, Jeanette, and certainly Axel, and to all the other members of the *FahrradBüro, KoMet, Oktoberdruck, Wuseltronick,* and *STATTwerke*. In particular, I wish to thank Sabine and Marlis for providing me with hundreds of documents about the history of *agitdruck* and *Oktoberdruck*.

My special thanks go to Janet Hall, who did a great job editing and correcting the manuscript, and to my friend Henk Raijer, who sacrificed his free evenings to help me produce the final typescript on the *taz*-computer.

B.M.

1

Introduction

In West Berlin, since the end of the 1970s, well-educated young collectivists have started experimental enterprises in which they are not only the experimenters but also the subjects of the experiment. Their aim is to prove that alternative forms of production can replace those of capitalism, even inside the dominant economy. They are attempting to reverse the objectives and constraints of the capitalist system. Instead of the maximisation of profit, the primary objective is the development of a new work situation of a non-hierarchical, unalienated nature — not separated from life in general but promoting the production of socially and ecologically useful items. How do they reconcile these political aims with their survival as business concerns inside a capitalist economy?

This book explores the creative tensions that arise when political ideas and standards clash with economic practice and constraints. It is not primarily an economic feasibility study, although relevant data will be considered. Rather, it is a study of deliberately created social structures, in which factors such as group size, recruitment, leadership, and stability not only provide the framework of the structure, but also play a part in the social action of members, which is oriented towards an aim, an ideal form.

Alternative collectives involved in economic activities are a fairly recent phenomenon: they are rooted in the cultural tradition of the anti-authoritarian movements of the 1960s. They can be found in almost all Western industrial countries, though they are largely concentrated in Scandinavia, the United States (Taylor and Case 1979), the Netherlands, and West Germany. The distinguishing feature of the Berlin collectives, though, is their high political motivation. The ideals which the collectivists pursue are not unique or particular to their specific form of production, but correspond to a larger current of thought and criticism of the dominant society. The West German political party *Alternative Liste*, sectors of the party *Die Grünen* ("The Greens"), and portions of the trade unions and citizens' action committees include in their programmes the need for a qualitative change in the work situation, self-determination for the worker, and the production of ecologically useful goods. The collectivists try to put into practice what political groups have proposed in theory. The problems that arise shed light not only on the tremendous difficulty of developing different economic relations inside the capitalist system, but also on the arduous task of holding together individualistic human beings in a collective context.

The method I employed was essentially one of participant observation. I participated in the work of three collectives (*FahrradBüro*, *KoMet* and *Oktoberdruck*) for about two months each and kept in close contact with the fourth one (*Wuseltronick*). To supplement the information obtained by direct participation, I analysed records of collective meetings, legal and productivity charts, and correspondence, which amounted in the case of *Wuseltronick* and *Oktoberdruck* to more than 300 documents per collective.

I visited other collectives in the same trade regularly and collected comparative material through informal interviews and questionnaires (see Appendix). The first questionnaire inquired into the legal form, debts, investments, and market situation of collective enterprises; the composition, turnover, and history of the personnel; and the development of the organisation of work. I gave the second questionnaire to persons with whom I had actually worked and who knew me well. This questionnaire was rather short and served as a guideline for an interview rather than as a detailed and exhaustive set of questions. I asked questions about the type of work they were doing, their educational and employment history, their domestic situation, their opinions on the work, their aspirations, and their political ideas and expectations.

I use the concepts of social anthropology for my analysis, and bring the material from the Berlin collectives into the framework of that discipline. Social anthropologists have long felt that they had something to offer in the analysis of industrial society, even if only to bring into question the common belief in the universal validity of Western industrial society's values of efficiency, maximization of gains, and the rule of law. This book stands in that tradition.

My primary intention is to demonstrate the complex inter-relationships between political thought and economic practice, and to show that, to some extent, it is possible both to hold revolutionary ideas concerning social and economic relations and still to compete as a viable business venture. Thus, collectivists wishing to abolish competition as an economic and social principle compete fiercely, even amongst themselves, while they are aware of this and reflect self-critically about it. To consider this perplexing contradiction, I analyse the structural principles with which the collectives experiment (such as abolition of the division of labour, no separation between work and leisure time, unitary pay, and non-hierarchical structures of decision making) and the economic constraints that inhibit these principles.

Another area for consideration is the extreme complexity of internal collective structures. If not only business considerations but also private and political attitudes become the subject of formal decisionmaking, or at least of debate, if each and every person is called on to voice his or her opinion, and if all decisions are made in common, each member will be confronted with a continuous need to make decisions. Decision-making processes become long and unpredictable and cause frustrations with which collectives have to cope. I analyse the extent of collective and individual withdrawals to less complex forms of organisation; the emergence of a new division between private, political, and business spheres; the delegation of decisionmaking; and new divisions of labour and responsibility.

Another intention of this book is to consider these collectives as an alternative to the system of human relations and relations of production that they criticize. Collective enterprises have been carried on the wave of a social movement of protest: against the dominant industrial society, and against the concept expounded by dogmatic and authoritarian left-wing groups that social change must be initiated by the state. Without firmly constructed ideological principles, this movement follows a utopian dream, resembling similar currents of past centuries. Issues such as striving for harmony with nature, communist community, reunification of time, and the belief in the "explosive power" of the utopian experiment link Berlin collectivists to their popular utopian predecessors. The vagueness of the utopian dream made different and sometimes conflicting views about society compatible.

The *leitmotiv* of my investigation has been the question of how this utopian dream and the optimistic eagerness to experiment can survive when faced with economic constraints and individual needs. How strong a force is hope (Bloch 1982) and how can it affect social change? From the investigation of this question in the Berlin context, inferences may be made concerning the development of social movements in general and their consolidation or collapse.

In my treatment of the political ideas of collectivists, a problem arises in that the majority claim not to follow, nor to have their actions determined by, any fixed ideology. In the 1970s, as members of small left-wing parties, some of these collectivists used propaganda techniques to politicise workers on the shopfloor. In contrast to this political strategy, however, they now mainly want to gather practical experience. Pragmatic problem-solution on the one hand and remnants of previous political theories on the other provide a complex blend of ideas that form the basis for the way they understand the essence of collective enterprise.

A large and still growing section of the discipline of social anthropology is now concerned with the meaning of, and with the debate about, the economic and the social and ideological embeddedness of the economy. Instead of analysing human economic behaviour quantitatively in terms of gains and losses, they consider the complex social relationships that underlie it and try to understand it through qualitative analysis. Even before Sandra Wallman's (1979) book, *The Social Anthropology of Work*, it has become obvious that there is a strong connection between ideological convictions and economic behaviour. The wish to belong to a community, to gain prestige, or to satisfy a transcending principle, be it a belief in gods or spirits or in a utopian model for society, can be stronger than the desire to maximize gain.

The abolition of the division of labour and of the principle of competition was one of the primary driving forces behind the setting up of collectives. Marx's writings on the subject of the alienating quality of the capitalist division of labour, and collectivist's own experience as wage labourers, inspired the creation of structures in sharp contrast to existing business enterprises, the collectivists main objective being the self-realisation of the worker rather than the maximum accumulation of profits. The question raised by this attitude toward production has occupied social scientists and economists and concerns the nature of human economic behaviour: Are collectives an example of the falseness of the neoclassical concept of "economic man," or, to the contrary, does their development show that the drive to maximize gain only lies dormant at the commencement of the initiative and eventually breaks through after a phase of non-materialistic idealism?

Vernant's observations (1965: 28-36) on the concept of work in ancient Greece show that the division of labour was not always considered a means to give work its maximum productive efficiency. It was regarded as a necessity inscribed in human nature and, as Plato expressed it, was one of the founding principles of society because every individual, far from being self-sufficient, needed a large number of people to mutually exchange the goods they produced. Man would do a given task the better if he would do only it and if the different individual talents were allowed to exercise themselves and create objects as accomplished as possible. The ancient concept considered less the process of fabrication than the use that was made of the object. The perfection of the object consisted in its adaptation to the need that it was supposed to satisfy. The craftsman entered with the user into a relationship of natural dependence and served the users needs.

The idea of the ancient Greeks that the work of the artisan was to serve primarily the needs of the consumers is consistent with one of the principal preoccupations of the alternative movement: the responsibility of the worker for the quality of the product he or she is producing — an issue that in the labour movement took second place behind the issue of the forms of social appropriation of the factors of production and the social distribution of the products. In this, the Berlin collectivists stand in the tradition of the anarchists of the turn of the twentieth century, such as Nettlau and Kropotkin, who claimed that workers should refuse to waste their energy on the production of low-quality or even damaging objects and go on strike against the useless gesture (Ribeill 1980: 89).

Since the writings of Chayanov (1966) and the historical reflections of E. P. Thompson (1967), social scientists have rediscovered the fact that once certain essential needs are satisfied, people are often not willing to increase their work effort. Thompson also pointed out that a strong division between work and leisure time is not universal nor was it common in our own past. Berlin collectivists try to link up in this respect with non- and pre-industrial attitudes toward work. Spittler (1989), modifying to some extent Thompson's distinction between "natural" time in pre-industrial and "clock" time in industrial societies, pointed out that the the work-rhythm in pre-industrial societies was not only structured by natural factors like daylight, seasons, and weather but was also culturally defined. "Time discipline" (determining the span between beginning and ending of work) and "work discipline" (defining the continuity and intensity of work) follow cultural rules and norms that are transmitted through learning (Spittler 1989: 5-7). The "pre-industrial" culture of work-time that collectives now consciously develop, in spite of economic pressures and the constraints of industrial society, may teach us about the cultural embeddedness of economic choices.

For André Gorz, the increased efficiency of industrial production due to automatisation leads to an unequal distribution of well-remunerated productive work, leaving more than half of the economically active population with a precarious job situation or with no job at all. For those who retain their jobs, the microelectronic revolution might effectively improve the work situation. "Repetitive tasks tend to disappear, ... work tends to become more engaging, responsible, self-organized, diversified, requiring autonomous individuals capable of taking initiative, of communicating, and of learning to dominate a diversity of intellectual and manual disciplines" (Gorz 1990: 22). For the others an identification with the work they do becomes impossible as "the industrial society has no need or no regular need for their work capacities" (Gorz 1990: 22). From this he concludes that in contemporary society "work is no longer the principal social cement, nor the principal factor of socialisation, nor the main occupation for everybody, nor the principal source of wealth and well-being, nor the meaning and centre of our lives" (Gorz 1990: 22). Has the emphasis collectivists put on a new culture of work therefore become anachronistic, or is it rather an appropriate response to the requirements of post-industrial society? Can their concept of work be generalized, or are they rather carving for themselves a niche in the capitalist market to become part of the privileged, highly qualified few?

2

Ethnographic Introduction

Transformations must start with the individual without renouncing, however, a critical engagement in the (political, social, economic and natural) environment.... Within the maxims of "self-determination, co-operation and no private profits" we are knitting our own cultural, political and social network... which spreads over the whole town. It is not a ghetto nor a "free state" but the sum of attempts to develop, within this society, the seedling of a new one.... In this network... is space for everyone who wants to strive towards an ecological and socialist form of life.

Written as the introduction to the STATTbuch 2 (1982:5), the alternative resource directory for West Berlin, which included 1,800 self-descriptions of alternative projects, this quote expressed a minimal level of consensus on which projects related to one another. The book itself gave an impression of everything that was understood by the term "alternative." The projects presented ranged from research groups concerned with new technologies to groups advising tenants on their legal rights, from pubs for gays to Third World solidarity groups, from groups giving information on medical treatment to small workers' collectives. Some of the projects included operated on an entirely benevolent basis, like the German-Turkish Initiative against Fascism, the centre for alternative medical advice, or the women's centres. Others, such as the *DAYTOP* therapy centre for drug addicts, the centre of child psychotherapy, or the kindergartens where handicapped and able-bodied children played together, received money from the Senate (Berlin city council). Still others were financed by the contributions of a circle of militants, such as the group "Citizens observe the police" or the *Bildungs- und Aktionszentrum Dritte Welt*. Most of the alternative cafes, theatres, shops, repair shops, and small enterprises were self-supporting, and the members subsisted on the proceeds of their work.

An individual, whether attracted by some of the alternative ideas or just feeling lonely or lost, could find support and advice through this alternative infrastructure, take action against social or political injustice, or simply spend his or her leisure time in a pleasurable way. Most of the alternative projects were specifically aimed not only to reach and involve people who already had similar ideas and outlooks but also to contact their ordinary neighbours in the *Kiez* (neighbourhood). They intended to make ordinary citizens sensitive to some very precise and tangible social and political problems and aware that the possibility existed for them to deal with these problems.

Of all the cities in Germany, West Berlin is the one where small enterprises and the homes of the less well-off sectors of the population are most closely intertwined. In the traditional working-class quarters of Kreuzberg, Wedding, Moabit and Neukölln, which cover approximately one-third of the residential area of West Berlin but house more than half of its population of 1.8 million, blocks of flats and business premises are constructed around open courtyards. The first courtyard is surrounded by flats, a second – and sometimes a third – by workshops. In the nineteenth and the beginning of the twentieth century these courtyards were the centres of small-scale productive activity. But increasingly, small enterprises are dying out now, and the workshop areas are instead occupied by communal households *(Wohnge-meinschaften)*, which transform them into residential spaces. Rents are relatively low for these premises as they are often in very poor condition and need to be entirely refurbished.

It was in these courtyards that, around 1977, small collectives started to develop, taking over more or less the same types of production as the old ones – such as woodworking, metalworking, the manufacture of industrial components, printing, plumbing, etc. – often using the old machinery left from previous enterprises. At the same time, others were opening up new areas of production, starting to develop ecologically preferable alternatives to the conventional systems of producing food, housing, and energy. Although their outward appearance was not distinguishable from the old enterprises, except for the fact that the workers were on the whole younger, collectives claimed to have a radically different organisation and attitude toward work but a similarly intimate relation to the *Kiez* (neighbourhood).

Originally, *Kiez* meant the dwellings of feudal vassals belonging to a castle or manor. Today, it basically denotes "neighbourhood." A social

A typical second courtyard in Kreuzberg, where Oktoberdruck and several other collectives are housed. Usually the first courtyard is surrounded by flats and the second one by small enterprises (photo by author).

rather than a geographical unit, the coherence of the *Kiez* depends on the feeling the inhabitants have of "belonging" to one another and to their part of the town. The *Kiez* often consists of a small cluster of side-streets with restricted traffic, often grouped around a popular street or a square (*Crellekiez, Winterfeldkiez, Lausitzer Kiez*, etc.). The *Kiez* was traditionally, and still is today, the basis of social life in that part of the town. West Berlin is a city with a high percentage of elderly people who have lived in the city all their lives and are closely attached to it. The alternative movements adopted this attitude, revived street feasts, took measures to control the traffic in residential areas, and initiated citizens' action committees (*Bürgerinitiativen*) on the *Kiez* level.

The collectives in Kreuzberg see themselves as the continuation of the traditional *Kreuzberger Mischung* (Kreuzberg mixture), a term that describes the close interrelation between living and working quarters, and the cooperation that exists between small traditional enterprises of the same trade or of different trades situated in the same *Kiez*. Today, it also designates the mixture of nationalities, especially German and Turkish, which is characteristic of Kreuzberg. In the first phase of their collective enterprise, members often lived, together or singly, close to their workplace. They and their supporters saw the close cooperation between collectives, which they call *Vernetzung* (networking), as an important step toward a different economy. Returning to the concept of neighbourhood, redeveloping forms of solidarity at the "roots of society" which had been eroded by the mechanisms of "mass-society," was one of the programmatic aims of the alternative movement.

Many hopes and expectations arising from people sympathising with, or involved in, "the movement," were focused on collectives. Their success or failure was seen to some extent as a measure of the success of "the alternative" as a whole because there existed the conviction that capitalist, industrial society could only be effectively transformed if new forms of working together and a different quality of product were successfully developed. Founders of collectives accepted this task and called their collective "a living utopia" or a "social experiment," comparing it to the inventor's shed where ideas that change the world are born.

In 1984 in Berlin, there were about fifty productive collectives, varying in size from three to fifteen members, that called themselves and were regarded by others as collective enterprises. Following heated debates about how to distinguish "collectives" from "ordinary enterprises," collectives were defined as enterprises where the means of production were controlled by the people working in them and which had no external owners. Without formal hierarchies and without differential pay, they wanted to be different from labour-managed enterprises that were owned by the work force but that had no egalitarian structures and unitary pay and were employing outside temporary workers. In 1990, the number of enterprises to which this definition would still apply has become difficult to assess as many have since changed their ideals and their organisational structure.

Within their sphere of economic activity, it is possible to distinguish, first, between production, service, and trading, and second, according to the nature of their activities: building, printing, metalworking, electrical work, electronics, the preparation of wholefood, and the like. In 1984, their organisational structures ranged from disordered groups of four people who each performed each and every task in the enterprise, to groups of twelve people with a formal division of labour. The different types of economic activity predictably attracted different kinds of people from varying educational and professional backgrounds. The metalworking collective, *KoMet*, for example, seemed to draw skilled toolmakers who were fascinated with the possibility of taking part in the organisational running of the enterprise and the development of their professional skills. The *FahrradBüro*, a bicycle collective once well known for its involvement in the politics of transportation but which then became merely a bicycle repair shop, seemed to attract former teachers who were disillusioned with the teacher-pupil relationship, or who were subject to *Berufsverbot* (dismissal from civil service for political reasons) and wanted to retrain in a useful craft.

The different collectives formed a patchy network of economically independent enterprises, which sometimes cooperated. Their common political convictions led them to undertake joint political action, such as collecting money and materials to support the revolution in Nicaragua, or helping squatters in Berlin. They also supported workers who, having been made redundant, occupied their factories. Although these actions found strong support in the collectives, they were not part of a general strategy to transform the social system, but were rather a spontaneous form of protest.

Oktoberdruck (October-printing)

The printing collective — in the summer of 1983, with twelve members, the largest in West Berlin — is situated in one of the typical courtyards of Kreuzberg in the premises of an old chocolate factory. When the collectivists moved into the first floor, they had to scrape chocolate off the walls and move out tons of old machinery. From there, the collective slowly expanded onto the second and third floors as the old traditional enterprises, a cardboard manufacturer and a *passementerie* workshop, went bankrupt or moved away. *Oktoberdruck* rented all the available space and sublet it to "alternative projects," an ecological magazine, and a consulting office for alternative enterprises, *STATTwerke*. The courtyard has since become one of the centres of collective activity.

In the large storage area on the third floor, the people working in the building hold their parties, and the collective's band practises there once a week. On the second floor is the social area of the collective; the kitchen, with a large table for lunches and meetings, is clearly separated from the space for dealing with customers. The swinging door that divides the two areas bears the inscription: "Customer, your road ends here."

In the month following the end of my work in the collective, the table at which customers were received was moved out of the office, the office space reduced, and a reception area created next to the entrance; this became the most elegant part of the enterprise. The changing of the space allocated to customers mirrors the relationship between them and the collective. In the early days of the enterprise, the customers were for the most part political groups, whom the printers were supporting with cheap printing services, or left-wing publishers and newspapers. The intertwining went furthest in the years 1975 to 1977, when the enterprise printed free of charge all the propaganda material for the Trotskyist group *TLD* (*Trotzkistische Liga Deutschlands*) and employed its unskilled members at a good salary.

At that time, the various activities of the repro-mounting department, the printing, and the office work were still carried out in a common area on the first floor, the office informally separated from the remaining space by two bookcases. *TLD* members at times kept the books, while customers went in and out amongst people working there. Today, the role of the customer is in accordance with their economic importance for the enterprise. Although most of them still come from artistic, "alternative" or left-wing circles, they now require better quality work, and no longer expect "solidarity" prices. Nevertheless, the name of the enterprise, referring as it does to the Russian October Revolution, stands for a political tradition that discourages right-wing or purely commerical clients.

Passing through the swinging door and crossing the social area consisting of kitchen, changing rooms, and showers, one enters the repro-mounting department equipped with six light tables. During the period of my fieldwork, five people were working there and in the darkroom. Two of them were trained repro-photographers, one was a printing engineer, and the other two were former students who had acquired their skills on the job. Every repro-monteur had his own box of tools with menacing inscriptions or death skulls painted on them to discourage colleagues from using them. The walls were covered with slogans, posters, encouraging statements, or complaints. This decoration disappeared when all the repro-monteurs left. During the transition period of 1983, when the new workers had not yet settled in, the walls were left bare; and they were only painted and redecorated a few months later, testifying that the new group had consolidated itself.

In the summer of 1983, in a small office next to the montage room, a typesetting facility was set up by an individual typesetter, who had hoped to become integrated into *Oktoberdruck* after he left his previous typesetting collective, *Gegensatz*, as the result of an argument. However, most members of *Oktoberdruck* were unwilling to accept him because they knew of his irregular hours of work and his general lack of commitment.

On the first floor, the printing section was equipped with a large modern A1 two-colour, or perfecting, *Miller* printing-press and a small new A3 two-colour *GTO*-press. Three of the six people working in this section during my fieldwork in the summer of 1983 had formal qualifications as printers. Donald had several years of work experience in business enterprises, while Thomas and the only woman in this section, Andrea, had just completed their apprenticeships. The other two printers, Jürgen and Werner, were former students who had learned to print on the job.

Oktoberdruck was founded in 1974 by Dieter, the co-owner of a small graphics enterprise, and Marlis and Constantin, two members of a printing collective, *agitdruck*, that they had to leave because of a dispute over investment decisions. *Oktoberdruck* was conceived as a collective, and the three founders decided upon a collective charter; but legally the enterprise belonged to Dieter and Constantin. From 1974 onwards, the enterprise was supporting Trotskyist groups. The founders wanted to combine membership in a political organisation with involvement in the collective, but the activists of the *TLD* were not interested in becoming fully involved in the collective enterprise. The Trotskyists sent an increasing number of their unskilled members to work in the enterprise. The professional revolutionaries were paid far better salaries than the founders dared to take for themselves. It proved impossible to uphold production when dependent on the unskilled temporary labour of the political activists. Finally, the *TLD* convinced the founders to also employ skilled wage labour. When in 1976 the *TLD* members disagreed with an attempt by the three owners to cut wages in order to save the financial situation, a conflict arose that ended in September of 1977 with a separation between the *TLD* party and *Oktoberdruck*, and complete political disillusionment.

The *TLD* members who left were replaced by wage-labourers experienced in labour disputes. After a while, they were each willing to continue the enterprise as a collective, even at the risk of taking DM 10,000 credit to avoid financial collapse. Their aim was the creation of strong personal bonds between people working together. Constantin, however, was not interested simply in bettering personal relations. He wanted the enterprise to become a model for workers in industry who aimed to take over run-down enterprises. He maintained, that to set an example, the enterprise should strive toward industrial dimensions. The interest in making it a "real collective" finally died out because of production stress, financial chaos, and the impossibility of making decisions collectively. From 1978 onwards, however, the group introduced unitary pay and regular meetings. In the summer of 1978, the founding group split, and Marlis and Dieter left the enterprise. Production collapsed when three of the four *Miller* printers left as well and an important source of credit was discontinued.

The financial collapse finally occurred in 1979. It reverberated throughout the "alternative scene," stimulating discussions on the question: "What really constitutes a collective?" Collectives of left-wing editors, booksellers, printers, and typesetters came together to talk about how *Oktoberdruck* could be saved. *Netzwerk*, the newly created alternative fund, proposed organising a campaign to collect funds, provided *Oktoberdruck* became a "real" collective. In the collective newspaper, *die tageszeitung*, four members of *Netzwerk* outlined the structure that the *Oktoberdruck* collective should adopt (*TAZ* 15.8 1979). Their main point was that every worker should become an associate member after six months. The salary should be basically the same for every member but should take into account differing needs and should depend upon the overall monthly position of the enterprise.

The new collectivists of *Oktoberdruck* accepted some of the conditions but introduced, at first, a fixed unitary wage and adopted the legal form of a company with limited liability (*GmbH: Gesellschaft mit beschränkter Haftung*). Just as every person had to become an associate after six months, nobody was allowed to keep the status of associate without working in the collective. People leaving could only take away what they had brought in.

The enterprise's disastrous financial situation made it necessary for Constantin to keep his own one-man society which owned the machinery, and to conclude arrangements with the creditors. As the *GmbH* could not provide a guarantee for the debts of approximately DM 300,000, repayment was assured by the rent that the *Oktoberdruck GmbH* paid to Constantin every month. However, an informal contract made it Constantin's responsibility to transfer ownership of the machinery to the collective once the debts had been paid off. Nine years later, in 1986, this transfer finally took place.

During the two months of my first period of continuous fieldwork, in the summer of 1983, the collective was going through a phase of reorganisation and upheaval in protest against the informal authority structure. Constantin, the former head and ideological leader, had been sent on a year's holiday in order to learn to become an ordinary member like everybody else. He had been severely criticized for interfering with the work of the other members without doing his own tasks properly and for working overtime when the others had wanted to go home. The authority of the second remaining head, Helmut, who had dealt with a large number of external contacts, was also seriously questioned but for the opposite reasons, namely that he was identifying less and less with the enterprise and was becoming increasingly cynical about collective work.

In 1988, fourteen years after its foundation, *Oktoberdruck* was one of the wealthiest and most strictly organised collectives in West Berlin. The structure of *Oktoberdruck* seemed stable, and personal relations within it were good, although the turnover in membership was still high. Its numbers, however, increased to seventeen in 1988. Each newcomer brought fresh expectations and arrived with ideals that the older members had since lost. The structure of the collective has to adapt to this and is constantly being reshaped according to new requirements. Although the organisation of *Oktoberdruck* is more formalized than that of other collectives, it continues to react to changing membership and circumstances.

KoMet (Metalworking Cooperative)

In 1984, the ten members of *KoMet* adhered strictly to the ideal of an organisation with a minimum of formal structure. Even though the collective was operating under the most rigorous market conditions, as it manufactured tools and equipment for the business industry. By 1990, it had dissolved into several enterprises, each struggling with a work organisation that has little in common with their initial ideas.

The workshop was situated on a factory floor in a courtyard in a better-off part of Kreuzberg. It was spacious and light with windows on three sides. A visitor or customer who entered the workshop immediately found himself in the production area amongst the machinery with a number of busy people hurrying about. The glassed-in office at the entrance was seldom occupied, so he had to ask to find somebody who felt a responsibility for dealing with his query. The shopfloor was loosely divided into sections of drills, cutters, lathes, grinders, and saws. All the machines were designed to produce specialized single parts, not series of identical ones. In front of the windows overlooking the second courtyard, workbenches were lined up — one for each long-standing member. Newcomers worked initially at the bench of an older member who introduced them to the job. Later, people who liked one another tended to work side by side.

In the large communal kitchen, furnished with a sofa, table, and chairs from a secondhand shop, visitors and established customers were sometimes invited to take coffee or to participate in meals. Apart from the weekly collective meetings, the communal hot lunches were social occasions in which all members participated and where an informal exchange of information took place. Prospective members often visited at lunchtime to be given a searching examination by older members. In front of the large table, the timetable with small coloured cards for every order was hung up next to a pinboard with notices, invitations, and postcards.

"From everybody according to his abilities, to everybody according to his needs" was the motto of the founders in 1979 when, stimulated by the wave of new collectives, a group of metalworkers set up their own enterprise. Radically opposed to the working conditions in capitalist enterprises, they wanted to create — both for themselves and as an example to others — structures of production without fixed wages and working hours.

Most of the founders had been politically active in the seventies, though not all were members of political organisations. When setting up the collective, they emphasized the individuality of the members rather than the principle of equal distribution of rewards. That is, their intention was to create the opportunity for each member to realize his different needs and expectations. During the first year and a half, each member took from the collective cashbox as much as he wanted or needed without having to justify the use he was making of it. In actuality, this amounted to between DM 800 and DM 1,800[1] per month. It was understood that somebody who, for instance, loved playing the piano needed more money to purchase his instrument than somebody who played the flute and that both ways of making music were equally important for the musicians concerned.

The motivation of the members had shifted over the years from a highly idealistic sense of mission to the more pragmatic need to find an agreeable job. The first members wanted "to set an example to workers in industry and to show that small-scale decentralized production of industrial goods is possible." They dreamt of their own ecological product, manufactured in mass form without any formal division of labour. The tight market in Berlin, which led to several toolmaking businesses going bankrupt, did not allow for experiments nor for investment in production machinery. The collective had to switch in 1981, for financial reasons, to a fixed system of pay, namely, DM 1,000 per worker plus DM 200 for each child in the member's care.

The turnover of *KoMet* members was considerable. In the two years following my period of fieldwork in the spring of 1984, four of the nine had left and five new members had started work. Two of the four who left were highly skilled and were about to take the examination for the masters' certificate; four of the five newcomers came directly from their apprenticeships and had no other work experience. Only one of the founders was still working in the collective, and the new members did not have the same firm political intentions. The newcomers, who were younger than the original founders were when they set up the enterprise, were searching for a political orientation and professional experience and took working in a collective as a starting point. Qualified newcomers were difficult to find as the income in the collective was half that in a business enterprise. Even toolmakers without work experience earned less in the collective than they would have if they had found a beginner's job in industry.

KoMet was for years an all-male collective. The women who later worked in it complained that its structures continued to be very male-dominated. Up to 1984, no woman had worked there for more than a year, partly because of the difficulties created by their position *vis-à-vis* the all-male customers in the metal industry and partly because of the outright rejection they experienced from some of their male colleagues.

Although *KoMet* was not one of the most successful collectives in economic terms, it was certainly one of the most exciting to work in. The flexible working hours, and the fact that members carried out their tasks from beginning to end, made the work very satisfying, although sometimes chaotic. *KoMet* has proved incapable, however, of finding a compromise between economic pressures and their challenging form of production. In 1990, it ceased to exist as a collective.

FahrradBüro (Cycle-office)

As the name *FahrradBüro* (cycle office) implies, this collective was not conceived as an ordinary cycle shop. For years, it was one of the corner-stones of the ecology movement against official traffic politics. At the time of my fieldwork in the autumns of 1982 and 1983, its political role had been almost entirely taken over by ecology groups such as the Green Cyclists, and what remained was mainly a bicycle shop with a collective organisational structure.

The *FahrradBüro* is situated in the Crellestrasse, a part of Schöneberg with severe traffic problems. The street is sandwiched between a four-lane main road and an unused railway where the Senate of Berlin is planning to construct a highway. For years, the street was used as a short cut by drivers wanting to avoid the traffic lights on the main road. They raced through the narrow cobbled street until, in 1980, the inhabitants took the initiative and put a stop to this by building a huge sandpit in the middle of the road. The members of the *FahrradBüro* were active participants in this successful action for traffic abatement.

From the street, the *FahrradBüro* looked very much like an ordinary bicycle shop, except for the fact that it displayed not only bicycles and spare parts but also literature on traffic politics, cycling holidays and the like, some of which the collective published itself. It consisted of three parts: the shop, the neighbouring office, which had windows onto the street, and the repair shop in the courtyard. Crowded and teeming with activity in summer, the shop looked rather dismal and damp during the winter months. It was poorly heated by a coal stove, and during the coldest days of December even the toilet froze. Bernard, the longest-standing member, had a permanent backache in winter and manned the shop with a hot water bottle tied to his back. Because it was very busy in summer and uncomfortable in winter, working in the shop was certainly the most unpopular task from the collectivists' point of view. This work was comprised of taking care of the books, postcards, and cycling clothes displayed in the back of the shop and standing behind the counter in the front part, where the shop was filled to overflowing with bicycles and had spare parts hanging from all the walls and the ceiling.

In the small narrow office, the administrative tasks were performed: the bookkeeping, the ordering and the publishing. In 1983, a qualified bookkeeper had been employed to bring the accounts into order and to make them comprehensible to all the members in the hopes that they would then be able to keep them properly themselves. Every Tuesday morning, a meeting took place over a communal breakfast, and the tasks for the coming week were agreed upon. Every member had to work for two days a week in the shop, one day in the office, and one in the repair shop. Once a week the repair shop was open for customers who wanted to learn to repair their cycles themselves. They were assisted by a collectivist and allowed to use the tools free of charge. Any money they contributed voluntarily was given to the Green Cyclists.

The collective was founded in 1979 by four men who knew each other from their common political activities in the *BI Westtangente*, a citizens' action committee against the construction of a highway on the old railway line. They had all completed studies in construction engineering or in urban planning and were looking for jobs. Although they had no expert knowledge of bicycles, they decided to set up a shop that would allow them, as they thought, to finance their more theoretical work on traffic politics from the sale of bicycles as the "most sensible means of transportation."

In 1982, none of the founders were still working in the collective. The links with the citizens' action committee had been almost severed, as even Bernard, the last member to be active on the committee, stopped participating. All of the members in 1983 had studied at university; six of the seven had completed their studies, while Bernhard dropped out shortly before the final examinations. Most of them had worked as teachers or educationalists, or were trained as such, but were subject to a professional ban because they had been members of parties on the extreme left. During my first period of fieldwork, in the autumn of 1982, four people worked in the collective on a permanent basis, and one was employed part-time to administer the publishing work. One year later, their numbers had increased to seven permanent members, plus a qualified bookkeeper employed part-time. Four, including the bookkeeper, were women. Although the shop was prosperous and the income per person had increased from DM 1,000 to DM 1,300 net per month, the atmosphere was much more pessimistic than the previous year. Considerable tensions between the male and female members embittered the work atmosphere. The male members, Hans and Bernhard, tried to recruit a new member whom the women did not want. They were also trying to rationalise the organisation of work and turn the collective into a wholesale business.

The number of hours worked per week was low — twenty-nine in winter and thirty-four in summer — while the income was higher than the salaries paid in ordinary shops. Nevertheless, the teachers earned about DM 1,000 per month less than they would have in teaching posts. The loss of members was remarkably low for two and a half years, but in 1984 severe personal problems started to arise. Members were complaining about the lack of a proper perspective. Some were heard to remark that they did not want to spend the rest of their days in a bicycle shop selling valves. Some members feared that the good image of the *FahrradBüro* as an activist in traffic politics was gradually fading and with it the clients from the ecology "scene." *FahrradBüro* was no longer publishing anything new, and its participation in traffic politics was reduced to displaying Green Cyclists leaflets on the shopcounter.

Although the collectivists participated only occasionally in activities that opposed official traffic politics, they kept their aim of making the use of a bicycle instead of a car as attractive as possible to their customers. Their service to the customer included extensive advice on the choice of a cycle; they tried not to sell overpriced, poor quality machines and attempted to educate their clients and make them critical toward the products they were buying.

During the last two years, the bicycle collectives in West Berlin and West Germany have met frequently to develop a common strategy toward bicycle manufacturers by setting up their own wholesale group. They hope to exert pressure on manufacturers to build cycles that are robust and can be easily repaired. In January 1985, they founded the first national union of bicycle collectives, in the creation of which the *FahrradBüro* had played a major part. The *FahrradBüro* itself, however, was taken over in July 1985 and became the private business of Hans and Bernhard. Three of the other members who left because of the rising tensions set up a new cycle collective in another part of town.

Wuseltronick (Fumbling with Electronics)

Wuseltronick is one of the best known collectives in West Berlin and is considered by its numerous admirers to be the successful forerunner of a future wave of highly skilled collectives using the most advanced technology. It was initially financed by state research grants, and was therefore subject to no direct market pressures, but has recently entered into actual production of the products it has designed. In December 1977, the members started the collective with a set of ideological concepts in mind, and these have been constantly questioned ever since. The workings of the collective are continuously checked against the initial ideals in long discussions, of which hundreds of pages of written records are kept.

Since its founding, the collective has been constantly expanding into larger premises. During the time of my fieldwork in the winter of 1983/84, its administrative section was housed in the *Mehringhof*, together with thirty-seven other alternative projects, while the electronics and computer section was situated on a large factory floor in another part of Kreuzberg. The office in the *Mehringhof* was also the social centre of the collective. Collective meetings took place there, the members sitting around the large oval table. Organisational schemes representing the collective structure were painted on the walls in the form of a wiring diagram. A movable disc, with all the members' names and the rotating tasks written on it, indicated the duties everyone had to fulfill on that day. Members cooked, tidied up, and shopped in turn. At lunch, they ate together with members of projects housed on the same floor in the *Mehringhof*. One, *Ökotopia*, traded in ecologically grown food, and in tea and coffee bought directly from producers in Third World countries; another published a journal on Latin American politics. Here the latest events in the *Mehringhof* were discussed, as well as the gossip of the individual collectives.

The electronics section of *Wuseltronick* worked together with *Südwind*, a collective on the same factory floor, which designed and produced sails for windmills. *Südwind* was founded on the initiative of *Wuseltronick*, which needed aerodynamic sails for the windmill prototype it had developed. The laboratory was dominated by creative disorder. Some desks overflowed with wires, switchboards, and microcomputer components. Along the walls were coloured boxes of spare parts and tools for all kinds of purposes, from plumbing to soldering electric wires.

Next to one of the large windows, the pride of the collective, the prototype of a small windmill, was set up. This windmill had been developed over many years in cooperation with the Institute for Wind Energy at the Technical University of Berlin, and was equipped with very advanced electronics systems. The instruments developed to measure the performance of this prototype have become one of the main concerns of *Wuseltronick*. As they can be used to measure the performance of other kinds of rotating machines, the collective has sold some of them to industrial enterprises but has long been unable to produce them punctually and efficiently enough to satisfy the demand. The five members working in this section were all graduate electronics engineers, with the exception of Reiner, who acquired his skills in electronics after finishing his studies as an aviation and space navigation engineer.

The collective was set up in December 1977 by three students, Matze, Berni, and Reiner, together with an assistant lecturer, Hansi, in the sitting room of the apartment Matze and Hansi were sharing. The first pieces of equipment were purchased using personal savings and gifts, and loans from friends or acquaintances. The main impulse in founding the collective came from the founders' previous experience as engineers in academic research.

> Clients and the objectives of one's own work were fortuitous and anonymous and therefore the work itself, to an unbearable extent, was determined from outside. The collective work allowed one to refuse to do research, for example, for nuclear power stations. Scientific intelligence could be employed where it was politically useful in the development of alternative energy production. (*Wuseltronick-Kollektiv* 1984:31)

Reiner, who had been a member of the *KJS* (Catholic Students' Youth) for years, combined Christian ideals with Communist convictions. He wanted the collective to live and work in the way that the first Christians had. Private relationships and children should not be separated from, but united with, the work in the collective. "We are the revolutionary subjects ourselves" was his motto; to create collective structures was to give an incentive for revolutionary social change. Hansi, Matze, and Bernie came from a highly structured communist party, the *KBW* (Communist League of West Germany), and held far less idealistic views about the revolutionary role of the collective. For them, to run a collective meant "to learn Socialism," to experience for oneself what it meant to live and work in this way.

This very closed structure, where friendships and work coincided, was disrupted for the first time when Bernie's girlfriend became pregnant and wanted to move to West Germany. The suggestion that he follow her was condemned as a betrayal of the collective. With the move into the *Mehringhof* in 1980, three new members, Julius, Michael, and Brigitte, joined the collective; as a result, further relationships with people outside the collective had to be established. When the collectivists decided to move from pure theoretical research into the development of prototypes and were considering starting to produce series, they increased their numbers to ten. The integration of these new members posed serious problems for the still rather closed structure, which had to be abandoned. The newcomers were virtually left alone to find out for themselves their place in the collective. They did not know which tasks to take over or the extent of their responsibilities; and they felt trapped in a dependency relationship as they received no systematic introduction into the activities of the collective and had to rely entirely on what information they could obtain informally from the older members. The difference in status between the newcomers and the older members was cemented by the fact that the founders had invested their entire property into the collective, whereas the newcomers brought only their labour-power.

As the collective became larger, it began to split into two groups. In the autumn of 1983, the electronics engineers, working together on a certain project, especially Reiner and Eberhard, started to develop the idea of setting up a producers' cooperative with other collectives. They wanted to begin producing windmills and perhaps other products en masse. The other half of the collective was not involved in this planning and remained rather sceptical. At first, only a few of the collectivists were interested in spending their time in actual production, and even Reiner and Eberhard, the fathers of the idea, preferred to do research. However, in 1988 60% of *Wuseltronick*'s annual turnover already derived from production and marketing of small series.

Notes

1. DM 1.00 was worth approximately USD 0.35 in 1984.

3

Utopian Dreams and Cohesion in Membership

Collectivists share convictions and ideas that are in opposition to the principles of the dominant capitalist society, but these convictions do not form a coherent system. They also reject centralized planning, together with the authoritarian politics of the extreme left-wing groups of the 1970s. Some members have read Marx, Lenin, and Trotsky, but they do not accept the strongly dogmatic interpretation of these authors held by the small Marxist parties of the past. But they all share the conviction that the ecological destruction of the environment must be stopped, differing, however, in their ideas as to how this should be done. They agree that workers should be in control of both their labour and its product but do not agree on the question of whether the overall economic system should be a market economy, a decentralized, planned economy, or both.

Some members regard a market economy as being the most unconstrained and only aim to convert from large to small scale production; others think that the use of resources and the production of useful goods should be planned on a local or regional level; while yet others aim to see a mixed economy with both decentralized planning and a market structure. Collectivists want to abolish the dependency relationship between employer and employee but have varied ideas about how the ownership of the means of production should be handled. Their opinions vary between the claim that each collectivist should have an individual share in the enterprise, increasing in proportion with the number of years worked there, and the claim that collective capital should belong to nobody but rather should be "neutralized."

Some collectivists are inspired by Braverman's writings on the workers' loss of control in modern industry (Bravermann 1974), or by Yona Fried-man's theoretical essays about the maximal size of an egalitarian group (Friedman 1977), though they do not refer to these writings to solve their own problems. Their criticism of the separation of leisure and work time, and their conviction that self-realization and self-determination should be possible in the work-situation, have already been stated by Marcuse and others. Though some collectivists may read these authors, they do not take them expressly as guidelines for their actions.

Though their motives for joining may be highly diverse, members of collectives do share some convictions and ideals. In the first phase, that of construction, their common "utopian dream" to create in practice the seedling for a new social order helped them to overcome the initial difficulties, gave them the incentive to invest time and money in the collective enterprise, and contributed to the cohesion of the group. Elwert, following Ernst Bloch (1982:166ff), calls this inspiration to attempt the realization of social structures that have not existed before and that point the way for the positive transformation of dominant society "hope":

> Hope promises a reward that largely compensates the benefit of daily competition with fellow-men and that is drawn from established privileges.... It gives him/her (the individual) maybe for the first time a personal significance and makes his/her acts meaningful for the social whole. (Elwert 1983: 82)

In September 1982, when I started my fieldwork, the "utopian" message of the collective enterprises was already less strong than it had been in the founding phase (1978 to 1980). The importance of the ideological factor had diminished over time. By 1988, when I was concluding this research, the "utopian dream" had largely been replaced by institutionalisation and by generalisation of the collective experiment to wider sections of German society.

Political Background of Collectives and Their Members

The names and emblems of collectives are drawn from the anarchist, feminist, communist, or ecologist traditions. The first business letters sent out by collective enterprises were often decorated with black stars, the anarchist symbol. Trees, rainbows, and laughing suns, the ecological symbols,

DIE FREIE WAHL

THE FREE CHOICE

ZWISCHEN
DEM KAPITALISTISCHEN (1),
DEM ORTHODOX-KOMMUNISTISCHEN (2)
UND DEM ALTERNATIVEN (3)
WEG ZUR SONNE, ZUR FREIHEIT......

*between the capitalist (1)
orthodox-communist (2)
and the alternative (3)
way to the sun and to liberty*

1) "Jump!"

2) "The infallible Party has decided to take the great leap forward!"

*3) "Smoke a joint and float over it!"
"I would prefer a suspension bridge!"
"...or a balloon!"
"Theorizers!"
"Babblers!"*

Zeichnung: Fuchsi (FDGÖ)

appeared as part of the emblems of many collective firms. Black (anarchist), red (communist), green (ecologist), and violet (feminist) are the preferred colours. Puns on names, such as *STATTwerke*, [1] and *Gegendruck* ("counter-pressure" plus "...print"), express their intention to be different from established social and political structures.

Collectives, although part of a counterculture, are not isolated from the dominant culture but have constant interaction with it. One aspect of this interaction is that collectives take up practically every issue at stake in the ecology movement: pollution, the demolition of old housing, the poisoning of the environment through the use of chemicals, unhealthy food, and the like. One of the reasons for the setting up of collectives in the first place were the founders' wishes to switch from mere political criticism to social action, to attempt to produce viable goods with more attention paid to their effects on the environment.

The political party that best represents the viewpoints of most members of collectives is the West Berlin party *Alternative Liste*. In the political history of the ecology movement, a distinction has to be drawn between the West German party *Die Grünen* (The Green Party) and the *Alternative Liste* of West Berlin. Both emerged from a fusion of small political parties of the extreme left with ecology citizens' committees. The Berlin *Alternative Liste* claimed to belong to the extreme left, whereas the national party *Die Grünen*, founded in 1978, tried for some time to preserve a political profile outside of any traditional political tendency and to represent interests with which voters from all parties could identify. Both trends have since come closer together, and the more radical *Alternative Liste* of Berlin has now practically become a regional group of the national party *Die Grünen*.

The main points in which the programmes of the two parties coincide are on the questions of energy, traffic, housing, and pollution. They object to the construction of nuclear power stations but tolerate electricity plants run on oil or coal as long as they are provided with efficient air filters; but above all they promote the development of decentralized energy production. They aim to reduce the number of private cars in cities and favour increased use of the bicycle and an expansion in public transport services. The *Alternative Liste* went even further on this point and demanded a car-free Berlin in its campaign for the 1985 elections. In its housing programme, the *Alternative Liste* not only calls for the preservation of older urban structures but also demands the same legal status for communal households (*Wohngemeinschaften*) as for families. Both parties have proposed elaborate waste-recycling programmes and strict pollution regulations for industry, as well as tighter control of the production and use of chemicals.

The achievement of these aims through economic change is still under discussion. During the 1984 strikes in the printing and metal industries, which aimed to achieve a reduction in working hours, both parties were in favour of a reduction to less than 35 hours per week in order to guarantee full employment. They have recently shown sympathy with the concept of small-scale production and have allocated funds for the development of alternative enterprises in the regions where they form coalition government, with the Social Democrats. [2]

Criticism of the destructive effects of industrialization, which is the main issue of the ecology movement, is not a new theme but is almost as old as industrialization itself. However, the extent to which the industrial infrastructure and its waste products impinge on the quality of life and on the health of the population has become an increasing cause for concern to greater numbers of people since wholehearted confidence that the benefits of technological and industrial progress outweigh its disadvantages no longer exists. In their extreme politico-geographical situation, shut in by walls with no countryside in which to escape, suffocated by smog in winter and having to swim in polluted lakes in summer, Berliners were probably more sensitive to the arguments of ecologists than any other European population. While the major political parties still propose to build further highways through the centre of Berlin and allow power stations to run on coal without adequate air filters, the ecologists take a more radical view and receive some support: the *Alternative Liste* polled 10.7 percent of the votes in the last local elections in 1989.

The ecological criticism of industrial society is only one aspect of the motivations which inspired the collectivists. The other is the Marxist analysis of the relations of production in capitalist society; Marxist political thought of the 1970s was an inspiration to the founders, many of whom had been members of extreme left-wing parties. In the 1970s, these parties, small though they were, considered themselves the vanguard of a process of revolutionary social change that could bring an end to the capitalist system. They developed highly authoritarian structures, being convinced that only a small minority of party members was capable of fully understanding and interpreting Marxist, Leninist, Trotskyist, or Maoist ideology. They would lead, and a mass party would follow. The members were sent out to activate workers on the shopfloor, and some abandoned their studies to become workers themselves in an effort to identify more closely with the working class, which they thought of as the revolutionary subject.

By the end of the 1970s, disillusioned by years of unsuccessful struggle, persecuted by their bosses, and laughed at by their colleagues, they left these parties. Others were expelled as deviants because they began to contest their authoritarian and even repressive structures. Some of them returned to the studies, some joined the anti-authoritarian *Alternative Liste*, and some participated in the establishment of collectives. They emphasized the importance of going beyond mere criticism of dominant capitalist society and also the need to develop in practice a model for the transformation of society, trying to combine their political ideas with a satisfactory work situation. As a reaction to their previous authoritarian experiences, they welcomed the spontaneous character of collectives that, at the same time, fulfilled the minimal requirements for egalitarian cooperation, had no private ownership of the means of production, and did not offer payment according to performance.

Though not actual founders of collectives, Herbie and Rolf are typical examples of members who changed from the framework of a political party to the more informal structure of collectives, where they hoped to find common ground on which to realise some of their ideas concerning society.

Now an ex-member of *Oktoberdruck*, Herbie spent ten years as a member of *KB* (*Kommunistischer Bund*), a communist cadre organisation. When he founded a branch of the *KB* in Flensburg in 1970, he was convinced that the working class was the only power capable of overthrowing the "imperialism of the West German state." He decided to leave his studies and work as a repro-photographer in an ordinary printing shop, where he tried for four and a half years to activate his colleagues on the shopfloor but without success. After the "German Autumn" (*Deutscher Herbst*) of 1977 (the result of the kidnapping of Schleyer, the president of the employers' association, by the Red Brigade (*RAF: Rote Armee Fraktion*)), left-wing radicals became the target of both popular and state persecution. Anti-communist feeling grew to such an extent that Herbie was compelled to leave his job. He moved to Berlin, joining the branch of the *KB* there, but slowly realized that his notion of the working class as a revolutionary force had been mistaken. The motivation was gone, and he had to work as a repro-photographer simply to earn his living.

When he became a member of *Oktoberdruck*, Herbie felt this decision was a reconciliation of the ideas of his political past with a new lifestyle. His political standpoint was reduced to two principles: not to exploit others, and not to produce print for reactionary or fascist organisations. He wanted to work in a way he found agreeable, with people he liked, without imposing this work-style on others.

For Rolf, who worked in the bicycle collective *FahrradBüro*, it had already become clear in 1972, while he was a member of the *KB*, that he preferred to be involved in practical initiatives in the ward where he lived, rather than in abstract political discussions. He advised tenants on their rights and lived in a housing community financed by the Senate of Berlin, occupied by young people who had problems with their parents. These rather independent activities did not always meet with the approval of those who represented the official party line. Rolf and his friends were expelled and readmitted several times when they refused to carry out political propaganda on the shopfloor, preferring to place their main emphasis on political activity in the ward (*Stadtteilarbeit*). In 1980, Rolf left the *KB* and joined the *Alternative Liste*.

After seven years as a social worker dependent on Senate money, Rolf hoped to find in the bicycle collective more freedom to put his ideas into practice. Unlike Herbie, he did not lose faith in his previous convictions, which were not as closely linked as Herbie's to the official party line. However, both lost their hope that industrial workers could become the driving force for profound social change. For neither of them did their work in the collective constitute political activity as such. Rather, it was a satisfactory framework that allowed Herbie to retreat from politics without too bad a conscience, and Rolf to engage in political activities outside the collective while feeling that his ideas were also supported inside it.

The issue of whether work in a collective constitutes political engagement is heatedly debated amongst members, whose opinions range from strong affirmation to outright rejection.

> We are just like an ordinary capitalist enterprise.... We try to survive in the market, sometimes we do work for ordinary customers with whom we disagree... I have no hopes of changing society. I try to help small initiatives that have the right ideas. It is the work itself that is so important to us. It is 'creative' because we carry out every step of a given job ourselves. We are all fond of each other in one way or another. We are like a cell, with no intention of forming other cells in its own image. (Heinz, *Graph Druckula*, 12.9.1983)

> The aim of work in a collective is to offer an alternative to the society of waste. We want to provide a yardstick for change.... I don't want to live on an island.

I want to keep in touch with people whose aim is to change society at other levels, such as those who fight for self-management for workers." (Marita, *Oktoberdruck*, 13.7.1983)

The political motivations of collectivists differ as widely as these two statements, made by members of two printing shops. The first regarded his job
as fulfilling an aim in itself because it satisfied his need for interesting and
varied professional work alongside workmates he liked. He regarded it neither as a stimulating example to be emulated nor as different in principle from
an ordinary business enterprise; for him, work in the collective was simply a
job, and he "made politics" at citizens' committees or by taking part in de-
monstrations in his free time. His view was that a collective is mainly good
for the collectivists themselves, and this view was widely shared by those
who did not represent their collectives in the outside world for example, by
writing newspaper articles or broadcasting.

The second statement tends to imply "any work in a project already as a
political action" (Makowski 1984:16). It corresponds to the image collective enterprises present in public, though fewer collectivists dare say now
that they are providing a yardstick for social change. Those who believed
that collective work had a political significance — either because it proposed
new relations of production as an alternative to the established onesor because it promoted an ecologically sound product — claimed, however, that
they did not see themselves as leaders in the process of social change. They
did not want to repeat the mistakes of the 1970s, when left-wing party members had tried to activate workers by promoting themselves as the vanguard
of a forthcoming revolution. The idea of a consciousness-raising ideology,
which formerly held such a central position in propaganda and agitation, has
been abandoned in favour of "no ideology."

A member of the publishing collective *STATTbuch* summed up these
views:

> Doing something concrete here and now, that is the practical orientation of
> this movement.... We want to learn to give expression to opinions, hopes, de-
> sires, information, goals, knowledge, and we no longer let others do this for
> us. We oppose domination. We do not want to have anyone in our power, and
> we do not allow anybody to exercise power over us. (Jungk and Müllert
> 1980:176)

Collectivists referred to sets of ideals held in common which they wanted others to share. But they consciously rejected any theory or system of thought systematically imposed on other people. In their work, they intended to experiment with different forms of cooperation, hoping to find solutions that could point the way to a new society.

In fact, their concept of "no ideology" in the sense of ideas growing out of practice corresponds to the quality Burawoy, following Althusser, attributes to "ideology." He maintains that it is lived experience that produces ideology and not the other way around. Ideology is rooted in and expresses the activities out of which it emerges (Burawoy 1979:18). In their striving to give impetus to the creation of a new social order neither do they contradict Gramsci's definition that qualifies historically grown ideologies as a "creation of concrete phantasy which acts on the dispersed and shattered people to arouse and organise its collective will" (Gramsci 1975:869).

The ideals they considered can already be found in the radical social utopias of antiquity, such as the *Sun Island* of Jambulos where in a fabulous natural environment utopian society was organised according to collectivist ideals: a life of peace and harmony, the abolition of private property and the division of labour, and the regular rotation of tasks (Bloch, E. 1982:568). Many of the Berlin collectivists' ideas resembled Robert Owens' 19th century thoughts about utopian communities. His belief was that small federated communities whose members were involved in establishing close human relations without the division of labour, even between town and country, and without bureaucracy would spread and change humanity (Bloch, E. 1982:650).

The utopian communities of the past, such as *New Harmony* in Indiana, the only Owenite community, or the religious community *Oneida*, founded in 1848 by Noyes, were stimulated by politico-economic criticism of the established social order but held the belief that major improvements could become possible here and now and did not require major political upheavals (Kanter 1972:62). Unlike these, the collectivists intended their example to be a stimulus to radical political change. For them, the collective experiment as such did not represent a major change in itself but simply pointed in the right direction. Unlike those utopian communities, which either followed a charismatic leader or strived to put into practice a fixed set of pre-established ideas concerning the perfect institutional structure of the community (Kanter 1972:6), the collectivists experimented with structures, constantly changing them in order to move toward the desired result: the "model collective" or "concrete utopia." This model should be as perfect as possible for the collective developing it and adapted to its particular situation. Other collectives were not intended to imitate it but to be stimulated by its example to develop their own structure adapted to their own situation.

Four Ideal Types of Collectivist

Of the thirty-six collectivists who I interviewed concerning their political histories, only six had no previous political experience at all. The others had all participated in one or more political organizations. They had been organized in parties of the extreme left (nine people interviewed), in trade unions or action groups on the shopfloor (seven), in feminist groups (four), in environmental politics (two), in university politics (six), and in student Christian associations (three). Some had been squatters (three), another had attended an experimental school for adult pupils, and another was a political emigrant from East Germany. Compared to other social groups, these people had a very high level of political consciousness; they judged contemporary German society more critically and were more ready to participate in political actions to defend either their own or others' interests.

Nevertheless, not all collectivists were equally motivated when they joined. Some had virtually no alternative, others were dissatisfied with their previous work situations, yet others hoped to make a special contribution to a more ecologically based society, and a few believed they were setting up a model, a real utopia, that would provide an impetus for overall social change.

The Aussteiger *(Drop-out)*

The German term *Aussteiger* does not have the same negative connotation as its closest English translation, "drop-out." *Aussteiger* refers to someone who consciously decides to opt out of a social system that he or she finds insupportable. For different reasons, Friedel, Conny, and Thomas all belonged to this category. They started to work in collectives because they found it impossible to become integrated into the official labour market.

After working for ten years as a toolmaker in a West German enterprise, Friedel came to Berlin to live with his girlfriend and two children in a squatters' house. He looked for a job but could not find work in the trade he had learned. Employers turned him down because, with his long hair, he looked too like "a guy who would bring too much disorder to the firm." The only job he could find was as a toolmaker with *Siemens*,[3] but he was compelled to leave after a disagreement with his Yugoslav colleagues, who were offended by his going to lunch with an unskilled Turkish labourer who had far lower status in the firm's hierarchy than the skilled Yugoslav toolmakers. When Friedel visited *KoMet* for the first time, he was immediately offered a place. In 1984, he was still enthusiastic about work in the collective and had no wish to return to a business enterprise.

> I hate all that's straight. Here you can work much more freely and pleasurably. If I produce a piece of work I know who it's for and why I'm doing it. This is something you would not know under normal circumstances.... This is no ordinary job here. You have to identify with it. If you don't, you'd better leave it alone. (Friedel, *KoMet*, 15.8.1984)

Conny was a teacher who, whilst training, had been a member of a Maoist student group. She was banned from her profession for two years because of her political convictions. After taking her case to court, the ban was revoked, but she was only able to find temporary jobs and finally became unemployed after a disagreement with the director of her school. In 1983, she was living in a communal household (*Wohngemeinschaft*), separated from her husband, but raising their child jointly with him. She worked in the *Fahrrad-Büro*, as she said, partly for fun and partly out of necessity.

> I got the job purely by chance. I was unemployed when I met Ulrike, whom I knew from the *FahrradBüro* self-help day, in a pub. I asked her whether by any chance they had a shortage of young talent, and she said they needed two more people. So I decided to have a go. My dream has always been to be a motor mechanic, not because of the cars but because of the technical aspects. That's something a woman is not supposed to learn about, either at home or at school, while it's the done thing for a boy of fifteen to take apart his pistons and cylinders himself. I enjoy fiddling about with my hands, but I am not at all keen on getting involved in any big political debates here. (Conny, *Fahrrad-Büro*, 17.1.1984)

Thomas started work as a printer with *Oktoberdruck* because he could not find any other printing job after finishing his traineeship. After slowly acquiring some work experience in the collective, he left for a better paying job in an ordinary enterprise. In an interview in 1983, he said:

I got the job here through two people from the printers' trade union, Andrea and Donald,[4] when I was unemployed after finishing my apprenticeship.... The real advantage here is not so much the work itself, because to a certain extent you have to work much longer hours under worse conditions than in an ordinary job. The actual advantage is that you're not working for other people, you have the final say regarding your own work.... If I eventually make a change, it will be for technical reasons, because I want to get to know other, bigger machinery, which we do not have in the collectives. (Thomas, *Oktoberdruck*, 13.7.1983)

Friedel, Conny, and Thomas dropped out of the system of regular employment either because of a lack of formal qualifications and sufficient work experience or because of conflict with the established authorities. They turned to work in collectives because the criteria for recruitment there receive different emphases, with personal sympathy and the capacity to work independently being considered more important than formal qualifications or previous experience. Indeed, the fact that a prospective collectivist had been in opposition to authority and held strong individualistic opinions concerning work-style and aims was a welcome characteristic.

In an economic situation of increasing unemployment, ordinary firms and the State as an employer have a wide choice — even among qualified workers — and tend to select and keep those workers who seem most loyal to the employers' interests. With a scarcity of work, even among experienced workers, young people and the inexperienced have the greatest difficulty getting started in the careers of their choice.

In Britain, this situation has led to the establishment of state-sponsored cooperatives to provide employment, especially for unskilled and inexperienced young people. The encouragement of cooperatives by the CDA (Cooperative Development Agency) is a feature of the even more stringent labour situation in this country. However, in Berlin, genuine need and lack of alternatives is only one, and possibly the weakest, motive for joining a collective. Only a small minority of collectivists have actually been unemployed, and even those who have been so involuntarily still tend to possess a better education and higher qualifications than the average unemployed young person in Germany. For the latter, the collective is scarcely a viable alternative as they lack the minimal qualifications for joining an established collective and also the minimal capital for setting up a new one. The situation was different in Britain in the beginning of the 1980s when central or, more usually, local authorities provided state-sponsored cooperatives with initial fixed and movable capital and advised members on their operation. The subsequent structure of these cooperatives depended to a large extent on the political orientation of their sponsors and advisors, ranging from common ownership with equal salaries to strongly hierarchical cooperatives. In Berlin, collectives depended mainly on their members for their initial financing, and the members therefore determined the organisational structure.

The members who joined a collective mainly because they were unable to find any other job are often pragmatic about the work. They try to avoid conflicts, have an aversion to long discussions, and support efforts to increase pay and reduce hours. For them, collective work does not embody any message for social change but, rather a solution to personal problems.

The Dissatisfied Worker

Wolfgang, Noppe, and Donald joined collectives because they were dissatisfied with the monotony of their previous work situations.

Wolfgang, a skilled toolmaker with ten years' experience and a member of the Social Democratic Party (SPD), left his job in an ordinary firm because he wanted to care for his small child while his wife worked full-time in her own hairdressing business. He criticized his former working conditions, maintaining that everything — from the drawings to the planning of the step-by-step production — had been imposed on him.

> I did not get on very well with my colleagues, because they were mostly much older and had the usual political convictions. I often quarrelled with them. The foreman and the boss interfered in my work. They wanted to impose their own ideas about how to do it. I would be given a ready-made drawing and a finished construction, and I was more or less told what order to do everything in. (Wolfgang, *KoMet*, 15.8.1984)

When his child was old enough to go to nursery school, Wolfgang joined *Ko-Met*, which one of his former colleagues had co-founded, because of the independence it allowed and the possibility it offered of acquiring new skills.

Noppe had worked as a toolmaker for seven years in the same firm where he served his apprenticeship, which he began when he was fifteen. Originally from a working-class background, he became a member of a shopfloor action group (*Betriebsgruppe*), independent of the trade unions, set up by former university students who had become workers in order to advance the class struggle. When the action group was dissolved, following the loss of most of its members through dismissal or return to university, Noppe left the enterprise as he felt relationships with his remaining colleagues had become increasingly dull.

> I wanted to leave straight after my apprenticeship. Then I got involved in this action group. When that fizzled out I was no longer keen on working in a firm where I had a secure job but where the social aspects were increasingly dull. After that I repeatedly stayed away from work on the pretext of being ill. The days when I could not bring myself even to go to work became more and more frequent, although the work was easy and we had a lot of breaks. Finally I went away on holiday, and from there I sent in my notice. (Noppe, *KoMet*, 8.8.1984)

Through acquaintances in his political activities, Noppe heard about the establishment of a toolmaking collective, *KoMet*, and joined. In 1984, he was the last of *KoMet*'s founders still to be working there. He enjoyed the company of the other members, the independence he had in dealing with technical problems, and the fact that he could gain insights into the administrative functionings of the enterprise.

Donald was, in 1983, *Oktoberdruck*'s most experienced printer. Before joining he had worked for many years as the second printer on the large press where he had served his apprenticeship. Bored by this very limited job, fed up with the hierarchical organisation of the work, he left to join a collective.

> I quit because of the total control, and the hierarchical division of labour between first and second printer .... and I was almost always second printer. On the rare occasions when I was first printer, there was always somebody trying to land me in a mess. And at some point I'd had enough. (Donald, *Oktober-druck*, 14.7.1983)

Donald said he was satisfied as his new job included five times the number of tasks he had been allowed to carry out in the large printing firm, with its high level of division of labour. He increasingly participated in the processes of decision making for the whole collective and also planned to gain insight into the production aspects of the repro-mounting department.

Wolfgang, Noppe, and Donald were experienced and qualified workers who could easily have found jobs in an ordinary enterprise that would have paid them twice as much as they were earning in their collectives. However, they decided to leave their secure jobs and work in collectives instead. For them, this decision meant sacrificing a certain amount of material comfort and even accepting longer working hours.

Most collectivists do not have such heavy financial obligations as their counterparts in industry, though, who may have dependent families and may be repaying loans on cars and houses. Generally, the lovers or spouses of collectivists do not depend financially on their partner, and both contribute to providing for eventual children.

When speaking of their previous work situations, Wolfgang, Noppe, and Donald described them as monotonous, constraining, and lacking in any possibility of gaining an overview of the entire productive process and of the functioning of the firm as a whole. They said they had been unable to relate to their work, as every step had been precisely prescribed for them. When they returned home in the evenings, they had tried to forget as quickly as possible what they had done during the working day. In spite of this, they had been interested in the technical requirements of their work and had wished to learn more about them but had found it impossible to satisfy their curiosity and initiative.

They became aware of an alternative through friends and acquaintances who were already working in collectives or who knew of them. Although some of them had participated in left-wing political groups — Noppe, for instance, on the shopfloor and Donald in the youth organisation of the printers' trade union — their decision to join a collective was an individual one that did not meet with their colleagues' approval.

Trade unionists generally denounce collective enterprises as capitalist firms under collective covers. They accuse collectivists of self-exploitation and of lacking solidarity with employed workers because they pay themselves wages below the agreed scale and often work unpaid overtime, thereby entering into "unfair" competition with those fighting for higher wages and shorter hours in business enterprises. For the trade unions, intercompany agreements on wage rates and hours are considered to be a success because they strengthen the unity of the labour-force, whereas the independent policy of collectives would weaken their position if they made a significant impact on the labour market.

Only a minority of trade unionists support the idea of workers' self-management, which touches on the crucial issue of workers' control over the production process. This minority is now starting to have an increasingly intense exchange with members of collectives and worker-managed enterprises. The leading union figures in the *Daimler Benz* shopfloor group, *Pla-kat-Gruppe* — well known for their commitment to workers' control and the conversion of their output from military equipment to socially useful products — were even excluded from the Industrial Union of Metalworkers in the summer of 1984.

Skilled industrial workers who join collectives, and even those who take over their run-down firms and try to continue them as self-managed concerns (such as the *Voith* workers in Bremen), are still the rare exception. The large majority of industrial workers believes that the issues of the quality of work and control over the production process have to take second place to the problems of increasing unemployment and diminishing purchasing power. The few worker-managed firms in West Germany still have a very good reputation among collectivists, although few of them believe that their own firm could become an alternative for most ordinary workers.

Wolfgang, Noppe, and Donald were privileged compared to the average worker as they possessed qualifications that were still in demand on the labour market, while their personal situations allowed them to live in reasonable comfort on a relatively low income.

The Ecologist

This type of collectivist is motivated by a particular concern for the ecological destruction of the environment and for the deterioration of personal relationships in large cities like Berlin.

Ulrike worked as a teacher for four years, while she was still very young. She hated her job because she felt that she was not given the opportunity to teach her pupils anything useful and that they were fawning in order to get good marks. At the age of twenty-six, she left teaching and joined the *Fahr-radBüro* in order to learn a useful technical skill and to be with people who "do something instead of just talking." She was convinced she was doing more meaningful work by helping to promote a sensible means of transportation and its conscious use.

It is very important that we all work in the bicycle shop because we are convinced that the bike is the right means of transport and that its use improves the quality of life. None of us would sell cars or motorbikes. We, or rather I, stand by this work. I think it makes sense. In a normal bikeshop people are only concerned with selling. We also have to make our living from this work, but we want more than that. (Ulrike, *FahrradBüro*, 16.12.1983)

Ulrike taught customers and pupils at evening classes how to repair their cycles themselves and fought hard against the development of power relationships within the collective. "Cooperation should be based on friendship" was her conviction.

Mathias had a degree in environmental technology and was very active on citizens' action committees for environmental politics. During his studies, he started to oppose the role of the type of engineer who, like a worker on an assembly line, invents new technologies without ever questioning their utility or their effects upon the people who would use them.

> The utility of technology is not questioned by the people who produce it. For example, you can produce a bike that is excellent to ride, or one that sells very well, or one that is manufactured very easily from the point of view of process engineering. These are the different aims to which the technology is subordinated, and the actual riding of the bike ranks last. (Mathias, *FahrradBüro*, 22.5.1984)

Mathias was convinced that the development of a technology that was comprehensible to those who would use it and that protected the environment would revolutionize the engineering sciences. Although for him work in the *FahrradBüro* was only a transitional job while he prepared a research project, he was interested in the combination of technology and environmental politics that it offered. According to him, the bicycle could raise the critical consciousness of its owner, impelling him or her to exert pressure on the manufacturers to produce machines that could be easily repaired. He was conscious, however, that in the interim they remained dependent on mass production and could only choose from the output of this.

During his studies of German language and politics, Bernhard participated in the same citizens' action committee as the founders of the *Fahrrad-Büro* but joined the collective only after it had been running for a year and could pay its members an income. At that time, he considered it a "natural continuation" of their concept of traffic politics, which radically opposed the use of cars in the inner city.

We came together in opposition to the highway, trying to develop a different concept of traffic politics, and the bike was part of that.... We did not have any direct effect, but we did influence certain things: change in the way of thinking about the importance of the bicycle, about a different type of traffic politics. Today all this is no longer current in the *FahrradBüro*, and also it has become rather superfluous because there are plenty of other traffic initiatives. (Bernhard, *FahrradBüro*, 19.1. 1984)

Bernhard felt nostalgic as he thought of the first years of the collective when, as he said, strong common interests and sympathy united its members, a common basis he now missed.

Ulrike, Mathias, and Bernhard had limited political concern, which focused on the protection of the environment. They were not organised as part of any political party with the aim of overall social change but participated in citizens' action committees that denounced and opposed specific ecological problems. Nevertheless, they believed the causes of these problems were escalating and the reason for the destruction of the environment by man himself lay in large scale industrialisation and its use of a technology that has grown beyond the human scale. Small-scale local initiatives would make it possible to re-establish a conscious exchange between people and their environment.

These collectivists tried to influence their customers to become more conscious of the environment in their daily lives. They told them about the advantages of cycling instead of motoring and encouraged them to learn to repair instead of throwing things away. Members of *Baubüro*, a collective of construction engineers, explained to their clients the danger of chemicals used in the building trade, while members of *Wuseltronick* suggested systems of decentralized energy production and reduced consumption.

However, the primary intention of all these people was to create a different environment for themselves, establish satisfactory personal relationships at their places of work, and then extend these to their clients. The intellectuals among the ecologists had suffered because during and after their studies they had been unable to apply in practice their ideas about society, and, therefore, they cherished the opportunity to actually develop a lifestyle about which they had speculated in theory.

The Revolutionary Utopian

These collectivists are probably the ones with not only the most radical but also the most utopian convictions. Their intention in setting up collectives was to establish models for new relations of production with a view toward bringing about fundamental social changes.

Fritz, who for years had been a member of a Trotskyist organisation, abandoned his studies of urbanism in order to train as a toolmaker and work in industry. By the end of his apprenticeship in a small toolmaking firm, he had revised his conviction that "the working class was bound to be the revolutionary subject" that was going to transform society. Instead, he wanted to come closer to his ideal of a free society by setting up a self-managed enterprise.

In 1981, during an early phase of the collective *KoMet*, he wrote about his concept of self-management:

> Self-management is the opposite of a representative model and it is incompatible in its essence with any other form of dominion. It is the basis of a free social order in which everybody owns the possibility and capacity — but is also confronted with the need — to take responsible decisions about his own interests and those of the social domains by which he is affected. (Fritz, *KoMet*, February 1981)

For Fritz, to work in a collective meant to experiment here and now with this future social system. The collective was to become a model that would give impetus to those outside it and would receive criticism and incentives in return.

Several years later, he came to realise that the equal sharing of responsibilities did not work in his collective and that it was he himself who took more decisions and carried out more of the disagreeable jobs than any other member.

> This joint has burnt me out. Very often I bore the brunt of certain jobs, and I did them because nobody else would. This was certainly a mistake, but I had no choice. Also it was usually me who had to be responsible for the problems in front of the customers. I have to get out of here. (Fritz, *KoMet*, 13.8 1984)

Marita was trained as a chemist and decided after several years of work to complete her A-Levels (*Abitur*) at a self-managed experimental school for adult pupils in the *Mehringhof*. Here, at "the centre of alternative activity," she became familiar with collectives. After working for a year in several different enterprises to get back into contact with ordinary people, she started work with *Oktoberdruck* as a bookkeeper. For her, collective work meant opposing the dominant social system with an alternative mode of coop- eration based on equality. The model developing in the collective, she thought, could become a yardstick for change that would incite larger parts of the population working in small- and medium-sized enterprises to strive toward self-managed forms of production.

Uwe worked for several years as an urban planner in parts of West Berlin that have acute housing problems. Simultaneously with his official job, he participated in citizens' action committees for better housing and advised tenants on their rights. The contradictions between the official planning poli- cies and his political convictions made him leave and search for work in a more practical trade.

He became one of the founders of *KoMet*, although he was not a qualified metalworker. He wanted the collective to become a model for decentralised and non-hierarchical production that could be extended to larger sectors of industry.

> I am in favour of an economy where the quality of the product plays a more im- portant role. Where good quality products are cared for, instead of shoddy goods that are soon thrown away. I am in favour of an artisan-style mode of production, maybe not that different even from the medieval guild system, where quality was monitored and competition limited... I have not thought so much about how to influence the relationship between production and consumption, but what I do know is that I reject any form of compulsion."
> (Uwe, *KoMet*, 17.5.1988)

The new social order Uwe wanted to initiate was to be the opposite of a synchronized society and was to consist of individuals with equal rights who could fully develop their differences.

Fritz, Marita, and Uwe thought that a radical change had to take place in the existing social structure. They used the word "revolution" to designate this change, although they no longer meant it in the Marxian sense, namely, through the revolutionary power of the working class. They aspired to bring about this change themselves. Their concrete plan for change was limited to one aspect of the social order that they considered crucial: working together in a self-determined way. In their efforts to conceive what they called a "concrete utopia," they wanted to show that different relations of production were not only feasible but already operational in the collective, which was to become a model for the future.

> The different ways in which we direct our attempts make them like a model.
> We have to display our endeavours in public to show the possibilities of orga-
> nising humane working and living conditions, and to get new impetus for our
> own discussions, widening our views beyond the limited scope of "the
> scene." I consider it very important to demonstrate the practical functioning
> of these new forms and to show not only the new quality of these attempts but
> also the ensuing difficulties. (Fritz, *KoMet*, February 1981)

Collectivists who share this far-reaching motivation tend to be influential
figures in the collective, if not among its founders. They often regard collective work as the hub of their lives, and sometimes as a substitute for their previous political activities. They are ready to sacrifice a successful career in
business because they believe in the principle of collectives. They are
conscious that their utopia cannot develop in isolation because the enterprise
is imbedded in the larger economy, but they tend to attribute its success or
failure to the strenght or weakness and level of commitment of the members,
rather than to external economic constraints.

The four ideal types outlined here are not mutually exclusive. Some collectivists could fit into more than one category, while others formerly belonged to one but now fit into another. Fritz, for example, lost confidence in
the "revolutionary" role of collectives and ultimately viewed the work simply in terms of his own position. However, the four ideal types are useful in
exemplifying the four basic categories of motive, which occur repeatedly in
collective enterprises and which explain some of the tensions that arise between members with very different aspirations and expectations.

Generational Turnover and Wearing Out of Utopian Ideals

The decision to work in a collective implies the choice of a certain lifestyle.
Incomes are extremely low: the average monthly income of a male worker in
the German metal industry in 1983 was about DM 2,650 gross, which is
about DM 2,000 net (*Statistisches Jahrbuch*, 1984), while the average
monthly income of a collectivist at the same time was between DM 1,150 and
DM 1,250 net [5]. So on joining a collective, members must adapt their standard and style of living accordingly. Most collectivists lived in communal
households (*Wohngemeinschaften*), where expenses for food, heating, and

rent were shared, and they had few external obligations. At the time when I conducted my interviews, no collectivist, to my knowledge, had to help support elderly parents, few were married, and any children were provided for by both parents.

The sense of allegiance to the collective, and the motives for working there, differed between older and younger members. The large majority of cases studied in 1984 comprised older collectivists, between 30 and 35 years old. The younger members, those between 22 and 26 years old, represented a maximum of 25 percent of the total number. The age group between 26 and 30 years was almost unrepresented. The average age was 32 years. Explanations for this striking age gap can be only tentative, as my sample does not permit definite answers to this question, but the data point in the following direction.

The older members grew up and were educated during the 1960s, in a period when established authority was being strongly questioned. These anti-authoritarian ideals were then introduced into the collectives. A large percentage of the members left socially valued professions, such as teaching or research, or better paid jobs, for example, in toolmaking or printing. Their choice of the collective style of work was motivated by criticism of established work situations, by a more or less well-developed political analysis and by some previous professional experiences.

The younger collectivists, on the other hand, are part of the "baby-boom" generation, born between 1959 and 1965, which is now seriously affected by increasing youth unemployment that blocks their access to a professional career. The job in the collective was often the only one they could find after finishing their apprenticeships, and they often joined a collective without having a clear picture of the work situation involved.

I would hypothesize that the 26 to 30 year-old group, which was so underrepresented in collective enterprises, was too young to have been influenced by the upheavals of the 1960s student movements and too old to have been seriously affected by the current youth unemployment crisis.

Collective ideals were mostly upheld by the older members, who stimulated the others. The younger members did not have equally pronounced political intentions; far younger than the founders, they were still trying to find their political and professional orientation and took work in a collective as a starting point only. Otto and Thomas, for instance, who were in their probationary period when I conducted my fieldwork, had heard of *KoMet* through an article in the journal *Der Spiegel* and had moved from West Germany to

Berlin expressly to obtain jobs there. Otto had difficulty finding work in his profession as a toolmaker because the employers in his native rural area refused to consider him because he was a conscientious objector. Otto and Thomas found it exciting to work with *KoMet* and thought it quite normal that there should be some members who had greater experience than others and so told them what to do. "There are no bosses, there are just some people who know more than others and its natural that we should listen to them," commented Thomas on the authority debate.

In the demanding building-up phase, the cohesion of the collective group depended to a large extent on the personalities who upheld utopian ideals. When this idealism weakened, differences among members tended to appear, though the areas of conflict did not necessarily coincide with the ideal types described earlier. When material conditions did not improve considerably, despite sacrifices of time and money, increasing consumption needs became a crucial point of conflict.

The lifestyle of some of the older members changed over time. They entered into stable relationships, had children, and therefore began to experience higher consumption demands. Some of them also felt the need to take up a socially recognized career. The turnover in membership accentuated the differences between generations of collectivists and between different political backgrounds. Responding to the attitude of the younger members and the changes in the developmental cycle of the older ones, the structures of collectives became characterised less by political idealism and more by a pragmatic self-consolidation.

Gunter (1982:379), analysing the replacement of ideas of utopian, "phantastic," socialism, after the first ten years of the Russian October Revolution, with "Scientific Socialism," calls this process the "wearing out of utopias" (*Utopieverschleiß*). He attributes the decline of utopian thought to an "eschatological delay, the "postponing of the expected communist condition" (Gunter 1982:378). Utopian dreams of ideal social and state institutions, of communism in production and consumption, were replaced by an enthusiasm for scientific work organisation, the Russian version of Taylorism (Gunter, 1982:382). In the Berlin collectives, the "wearing out of utopias" led to a stronger preoccupation with the systematization of the structures of production, and the creation of associations, networks, and organisations to defend the economic interests of collective enterprises. The cohesion and continuity of these enterprises is increasingly maintained by these structures rather than by common utopian ideals.

Notes

1. *STATTwerke*, derived from the word *Stadtwerke* (municipal services); *statt*, however, means "instead."

2. In order to complete this outline of the politics of *Die Grünen* and the *Alternative Liste*, it must be mentioned that they follow a policy of Third World development, which questions consumption habits in industrialized countries. They are also in favour of leaving NATO as they regret the logic of military blocks and strongly support the peace movement.

3. A large West German corporation producing machines electrical and electronic equipment.

4. In 1983, also members of *Oktoberdruck*.

5. A female worker in the metal industry earned DM 1,944 gross, a male print worker DM 3,000 gross and a female print worker DM 2,016 gross per month in 1983 (*Statistisches Jahrbuch* 1984) plus holiday payment, paid overtime, and a thirteenth monthly salary.

4

Political Consumer-Producer Relations

The creation of alternative economic networks — optimists would call it a "counter economy" — is not only one of the political aims of most members of collectives, it is also an economic necessity. One of the basic political aims shared by most collectivists is to transform the anonymous money and commodity transactions of the capitalist system into personal relationships between individuals. They wish to sharpen the critical attitude of consumers toward the product they are purchasing and the way it was produced. Their utopian ideal would be an economy where producers and consumers share the same interests and act in a complementary way. The inherent opposition of the capitalist market economy — with, on one side, consumers wanting high quality and low prices and, on the other, manufacturers striving for high profits — should be able to meet in a consensus without passing through the mechanisms of competition.

Alternative Forms of Financing

Most of the pioneering collective enterprises started in 1977 or 1978 with almost no initial capital. Members' friends and acquaintances helped with their personal savings to cover the most pressing capital needs, and many of the founders contributed all their own savings — and sometimes even a legacy — in order to set up the enterprise. Almost none started by having a long-term bank loan or a credit line. The first machines the collectivists used were second- or even third-hand, discarded by innovative business enterprises and often more than ten years old. This outdated technological equipment gave the enterprises a considerable handicap in getting started, and the members had to compensate by accepting low pay and long working hours.

Almost all the older collectivists reinvested in its entirety the money that was made during the first one or two years, while themselves subsisting on unemployment benefits or student grants.

The only loan available to set up an enterprise that cannot give surety of a reasonable amount of initial capital is the *ERP* (European Recovery Programme) credit system. This is intended to encourage enterpreneurs to set up businesses in economically and geographically disadvantaged areas, such as West Berlin and the border regions with East Germany. The *ERP* credit system, which draws on financial funds from the Marshall Plan, is accorded to individual enterpreneurs who are starting a business that promises to be profitable. Small enterprises asking for this form of credit should have the legal status of a *GbR* (*Gesellschaft bürgerlichen Rechts* or partnership) as the credit has to be taken up at the level of personal responsibility of the enterpreneur.

Collectives applying for *ERP* credit, as *KoMet* and *Wuseltronick* did, had to put forward two of their members as "entrepreneurs" and "owners" of the enterprise. This formal arrangement did not cause many problems for *Wuseltronick*, as the members in whose names the credit was acquired remained with the collective until after the money had been repaid. For *KoMet*, however, problems arose when both members who had been named as the formal borrowers left the collective after one and two years respectively — one of them, Hans-Christian, after a disagreement. He threatened to dissociate himself from the credit arrangement, thereby ruining the enterprise, unless he was paid DM 10,000 compensation. The collective had no choice but to comply with this.

Netzwerk

Finding alternative forms of financing, or gaining access to bank loans, has been a concern for collectivists and their sympathisers since 1977 and 1978, the years marking the commencement of many collective enterprises. In 1978, an alternative fund, *Netzwerk*, was set up to support alternative activities that were not assisted by state money and to provide payment for the political and social activities of teachers subject to a political dismissal from the civil service.

Since its foundation in 1978 until 1984 alone, *Netzwerk* has distributed no less than DM 2.5 million in loans and contributions to a wide range of projects. These range from the engineers' collective *Wuseltronick* to Turkish immigrant newspapers; from art exhibitions to the *Grey Panthers*, a radical initiative for old people. Most of the contributors to the fund are relatively well-off academics and those in liberal professions who have agreed to make a monthly contribution corresponding to one percent of their income (STATTbuch3 1984:716).

Only one year after its foundation, the alternative fund came under heavy attack from contributors and recipients alike. The advisory board[1] choosing the projects to be supported was accused of bureaucratisation and of losing contact with the those who contributed to and those who profited from the scheme. Representatives of alternative projects, and in particular the productive collectives, wanted *Netzwerk* to become a coordinating institution for collectives, in which only projects that were themselves eligible to be sponsored made the decisions concerning applications. The majority of *Netzwerk* sponsors, on the contrary, wanted to keep control over the purposes for which their money was used and wanted direct contact with the projects they were choosing to sponsor. The first general meeting of *Netzwerk* contributors was attended by several hundred people and evoked heated debates. The active involvement of contributors and projects has lessened considerably since then. While *Netzwerk* had 3,630 paying members in December 1982, membership had fallen to 2,066 by December 1987 (*Netzwerkrundbrief* 2.5 1988).

The amount of money *Netzwerk* can offer to productive collectives is generally insufficient for their capital needs. Since the summer of 1983, when a group of six female members of collective enterprises attempted – unsuccessfully – to get themselves elected to replace the acting managing committee and to make *Netzwerk* an instrument of the collective enterprises, the collectives have lost interest and turned for financial help and advice predominantly to the alternative advisory office *STATTwerke*. In August 1987, however, *Netzwerk* established its own advisory service for self-managed enterprises.

STATTwerke: *Direct Credit Procurement*

STATTwerke emerged out of an initiative by students of the economic, political, and social sciences at the Free University of Berlin, who had participated in the compilation of the first *Stattbuch*, the alternative directory for Berlin. Since the autumn of 1982, they have organised courses in bookkeeping and business management for members of collective enterprises, and since

STATTwerke booth at the Frankfurt Collectives Fair. Marlene, one of the founding members, is counseling a potential new collectivist (photo by author).

1983, they have acted as mediators between private sources of credit and collectives. In May 1984, they already had offers of DM 1.1 million, of which more than DM 250,000 was allocated to collective enterprises. Up to August 1985, they had provided DM 1.5 million for collectives, including shops and agricultural, service, and housing enterprises. In the meantime, however, the initiative was prohibited by the federal supervisory board for credit (*BAK: Bundesaufsichtsamt für das Kreditwesen*) because it was acting as an "investment business."

Credit procurement was aimed at creating a direct link between sources of credit and collectives in need of finance, thus overcoming the anonymity of ordinary banking transactions. In actuality, it attempted to institutionalise direct political support to collectives by means of low-interest credit from friends and supporters. The aim was difficult to realize, though, as only 25 percent of the creditors lived in Berlin, where 50 percent of the collectives in need of credit were concentrated. The procedure for mediating credit put great emphasis on personal choice. The potential creditors filled out a questionnaire in which they detailed the financial conditions under which they would give credit and the type of collective they would prefer to support.

Creditors seemed to prefer financing ecological farms and traditional handicrafts as Michael, a member of *STATTwerke*, pointed out: "They still follow the cliché that collectives should exclusively practise ecological agriculture and unalienated manual labour." Most creditors sponsored the collectives that *STATTwerke* proposed, therefore it was ultimately the *STATTwerke* members who determined the criteria according to which credit was provided. For credit of less than DM 50,000, *STATTwerke* invited members of the collectives needing loans to attend an informal discussion in order to find out "intuitively" whether or not they were organised as a collective. Only if higher credit was requested was the legal charter of the collective concerned checked to prevent ordinary enterprises profiting from the extremely low interest rates (3 to 6 percent) that the creditors were willing to accept. "Neutralisation" of collective capital was to be as secure as possible, so that individual members of collectives could not exploit the goodwill of their creditors for their own private gain. *STATTwerke* usually took only one percent of the sum provided, to cover its costs. Michael feared, however, that *STATTwerke* might deteriorate into a mere service agency if the collectives did not participate more fully in its decision-making processes.

This type of credit-giving created privileged access to cheap capital resources for the collective enterprises. The creditors voluntarily forewent a large proportion of the interest they would have received if they had taken out long-term savings agreements with an ordinary bank. However, the political ambition that underlay the initiatives of *STATTwerke* went further than the procurement of cheap credit for collectives:

> It would be possible to develop a completely new system of finance, through which the creditor would keep direct control over the use that was made of his money. Such a method of finance could approach the political goal of abolishing alienation. Decisions about loans would be made according to people's preferences concerning the specific products their borrowers were going to make and the system of organisation of production they would adopt. In this way, individual preferences would have a much stronger influence on the market allocation of resources than is possible through purchasing decisions alone. It would be interesting to know whether preferences revealed by lending decisions are different from those revealed by purchasing. Whether, for instance, the same people who give credit to an ecological bakery would eat "King Corn" bread, or whether people who support bicycles as a sensible means of transport would give money to a metal-working collective that produces moulds for the car industry. (Michael, *STATTwerke*, 16.5 1984)

In fact, Ulrike, a dedicated member of the *FahrradBüro*, gave DM 10,000 from her personal savings as credit to *KoMet*, which produced, among other things, moulds for the car industry. She decided to support *Ko-Met* because of its collective organisation of production, despite the fact that it did not manufacture ecological products although, as we will see later, it was unsuccessfully striving to do this.

The Ökobank

The next step in the creation of an alternative economic infrastructure was the establishment of an alternative bank, the *Ökobank*. The idea was born out of a boycott campaign against banks involved in arms deals and in trade with South Africa. At the alternative fair in Frankfurt in the summer of 1984, an association called "Friends and Sponsors of the *Ökobank*" (*Freunde und Förderer der Ökobank e. V.*) was charged with the task of raising the necessary initial capital. When the bank opened for business almost four years later, on 30 April 1988, more than 12,000 associates of the cooperative bank had raised the initial capital of DM 7.5 million (TAZ 2.5.1988).

The bank's foundation was preceeded by intense discussion among those involved in the alternative scene who questioned its principles. The activists of the *Ökobank* association confronted the staff of professional bankers who were to run the bank. While the former wanted a self-managed decentralised bank with democratic structures, a true "instrument of a counter-economy," the latter had to build up a structure according to strict German banking law, which implied for example that the bank manager had to have the ultimate authority. The Federal Supervisory Board for Credit (*BAK*) authorised the opening of the bank on the condition that the total volume of credit transactions was restricted to three times the equity capital (whereas in ordinary banks it can be up to eighteen times the equity capital). The established cooperative banks, members of the national Association of Cooperative Raiffeisen Banks (*Bundesverband der Raiffeisen Banken*), were even more skeptical toward the newcomers than the *BAK* was and will not allow them to become members of their deposit protection fund until they have proved over several years that they intend to be serious bankers. Since Raiffeisen founded, in 1864, the first cooperative bank, the *Heddesdorfer Darlehenskassen*, to safeguard the existence of peasants and small producers in the face of growing industrialisation, cooperative banks in Germany have become well-established but increasingly inflexible.

The special feature of the alternative bank, which distinguishes it from all other cooperative and ordinary banks, is the creation of structures that allow the investors a say in the use to which their money will be put. The bank offers specific long-term savings policies for financing predetermined sectors of the alternative economy and culture. The investor can give priority, for instance, to women's projects, projects for the protection of the environment, or those set up by the handicapped, and their money will be used accordingly. An advisory board, comprised people involved in the alternative scene, work out the details for these particular savings arrangements.

The objective of the bank is to become an instrument in the hands of politically motivated investors who want to promote an alternative economy and culture. In this perspective, the investors are called on to decide whether they are willing to receive a lower rate of interest on their long-term savings. For the wealthy supporters of an "alternative economy," this bank will probably only become a secondary deposit for their long-term savings, to be used as credit volume for alternative projects. In its building-up phase, the bank needs dependable borrowers and cannot run the risk of financing vanguard projects with no security. The bank's alternative principles depend, in fact, upon the "renunciation of interests" (*Zinsverzicht*) in order that it may eventually be able also to assist financially weaker projects and collective enterprises. Ordinary firms will be given credit at the normal interest rate as long as they do not produce goods (for instance for nuclear power stations or armaments) that contradict the ecological principles of the bank (*Contraste* April 1988:8).

Party and State Money: The Ökofond

Most members of collectives regard it as essential that collective enterprises remain independent from state funding so that their economic destiny does not depend upon the grace or disgrace of the government in power. In 1983, however, the Social Democratic party (SPD) and the party *Die Grünen* formed a coalition government in Hessen and set up a fund of DM7.2 million for the year 1984 to further "alternative economic funds." A rush for this money became imminent.

To avoid fierce competition between collective enterprises for the small amount of resources to be distributed, a committee of twelve representatives from all over Hessen was formed to discuss with the deputies of *Die Grünen* the use that should be made of the money. The members of the committee agreed that no new jobs should be created as long as some of the existing ones were still without social security payment and financed by unemployment money. Conflicts arose, though, as to whether the money should be shared with cultural and social projects, and whether it should be distributed in the form of grants or loans.

Members of collectives in South Hessen, who had in the meantime founded a union to represent their interests, insisted that absolute priority should be given to productive collectives and that the money should be used for developing ecological products, initiating credit with low interest rates, and helping build up the advisory activities of the union. As the collectives from North Hessen disagreed with this, the committee's discussions became increasingly irreconcilable, and no request for money was dealt with before the 1984 fiscal year ended on 5 December (Bergmann, 1984:11). *Die Grünen*, however, threatened to cease cooperation with the Social Democrats in November 1984, and the alternative fund was seriously endangered. It was saved only because eventually the two parties decided to continue their alliance for a further two years.

In the towns of Düsseldorf, Erlangen, Nürnberg, and Bremen, where *Die Grünen* formed part of the local governments, special funds were set up either for "alternative projects" in general, including cultural and social initiatives, or for encouraging the creation of jobs on the local market, regardless of whether the enterprises were collectives or not. In applications for these public funds, the regional *Netzwerke* often played the role of intermediary between the public authorities and the collectives, a role that to some extent revived the activities of the *Netzwerke*, which had diminished considerably. In Berlin, the new Senate formed by a coalition of the Social Democratic party and the *Alternative Liste* in February 1989 contributed DM 10 million to a credit guarantee association set up by *STATTwerke*, which assumed liability for private and bank loans to collective enterprises. This association, which had also received DM 1 million from the Protestant church and *ERP*-countersecurities, was one of the cornerstones for securing "Direct Credit Procurement."

The structures of collective finance, confusing as they might appear to the external observer, all have several common characteristics: in particular, they rely on the commitment of political supporters, and they try to make collectives as independent as possible from state and bank intervention. Especially in this last respect, alternative collectives distinguished themselves quite clearly from cooperatives in Britain, which depended in the beginning of the 1980s for financial support mostly on the state-funded Cooperative Development Agencies (CDA). Nascent British cooperatives applied through the regional CDA for founding and equipment grants, the level of which depended upon the sympathy of the regional authorities towards cooperative ventures and upon the number of jobs they would create. In 1982, for example, a toy-making cooperative in Lambeth received 13,783 Pound Sterling to set up an enterprise with seven workers.[2] The CDAs gave advice on the financial set-up and on the legal charter. Depending upon the political orientation of the agency, this advice pushed cooperatives toward adopting hierarchical or strictly egalitarian structures. As a "sensible occupation for young people on the dole," cooperatives in Britain were even advocated by the Thatcher government. They also fitted in well with the Conservative ideology of "workers having a stake in business" — profit-sharing was seen as the best incentive to work (Wajcman, u.p.:6).

In a socialist economy such as Yugoslavia, it was the rule that labour-managed enterprises were initiated and encouraged by governmental bodies, which determined the organisational form and decreed that property in capital and machinery must be socialised. Before 1965, a Yugoslav firm had to pay 60 percent of its income to government agencies, which then distributed it as credit and subsidies to the enterprises they wished to encourage (Comisso 1979:73). After 1965, this tax was reduced to 30 percent, and the autonomy of the firms increased considerably as they now had to bear the consequences of their business decisions in the form of profits and losses (Comisso 1979:74). As a consequence, tensions arose between the planned and market elements of the Yugoslav economy. As the capital: labour ratio began to vary considerably from firm to firm, the incomes they could offer also differed. Skilled workers were attracted by the wealthy firms, whereas the poorer ones lost out in the competition. The weaker firms, which were not competitive in the market, claimed state protection, while the more successful ones demanded greater market freedom, but at the same time also tried to profit from state support (Comisso 1979: 213).

The role of the state in respect to investment is subject to debate among theoreticians writing about labour-managed firms. Criticizing the actual Yugoslav labour-managed economy, Vanek sees an egalitarian political and economic system compromised by the increasing differences between firms and regions. He wants investments to be entirely financed from outside (Vanek 1977:172). Enterprises should contribute to a national fund, which would then set up new firms, equilibrate the capital-labour ratio in the national economy, and free the enterprises from the obligation to reconcile diverging interests with new investments.

More cautious in their assessment of external financing by banks and government authorities, Eger and Weise (1978:168), warn that labour-managed enterprises might lose their self-determination. While the workers are tempted to shuffle off some of the capital risks to the lenders, the credit-givers in turn want to keep control over the economic rentability of the enterprise. The firm is often obliged to submit to control mechanisms that interfere with its internal organisation. The British women's cooperative at Fakenham, for instance, was at first sponsored through loans from Scott Barber Cooperative Association on condition that a male director be employed (Wajcman 1983: 64).

Technological Standards and Competition

The degree to which collectives accept innovation and accumulation as "natural" laws of the capitalist market, which they must follow if they are to survive rather than ignoring the logic of the market altogether, can be used to differentiate collective enterprises and their market strategies.

In discussions between members of collectives with a low level of investment and those with a high one, the members of the "poorer" collectives readily claim that they are following the purer line because they make fewer concessions to the capitalist market and do not accumulate capital. Members of the "wealthier" collectives usually reply that not to replace old machinery means running down the enterprise.

Collectives like *Oktoberdruck*, *KoMet*, and *Wuseltronick* set out to compete on the open market with other business enterprises. *Oktoberdruck*, in particular, made large investments to raise the level of the technology to that of their competitors, and is now trying to enlarge its circle of customers to make the machines pay for themselves. Collectives like *agitdruck*, *Contraste*, and many others prefer to produce for a circle of politically inspired customers. They do not invest in new machines and therefore have fewer fixed costs. Without holding money in reserve, they basically live "from hand to mouth."

In the spring of 1984, at one of the *Lundkreis* [3] (the weekly meetings of Berlin collectives), the different standpoints were put forward in a heated discussion. Members of collectives had come together to discuss a request from the *Alternative Liste* to outline their economic interests in, and political standpoints on, an economic programme for West Berlin. A controversy arose over the question of Berlin subsidies (*Berlinzulagen*), subsidies of 30 percent granted to Berlin enterprises if they invested in new machinery. Members of financially weak collectives demanded that these subsidies should be abolished, as they favoured only those enterprises capable of buying new machines and placed at a disadvantage enterprises like their own, which bought exclusively second-hand equipment. They denounced this law as being a typical offshoot of the society of consumption, which subsidized the throwing away of old machines that still worked and could still be used. They argued that encouraging investment in more modern technology would only lead to rationalizing still more jobs out of existence and demanded that the subsidies for modern technology should be replaced by money for each new job created.

The better-funded collectives, and *Oktoberdruck* in particular, which were regularly replacing their machines as soon as they became outmoded, judged these subsidies to be important for any Berlin enterprise. The subsidies conferred advantages that were badly needed if a Berlin concern wanted to compete in the West German market. Their argument was strictly in terms of market-logic, a logic the poorer collectives fundamentally contested.

The discussion developed into a clash of principles. Referring to the ideological quarrels inside the party *Die Grünen*, the conflict was expressed in terms of "fundamentalists" against "realists." The fundamentalist current of the party, grouped around Rudolf Bahro, called for a radical change in social and economic structures without any compromise with the "System." It called for consumption abstinence and a radical opposition to the squandering of resources. The realists argued that change was only possible progressively and only if they managed to survive in the "System," thereby encouraging the population with practical examples of successful change.

Two Opposing Business Strategies

The split of *agitdruck* in 1974 is probably the most striking case of a collective being divided over the question of competing on the open market. The split created two independent enterprises, which have followed entirely opposite business strategies for fourteen years.

Even in 1972, the members of the small printing collective *agitdruck* were divided in their attitude toward investments. Two members who were studying printing engineering, Marlis and Constantin, wanted the enterprise to accept more orders for printing books and to switch from the occasional production of leaflets, booklets, and small newspapers to a more regular workstyle. They were investing more time and energy than any of their colleagues, for the other members did not regard printing as their career but based their professional prospects on their university education. For the latter, on the contrary, the printing of left-wing literature turned away by business printing shops, and the unpaid work for the political groups they were supporting, meant a contribution to the political struggle, not a job to earn a living. Furthermore, the collective charter established that priority was to be given to the members' studies. Members who were taking examinations continued to be paid without being obliged to work, and the usual work week was 20 hours.

When, in 1972, at the insistence of Marlis and Constantin, a second-hand R20 printing press was purchased for DM 20,000, the pressure of work increased. The student members, who had initially objected to this investment, were especially critical, saying that the incoming orders were becoming more commercial and that the production process was being subdivided. As most of the members worked part-time, the coordination of larger orders was difficult. Work on orders was started by some members, who had the relevant instructions direct from the customer, but had to be finished by others, who did not. The result was low quality products and a stressful work situation.

Nevertheless, a year later Constantin insisted on a fresh investment in a new and more powerful printing press worth DM 125,000. In a paper which he presented to the collective in the spring of 1973, he explained his reasons:

> Work in a collective is also work under capitalist conditions, as it means producing for the market. Because of the constant technological progress of our competitors, it is necessary to replace old machinery in order to survive. The socialist elements in *agitdruck* are limited to the printing of material for political propaganda and to a collective method of production and appropriation of the surplus. As a result, market mechanisms cannot be neglected, as left-wing customers go to capitalist printing firms if they are cheaper.

Constantin felt he was wasting a great deal of time producing commercial orders on the old, slow machines, and he was ready to put in a period of hard work to pay off the investment in new machinery. However, his argument did not meet with the approval of the other members. When he realized his inability to convince them, he and Marlis ordered the new machine behind their backs. This breach of collective conventions was answered by exclusion. Marlis and Constantin had to leave, taking with them the new machine and the accompanying financial obligations.

Printing as a Political Contribution: Agitdruck

For the past sixteen years, *agitdruck* has continued to exist without changing its attitude toward investments. All revenues from the enterprise are passed on directly to the members without setting aside any reserves for the replacement of machinery. The collective survived in a market-niche, printing mainly propaganda material for left-wing and, later, ecologist customers, who did not expect high quality products. Only a few members were capable of producing reasonably good quality output on the old printing presses; none had professional training, and in addition, the old machines were malfunctioning.

The collective would probably not have survived at all had it not become a victim of persecution in a 1978 political campaign. Having printed an extreme left-wing newspaper, *infobug*, which examined the use of violence in political action, the four printers were sent to prison for eight months. Their sentence was heavily criticized in liberal and left-wing circles, and the persecution of *agitdruck* became known throughout Europe as an example of West German censorship. Its case was supported by the *Russell Tribunal*, and large contributions were collected to continue the enterprise while the printers were in prison. In the meantime, the collective was run by former members who came back to help out. From the money collected, a new printing press was purchased, and the collective was for months well supplied with orders from left-wing publishers.

The ties of *agit*-members to "their" collective were marked by a great sense of generosity. A former member of *agitdruck*, Sabine, who had worked with the collective from 1972 to 1975, came back in 1978 to keep up production while the *agitdruck* printers were in prison. She worked for a year without taking any money from the collective, living off unemployment benefits, and even gave her signature as responsible for the bill for the new printing press.

Following the 1978 crisis and the subsequent period of relative economic success, no major improvements were made to the enterprise's technical equipment. Members who suggested the need for further investments were accused of "Constantinism," meaning putting the economic interests of the enterprise before its political ones. The majority still regarded their work there as a temporary occupation and did not want to be burdened with the financial obligations that would be incurred by purchasing new equipment. Those who wanted to make a career out of printing did not stay long, and those who remained were unskilled, so that the economic situation was frequently unstable. It only improved during large political campaigns, such as that against the population census of 1983/84, when the campaign organisors had a large part of their material printed by *agitdruck*.

Since the end of the 1970s, *agitdruck* members have ceased to divide their time between work and study. In 1984, they were working full-time for a monthly salary of DM 1,000 net, about DM 300 less than the *Oktoberdruck* printers earned. Despite this change, the business strategy remained basically the same.

Competing on the Open Market: Oktoberdruck

The investment policies of *Oktoberdruck* were influenced over the years by its founder, Constantin. From 1974 to 1978, he, together with his friend Dieter, was the only associate of the company. The central core of three founders — the third being Marlis, who did not have the formal status of associate — made the investment decisions, although sometimes up to twenty-four people worked in the enterprise. The other workers were treated like ordinary employees and were paid salaries as per tariff. They were mainly members of the Trotskyist group *TLD*, which *Oktoberdruck* supported with cheap printing facilities.

In 1975, the enterprise purchased an A1 two-colour, or perfecting, *Miller* printing press for DM 250,000. This purchase heavily indebted the collective as it did not possess any financial resources of its own. It was helped, though, by the 32.5 percent Berlin subsidy. From 1976 to 1977, the order inflow was excellent, as *Oktoberdruck* was printing the local newspapers *Zitty* and *Tip*, and the feminist journal *Courage*. The owners had to employ professional printers who knew how to operate the *Miller* press, which was run in shifts to make it pay its way. The enterprise was flourishing with the growth of the newspapers but was spending too much on salaries as the number of workers was constantly increasing. But in 1977 the newspaper *Tip* had become so large that its organisers decided to switch to a printing shop with roll offset. *Oktoberdruck* thereby lost one of its most important customers at a point when its financial obligations exceeded its reserves. However, the other newspaper, *Zitty*, filled the gap with its own growth, and the order inflow remained good until the financial insolvency of June 1979, as a result of which the firm had to be entirely restructured.

The present *Oktoberdruck* collective started in 1980 from the ruins of the old one. Only part of the newspaper *Zitty* remained a customer of the new collective, which disposed of the advanced technological equipment of the former enterprise and of a rather secure circle of customers. Constantin stayed the nominal owner of the *Miller* printingpress and all the equipment that the collective rented from him, this rent allowing him to repay the outstanding debts. As it was working with professional machinery and had indirectly taken over the financial obligations, the collective had right from the start to adopt a professional work-style. At the end of 1981, it purchased a smaller two-colour *GTO* printingpress in its own name, which was of the same technological standard as the *Miller* press. A new *Miller* press was purchased in exchange for the older one and remained Constantin's property. New members were chosen from among professional printers; two shifts at the *Miller* press were maintained; and the standards of quality were set comparatively high.

Oktoberdruck's customers came from much wider circles than those of *agitdruck*. Among them were publishers issuing photobooks and artprints, which required high quality printing. Even the left-wing publishers began putting greater emphasis on aesthetic criteria as the market for purely political literature became narrower. *Oktoberdruck* competed directly for their customers with ordinary business firms. For this purpose two members, Marita and Donald, went in October 1983 to the annual Frankfurt bookfair. They returned home with new contacts with prospective customers and the firm conviction that continuous advertisement was necessary in order to survive.

The Trademark: Creating a Market Niche

The specific links members of collectives establish with their alternative customers go beyond mere economic exchange. Favours and services, and the pursuit of common political aims, make these relationships multilayered and long-term, approaching what Blau has called "social exchange," characterized by unspecific obligations that "involves the principle that one person

"Could you please pay this time within three or four months! We are starving!"

does another a favour and while there is a general expectation of some future
return its exact nature is definitely not stipulated in advance... Only social
exchange tends to engender feelings of personal obligation, gratitude and
trust that purely economic exchange as such does not." (Blau 1964:91)

   While contemporary market transactions are dominated by depersonal-
ized economic relations, the collective enterprises build their market strategy upon the reintroduction of values of utility and morality. In offering
trustworthy product information, special repair services, and toleration for
delay in payment, collective practice is not very different from the customer
service of certain small modern business enterprises. The difference, however, lies in the common political aim of collectives and their politically motivated customers to create mutually supportive relationships in order to promote the production of socially and ecologically useful items and to favour
collective structures of production.

   To reduce competition and form a common stand against business enterprises that may intrude into their market niche, collectives form unions and
are planning to agree upon a collective label. Collectives of the same branch,
whose potential customers look for the services of a "collective" for political
reasons, have a far greater need to form unions and delimit their identity by
using trademarks than collectives producing for ordinary customers and bu-

siness enterprises.

Only a few months after their separation, *agitdruck* and *Oktoberdruck* ceased competing with one another and agreed to cooperate. Four new printing collectives have since been founded, and *Oktoberdruck* is one of those equipped with the highest technology. For all these printing collectives, politically motivated customers were, to a greater or lesser extent, the basis of their clientele, since some of the radical left-wing publishers have also taken to producing artbooks and novels. For printing collectives like *agitdruck*, there still seems to be more "value" in printing a leaflet for a political group with which they sympathize than in producing a commercial book. Printing collectives like *Oktoberdruck*, however, seem to have developed a more professional pride in the perfect completion of a difficult order. *Oktoberdruck*'s circle of customers is courted, too, not only by business enterprises but also by one of the new collectives, *Bloch und Partner*.

When *Bloch und Partner*, with their high-quality machinery, started to become a serious threat to *Oktoberdruck*, both groups decided that regular meetings of all six Berlin printing collectives should be called to convert latent competition into cooperation. In the first sessions in 1983, they compared prices, turnover, and results and tried to ascertain the advantages or disadvantages of their respective organisational forms. It was concluded that each would send customers they were unable to serve to one of the other collectives. They decided to make advantageous purchases in common and to keep each other informed about opportunities to buy second-hand machinery from bankrupt firms.

However, a conflict arose in the summer of 1983 after Constantin heard of a bankrupt screen-printing enterprise that was for sale at an extremely low price. He tried to find people willing to take it over as a collective but met with resistance from the only other screenprinting collective in Berlin, *Graph Druckula*, which dreaded a competitor and wished to buy the rundown enterprise's powerful screen-printing machine for itself. Without consulting *Graph Druckula* any further, Constantin found six unemployed printers, with little experience in screen-printing, who were willing to work together without having previously known one another. Constantin organised the purchase of the firm with money from the leasing society (see chapter 5).

The new collective, *akut*, became the first to be founded largely on the initiative of an outsider. However, the attempt almost failed when one of the most experienced members left it. Hidden tensions with *Graph Druckula* continued until the new collective turned to it for help and advice. *Graph*

Druckula then realised that *akut* was addressing a rather different circle of customers, as it was printing on much larger formats. It then readily offered to check their screen-printing machine and to advise them on the purchase of colours and papers.

When *Oktoberdruck* proposed to introduce a label for all printed goods produced collectively, relationships between the collectives became strained. The *Oktoberdruck* printers hoped that this label would encourage publishers with left-wing customers sympathetic toward collectives to give them preference when placing orders. However, the collective *Bloch und Partner* objected that they might lose customers — instead of gaining more — if they had to produce under the same label as *agitdruck*, which was known for its low quality output. They argued that products from alternative enterprises should be of high quality in order to prove that collectives were able to produce as good if not better quality output than ordinary firms. The discussion about the label for collective products reached an impasse as *agitdruck*, the oldest printing collective, could not be excluded.

The number of printing collectives in West Berlin is still sufficiently small so they do not inhibit each other seriously in the market and are able to turn their latent competition into cooperation. The situation is more severe, however, among the collective wholegrain bakeries. The first ones were founded in the mid-seventies by people wanting to promote healthfoods, and especially wholegrains, as a first step toward a more natural and healthy lifestyle. The bakery collectives multiplied considerably in the 1980s, and their products were increasingly imitated by ordinary noncollective bakeries. The result is an overcrowded market where each new bakery collective is felt as a threat to the existing ones.

In January 1985, the five bicycle collectives in Berlin, together with a number of West German bicycle collectives, founded a union that organises regular meetings and common wholesale facilities. By buying bicycles in larger quantities, they are able to obtain better conditions from the manufacturers and to be more successful in their own local markets, where they have to compete with a dense network of ordinary cycleshops. Some of the bicycle collectives were actively involved in traffic politics, which brought them the sympathies of ecologist circles and a stock of regular customers.

For the members of the *FahrradBüro*, the customers were their central interest, and the political aim of their work was to educate them in traffic politics, transmitting a critical attitude toward the product and a basic knowledge of the technology they were buying. Apart from the more politically aware customers, the people who preferred to buy the more expensive cycles in the *FahrradBüro*, instead of going to the cheaper department stores, were well-off, middle-class customers who esteemed the repairs service and honest advice available. They created a relationship of diffuse commitment and reciprocal obligation still typical of some traditional handicraft and neighbourhood industries that follow the maxim: "Honesty is the best policy" (Fox 1974 :157).

To help familiarise their customers with the simple technology of their bicycles, the collective gave them the opportunity to use the repair shop and its tools free of charge once a week and to repair their bicycles under the instruction of a collectivist. The members hoped their customers would develop a preference for goods and spare parts that could be repaired, instead of having to be thrown away at the slightest defect.

> Starting with the bicycle, a new consciousness could develop, a new approach to technology; we want to encourage a new stratum of buyers who are very critical in their purchases and who might influence the development of a different technology. So that we can pressure the wholesaler to sell, for instance, adjustable pedals instead of the non-adjustable ones, to pressure in turn the manufacturers, so that they at least make repairable parts. Another collective in the Waldemarstrasse held the principle of selling only good locks, because they took the view that bad locks were mere deceit. Now some customers want cheap locks, and I don't know whether I should relieve them of the responsibility for their purchase and spoonfeed them each time with information, or whether I should give it to them only if they ask. Information is also part of the self-help day, however, we don't get paid for giving information in this society. (Mathias, *FahrradBüro*, 22.5.1984)

The members of the *FahrradBüro* explained that they were trying to make an active contribution toward a criticism of "the society of waste" by repairing bicycles, or their parts, which other shops would not be willing to undertake. They did this despite the fact that it is much more profitable to sell an entirely new rear wheel than to spend two hours repairing its hubspindle. The department stores in the ward profitted from this attitude. As it is unprofitable for them to maintain a service section, they send their customers to the *FahrradBüro* to have their carelessly treated, low-quality cycles repaired, and they afterwards refund the customers for the cost of the repairs. The collectivists have to cope with the dilemma of, on the one hand, refusing to be exploited and, on the other, not wanting to turn away a customer with a broken cycle.

> There is no doubt that we repair bikes sold by specialized dealers. But it's get-
> ting problematic with the department stores and with *Eduscho*.[4] None of us is
> really consistent in that respect. Even Bernhard takes in the repairs if the cus-
> tomer stands in the shop with tears in his eyes. (Ulrike, *FahrradBüro*,
> 16.12.1983)

This attitude stands in striking contrast to what Gouldner regarded as one
of the specific features of economic exchange.

> Contempt for sentimentality is the hardening of the self to endure isolation in
> order that one's market options should not be pre-empted. (Gouldner
> 1971:387)

The special non-economic relationship between customers and collectivists
is two-sided. Not only do the customers support collectives even if they are
slightly more expensive or slower in filling an order, but the collectivists also
feel personally responsible for their customers, in a way similar to good traditional craftshops, which still have a personal relationship with their clientele and take pride in what they make or sell.

Producing for Ordinary Customers

There is no clear-cut boundary between customers who are politically motivated and those who are not. Most collectives serve both, though they generally prefer to produce for the "alternative market." The most recent developments have brought into existence collectives that coyly hide their identity
behind an entirely neutral name so as not to prejudice their chances among
ordinary customers. The printing collective *Bloch und Partner* is an example. Instead of choosing a provocative name like its fellow collectives *Oktoberdruck* or *agitdruck*, or a flamboyant one like *Graph Druckula* (derived
from the famous vampire, Graf Dracula), it selected the completely neutral
Bloch und Partners, which appears in every classified directory just like any
ordinary enterprise.

Another example is the newly founded cooperative for wind-energy and
electronics, which groups together *Wuseltronick* and three other collectives.
After long discussions, they decided to give themselves the conventional

name *Eutek*, derived from the Greek meaning "beautiful technology," which stands in striking contrast to the name *Wuseltronick*, derived from *wuseln* ("fiddle," "fumble around") and electronics. The new name — well designed to encourage respectable customers — promptly raised criticism among the other collectives working with *Wuseltronick* in the *Mehringhof*. They believed that the prefix "eu-" had been misused far too often in naming *Nazi* institutions for a collective to include it in its name. Furthermore, technology was not beautiful in itself but often quite the opposite. The cooperative accepted the criticism and promised to find another name. They finally decided upon the neutral name *Genossenschaft Berliner Ingenieurskollektive* (Cooperative of Berlin Engineers' Collectives).

There is no explicit rule about the customers collectives are supposed to work for, but there is a firm tacit agreement that they should not produce any military equipment nor output for the police force or the prison service. *Ko-Met* lost its most important customer in 1981 because they refused to build the mould for shaping the housing of a police walkie-talkie. *Wuseltronick*, however, entered in 1984 into negotiations with *Messerschmidt Bölkow Blohm (MBB)*, then the largest West German armaments combine, when it was approached by them to develop a power transmission system between a diesel engine and a windpowerplant for one of its subsidiary companies. The collective decided, with reservations, that they would enter into the deal only for the sum of DM 400,000 — far higher than their usual rate — and only if they remained the owners of the expertise. The contract would have filled their order book for the coming year, but ultimately it failed because the parent company refused to pay such a high price.

By negotiating with *MBB*, *Wuseltronick* violated one of the fundamental principles of alternative production. Although the product they were asked to develop was an ecological one, it meant transferring skills and expertise to a firm that was following "ruthless capitalist business strategies," including arms sales. However, instead of refusing the deal outright, they asked an excessive price. Being politically opposed to their business partners, they wanted to make as much money as possible out of them, asking, as it were, a politically motivated surcharge. They also justified their decision with the argument that the product itself was not harmful. They predicted that the production of wind-powered plants was not going to be profitable for *MBB* and that it would therefore not be able to transfer returns from this production to other, harmful ones. They did not treat *MBB* as an ordinary business partner for, when the parent company turned down the high price accepted by the subsidiary company, the collectivists refused to modify the amount asked. *Wuseltronick* finally developed the power transmission system in coopera- tion with the German car manufacturer *Volkswagen* and sponsored by the Federal Ministry of Science and Technology (*BMFT: Bundesministerium für Forschung und Technologie*) and by the Senate of West Berlin. Accor- ding to Eberhard of *Wuseltronick*, it was the long negotiations with *MBB* that had attracted the interest of the sponsors.

Nevertheless, when other collectives came to know of this, *Wuseltronick* was severely criticised, and the collectives working on the same floor in the *Mehringhof* called a meeting to discuss their business activities. *Wuseltro- nick*'s members justified their reactions by saying that they had acquired va- luable experience from their negotiations with *MBB*. They stressed that cer- tain business decisions had to be taken by the members as a body because they alone had to accept the consequences of these decisions. They also argued that it was difficult to draw the line between rejectable and acceptable pro- duction. Eberhard even maintained that "all productive activities inside the system were stuck in its filth." For the future, they were unwilling to agree to disclose their business deals beforehand but promised to discuss and explain them afterwards.

This did not cause the expected degree of trouble. Those collectivists who had come to severely criticize *Wuseltronick* and to lead them back to the "straight and narrow" were disarmed by feelings of helplessness, as they were able to offer no alternative market strategy. Only three years earlier, *KoMet*'s production of tools for the making of crown-caps stirred up opposi- tion in alternative circles; but in the meantime, the collectivists became more aware of the problems of having to survive in a market situation and seem more wary of criticising each other.

Toolmaking collectives like *KoMet* cannot choose their customers ac- cording to whether or not they produce ecologically sound goods. The mar- ket for industrial tools is narrow, and many West Berlin toolmaking firms have had to close down in recent years. Although *KoMet* members dreamt of their own "useful" products, in the meantime they made cutting tools for ma- chines that produced 200 plastic containers per hour, or moulds for the tail- lights of cars. One of the few customers with whose products they could iden- tify was *Mirotec*, a firm manufacturing dialysis instruments.

Business firms came to *KoMet* because the toolmakers were fast and flexi- ble in the execution of orders and willing to put in some overtime to attract and to keep promising customers. The businessmen seemed to enjoy being treated in a more informal way. It was not only the "alternative" clients who were used to addressing the collectivists by the informal "*Du*" and who were on first name terms with them. Some of the "bourgeois" customers felt at ease in the collective and enjoyed being shown the machinery or having a coffee in the kitchen. Some of the *KoMet* customers who were employed in well-paid positions in business came to relive their own left-wing pasts and admired nostalgically the collective forms of work. They became the most faithful and comfortable customers a collective could have.

The dilemma in dealing with ordinary business firms lies, for some collectives, in the fact that, even if they do a reasonable job for which they can be proud, this is then used for ends with which they disagree. The woodworking collective, *Moabit*, for instance, renovated an old building in *Kreuzberg* for a building society. The joiners enjoyed the task of preserving the old wooden structures, but they were upset about the building society's speculations, which would increase the rents on these premises to such an extent that the old tenants would be unable to remain in the flats.

Conclusion

Collectives have to balance their ideological aims carefully against economic profitability. Some collective enterprises, like *agitdruck* and the *Fahrrad-Büro*, managed to attract a stable circle of loyal customers, which protected them to a large extent from market pressures. Others, such as *KoMet*, had to rely on ordinary customers for their economic survival. Most other collectives tried to maintain a market-niche of "alternative" customers as their secure basis and open up toward ordinary clients to increase their profitability. They follow a similar economic strategy to the *Merina* of Madagascar, whose strategies for finding cooperators for agricultural tasks were analysed by Bloch (Bloch, M., 1973:83-85). The *Merina* use the labour of kinsmen as a secure labour force in reserve but try to engage as many nonkinsmen as possible to cultivate the fields. They can make a larger profit by manipulating these short-term contracts, but they try to uphold primarily the more stable and reliable kinship ties. The same is true for collectives, which have to keep up the moral links of political commitment if they want to be certain of reliable financial help from political supporters and of a stable circle of "alternative" customers. One of the basic principles upholding this morality is that the profits of collective enterprises cannot be individually appropriated.

The nineteenth century theoreticians writing on the economic behaviour of cooperatives agreed that their ultimate interest is to maximise the returns of their enterprises at the disadvantage of the consumers and that this tendency can only be restrained by putting them into competition with one another (Webb-Potter 1893:136; Oppenheimer 1922:131). The experiences of Berlin collectives contradict this assumption at first sight. However, Berlin collectives are still a small minority among enterprises of their trade, and they rely on cooperation between each other and on support from politically motivated customers for their survival on the market. On the other hand, the experience of the Yugoslavian economy, where labour-managed enterprises are dominant, showed that competition became critical and led to extreme inequalities and tensions when the government released its control over internal business decisions (Comisso 1979:74).

Notes

1. Composed of five representatives of projects, five elected contributors, and five contributors chosen randomly.

2. Malcolm, Hackney CDA: personal communication.

3. *Lundkreis* is the informal meeting of members of collectives, which organised national meetings and fairs and initiated the collective bulletin *contraste*. It was started by collectivists who had participated in an international meeting of alternative projects in Lund (Sweden).

4. *Eduscho* is a chain of coffee shops that sold extremely cheap bicycles for a few months to promote their coffee; customers had to assemble these cycles themselves.

5

Investment and Consumption

Collective property — machinery and equipment — should not belong to individual members of collectives as their marketable goods but should be used and controlled by them only as long as they work in the enterprise. If they leave, even after years of work, they are not allowed to take with them any share in the "neutralised" (*neutralisiert*: not attributed to any owner) company capital, which should be exclusively used for production. This was the principle decided upon by most collectives at their foundation.

In building up the enterprise, maintaining and increasing its capital and improving the technological standard of the equipment, all members have to forego earnings that would have been spent on immediate consumption. The capitalist opposition between capital and labour expresses itself as the opposition between investment and consumption. Tensions arise between those members whose aim is to expand and build up the enterprise and those who want a decent salary now and do not care so much about investments for the future.

This contradiction appears in all labour-managed enterprises in which the equipment and capital funds cannot become the private property of the members but is "productive property" which can be used but not sold. If an investment is to be entirely self-financed, capital for new purchases has to be accumulated by members who may then have left the enterprise by the time the new equipment is bought. The readiness to forego personal spending for collective accumulation differs considerably, depending on personal commitment, consumption habits, and the length of time a person expects to remain in the enterprise.

Over the years, some collective enterprises have acquired considerable wealth through the efforts of their members. Some are now worth several hundred thousand German marks, a sum which is not great for a medium-sized firm but which represents many times what any of the members has ever privately owned. Problems of private appropriation arise when members leave the collective to become reintegrated into the dominant economy and its logic of private ownership.

Legal Forms of Collective Property

"Abolition," "neutralisation," and "socialisation" of property were frequently used concepts among collectivists — who owned hardly anything — and among intellectuals — who sympathised with the idea of an alternative economy. One of the latter, Marlene Kück, defines neutralised property as "no title to property at all, neither individual nor collective. The enterprise belongs to itself and the staff holds it in trust" (Kück 1985:23). In the beginning, the few resources possessed by enterprises were not generally claimed as the private property of any individual. The accepted principle was that "the owner is anyone who works here." This principle, however, was not secured by any corresponding legal form in the German legislation applicable to enterprises. Most collectives, therefore, were set up with one or more formal owners, in the conviction that the principle of "socialised" property would be respected. A deep-rooted suspicion of the existing legal system and the rejection of "bourgeois laws" made collectivists think of legal forms as administrative chicanery.

The first model project to develop truly socialised property was *Mehringhof*, a complex of old factory buildings in Kreuzberg. It was bought in 1978 for DM 2 million to become a centre for alternative activities. Today, *Mehringhof* houses thirty-eight projects, ranging from a school for adults, a theatre, and a printing collective to the electronics collective, *Wuseltronick*. The money for the purchase was donated anonymously by wealthy sympathisers. *Mehringhof* took the legal form of a company with limited liability (*GmbH*); it did not belong to named owners and was managed by the assembly of tenants, who paid rent to the society for the maintenance of the buildings. The tenants made common decisions about the admittance of new tenants, rent increases, and joint maintenance work.

Although the productive collectives admired *Mehringhof*'s model, they were unable to imitate it as they had no donated initial capital. Most of the collectives started with almost no initial capital at all. They went through a slow process of accumulation, having to rely on small gifts and loans from friends and relatives. They used second- or third-hand machinery and compensated for their lack of capital by investing their own unpaid labour. Most could not obtain ordinary bank loans as they were unable to offer sufficient guarantees. Neither were they able to choose the legal form of a company with limited liability (*GmbH: Gesellschaft mit beschränkter Haftung*), as to do so minimum equity capital cover of DM 50,000 is required. The most widespread legal form taken by collectives was that of *GbR (Gesellschaft bürgerlichen Rechts*), the society of civil law.[1] For this, no initial capital had to be raised but all associates had to use their private property as a guarantee. Associates of societies of civil law had the legal status of employers, had no social insurance, and had their incomes taxed at the same high rate as company profits. Because of these disadvantages, generally only one or two of the members became associates. They were the formal owners, financially responsible, while the others had the status of employees.

Although in most collectives all members initially agreed that this legal arrangement would be simply a formality — everybody was paid the same net wage and therefore felt themselves to be equal owners of the enterprise — the real legal owners had more effective power than other members and often felt more responsible for the enterprise and its financial success. To a large extent, they were the informal spokesmen and initiators, more at ease in dealing with other organisations. The legal status of owners not only reinforced their position as informal leaders, but sometimes led to them transforming the collective into their own private enterprise. The short history of alternative enterprises is full of examples of formal owners becoming the actual ones. Describing a conflict over property in a West German community, Jarchow and Klugmann (1980:35) review the problem: "The conflict made obvious to the others that the community had been built on personal feelings — and therefore, in the case of conflict, built on sand. When feelings and relationships no longer coincided as in the past, somebody had to go — and it would not have been the owner."

Many of the present collectives have learned from the negative experiences of their predecessors, and accord greater importance to the legal form they adopt. Some collectives have now changed their legal status to that of a society of limited liability. With this status, all members can become associates as well as employees, and this legal form provides a certain protection of company property against the individual claims of associates while also protecting the individual members against outside claims in the event of the enterprise's financial collapse. Special clauses can be inserted into the charter that make unanimity or a three-quarters majority necessary to dissolve the company. But, as the whole charter can be changed, these clauses cannot protect the property of the collective once and for all from privatisation.

Unlike British legislation, West German law does not make provision for protecting from private appropriation enterprises that are not privately owned. The legal backup the Berlin collectives wish to achieve, to guarantee democratic decision-making and "socialised" property, exists in Britain in the legal form of "common ownership cooperative," introduced by the Labour Government in 1976 (Industrial Common Ownership Act, 1976, Chapter 78). This prescribes that the enterprise is wholly owned and controlled by its workforce. Outsiders are not allowed to own a share in the firm. Each member has one vote and one share worth one pound only. Cooperative property cannot be acquired for personal gain, and if the enterprise is sold the money has to go to a charity. Although even this legal form does not provide a complete guarantee against private appropriation — members can, for example, decide to pay each other such high salaries that the cooperative capital is used up — it protects the collective principles if the majority of the members remains dedicated to them.

The legal form in Germany that comes closest to the British common ownership cooperatives, the *Genossenschaft*, [2] has been increasingly adapted to the form of a shareholding company (*Aktiengesellschaft*). In the *Genossenschaft*, provisions can be made so that each member, the minimum being seven, has only one vote in the general meeting of the shareholders, consequently a leaving member cannot take out more than his or her nominal share. However, the amendment to the legal form of *Genossenschaften* in 1973 included the possibility both of a plural vote and of paying interest on invested capital. The general meeting of shareholders lost its authority to issue directives, and the autonomy of the executive board was reinforced in a manner similar to that of a shareholding company (Flieger 1984:258). These last two legal conditions have proved incompatible with the democratic principles of collective enterprises. The attempts of most collectives to have their democratic charters accepted by the cooperative union (*Genossenschaftsverband*) were rejected because they had accorded overriding authority to the general meeting.

The cooperative unions, the senior organisations grouping all *Genossenschaften*, are today dominated by the large *Genossenschaften*, such as the cooperative banks *Raiffeisen* and *Volksbanken* and the cooperative retail chain *Konsum*, which function in a similar way to ordinary shareholding companies. They are not very interested in the integration of small, economically weak members with radically left-wing views. They are afraid of losing their reputation for respectability and therefore examine very closely the viability of every enterprise wishing to become a *Genossenschaft* (Flieger 1984:259). Numerous newly founded collectives have been unable to overcome this resistance.

However, the beginnings of the cooperative movement in Germany were much more radical. In the nineteenth century, *Genossenschaften* were considered one of the past achievements and present pillars of the labour movement. Although at the end of the century they were discarded by the socialist party as irrelevant for furthering radical social change, a few continued to exist in a more or less pure form until the National Socialists came to power and eliminated them. The years of *Nazi* rule destroyed the structures and traditions of the cooperative movements. Some consumer cooperatives were founded after the war, but they never gained the same political importance as the earlier ones, although they were economically successful.

The cooperative movement in Germany started in the nineteenth century on a very small scale and was seriously undercapitalized. However, as Oppenheimer (1922:71) points out, the small size of the *Genossenschaften* was an important factor in their success. Small groups with fewer than twelve members lasted longer and were less caught up in the "iron law of transformation" into capitalist enterprises (Oppenheimer 1922:64). Many *Genossenschaften* developed slowly into associations of entrepreneurs, as the sharing out of profits was exclusively linked to capital shares, not to work performance. If a member left, he or she could still remain an associate, or even sell his or her share for a higher price. So after a few years of fluctuating workforce membership, many shares were held by people no longer working in the enterprise. If the *Genossenschaft* became affluent and able to pay a high dividend on its shares, the members became reluctant to divide the profit between more associates and therefore restricted access to the shares by employing wage-labour instead. Less profitable *Genossenschaften*, on the other hand, had many members but few of them were actually producing; in addition, they employed a few wage-labourers.

In both developments, the capital became dissociated from the labour. The surplus produced by the members and nonmembers who were actually working in the enterprise was largely taken by nonworking associates. This emergence of new capitalists is what Oppenheimer (1922:16) means by the "iron law of transformation," suggesting that the cooperative movement had done nothing to better the lot of workers as a whole. In 1892, of the seventeen German *Genossenschaft*, only one had kept its ideal form with all the workers as shareholders and all the shareholders workers. Oppenheimer (1922:163) proposed that working in a *Genossenschaft* should be closely linked to being an associate, so that shares in the profit should be distributed according to the work done and not according to the capital brought in.

The present collectives in West Berlin are structured in the way that Oppenheimer would have approved of. They follow the principle that everybody who works in the enterprise must become an associate and loses his right of ownership if he stops working. Capital brought in does not "work." It is not remunerated but paid back with simple bank interest. As no formal legal structure exists to embody these aims, collectives have started to experiment with complicated legal constructions, such as leasing societies, associations acting as holdings for societies of limited liability, *Genossenschaften*, composed of several collective enterprises.

The collective daily newspaper *die tageszeitung*, for instance, consists of four societies of limited liability, all of whose capital is controlled by an association of trustees composed of the permanent working members and of people who work occasionally for the newspaper. The relatively high initial capital needed to start a daily newspaper was raised through donations, collections, and later, by subscription; this is now considered "socialised" property, which means that it does not belong to anybody. The actual working members do not own it; they manage the finances but cannot sell the newspaper or any part of it without the consent of the association. The weak points of the structure, however, are the societies of limited liability, some members of which have to be shareholding associates. They might be able to claim their purely nominal share as private property if they contested this in court. According to the collective's accountant, fortunately, nobody had ever thought of this possibility, let alone attempted to put it into practice.

To protect the property − machinery and equipment − from financial breakdowns and private takeover bids, members of the alternative advisory office *STATTwerke*, together with Fritz of *KoMet* and Constantin of *Oktoberdruck*, founded a collective leasing society in 1983. Collectives can become members by donating their machinery to the society or by purchasing new machines through it. After a probatory period, the collectives then lose direct property rights over their machines but can still decide to replace them with new ones. The maintenance of old machines and the purchase of new ones is financed by the leasing rates paid by members to the society.

Members must respect certain organisational principles: they are not allowed to employ wage labour, they should not have hierarchical structures within the collective, etc. Breach of collective conventions, such as attempts to privatise collective property, entails the confiscation of the invested assets without compensation. Up to 1988, only two collectives had joined the leasing society, one because of serious financial difficulties and the other to finance the machinery it needed to get started. Not even the collectives to which the initiators belonged, *KoMet* and *Oktoberdruck*, had become members, as they feared the extra administrative work involved when serving on the board of the leasing society and the possibility of losing control over their property.

West German business legislation protects the capital and its holders. Even if in a shareholding company, the owner of shares no longer personally takes part in the decisions of the enterprise; his interests are upheld by law and the almost impersonal capital shares are "served" with dividends. The law prescribes that the ultimate responsibility for and control over the enterprise lies with those who own it. Most collectivists, on the other hand, want to "neutralise" the property of the means of production and give control over the enterprise to those who work in it. If the primary aim of law in capitalist society is to "protect the sanctity of individual life and the sanctity of property," as Leach (1977:32) has pointed out, and if the most important goal of collective agreements is to protect the basic equality of the different individuals and to abolish property as capital and as an instrument of labour, then the two systems of values are contradictory. As Leach (1977:29) wrote, "Formal law presupposes the existence of a degree of public consensus which does not in fact exist." Although collectives do not move outside the law, as do the terrorists in Leach's example, they cannot protect their interests and values entirely by means of the legal system controlled by the state.

As Pospisil (1971:101) has pointed out, several legal systems can coexist within a single society and complement, supplement, or conflict with each other. If collectivists attempt to secure their concept of "neutralised" property against the dominant social and legal practice, they act on a different legal level. They can enforce their concept of property inside the subgroup composed of collectives and of their political supporters. But the sanctions they can use are "jural" and not "legal" ones — to use Radcliff-Brown's distinction (1952:205-211). Whereas the dominant West German law can be enforced by a tribunal backed by a monopoly of force, the ultimate coercive means a collective can employ against a deviant member is his or her exclusion from the group and exposure to ridicule and criticism in the alternative scene. When members break entirely with the collective ethos, they can switch back to the legal level. They can then try to impose the dominant social concept of private property through the courts, claiming that part of the collective property should be paid out to them individually.

The most common attitude, however, is to regard the enterprise's productive property as "neutralised," and therefore inalienable, and to allow for personal and alienable property in the members' private domains. Discussing the legal principle of inalienability of land and tools in early Roman law, Goody (1962:301) found a similar distinction between inalienable productive resources and alienable consumer goods. He pointed out that linked to land were certain political rights: the right to compose the domestic group and rights in residence that went further than the simple economic aspect of securing a livelihood (Goody 1962:298). The inalienability of the collective machines and capital has a similar political importance. A collective is regarded by its members as a "free enclave" inside the capitalist system, where they can experiment with economic and social relations that contradict the dominant social and political order. Or, as Andrea of *Oktoberdruck* put it: "The selling of a collective enterprise is a political mistake, it means giving an enterprise back to the "system" that has been conquered for the people actually producing." But, as private property is maintained in the domain of domestic consumption, tensions about the private or collective allocation of resources arise.

Immediate Expenditure Versus Long-Term Investment

Most collective enterprises are undercapitalised; they have few financial resources as reserves. As labour in a collective is not remunerated at a market-determined wage rate but is dependent on the residual of income over expenditure – as the economists Ireland and Law point out (1982:2) – a new investment in machinery or equipment often has the immediate consequence of reducing for months or years the money available for immediate distribution as individual income. To uphold product quality and productivity, old machines have to be replaced from time to time, as the capacity to compensate for low productivity rates with longer working hours is limited. Members are generally aware of this dilemma, though not always prepared to sacrifice part of their income or to work increased hours to pay for a new machine. "Self-exploitation" became a term not infrequently used in political discussions among collectivists. The question was repeatedly raised: if collectivists are certainly not being exploited by a capitalist who would benefit from the surplus they produce, are they not exploiting themselves by overworking? The tension between those members willing to invest and those reluctant to do so splits collectives, and the outcomes of these struggles differentiate enterprises that invest a great deal from those that do not.

The readiness of individual members to engage in long-term investment depends on a large variety of factors, from material constraints, the number of their dependents, and their consumption habits to moral and political considerations. Investments may be to the advantage of those members who expect to stay with the collective long enough to profit from the new investment and increase the quality of their products. Members who intend to stay for only a short time, however, must renounce a part of their income for the sake of future investments from which they will not profit, as any leaving member cannot take "his" part of the accumulated capital with him.

Level of Payout

Numerous collectives started out with their members receiving no pay at all for the first one or two years, or alternatively, being paid according to need, which meant that the scarce resources were given in preference to the most needy. Most members subsisted on unemployment benefits or student grants. After the first building-up phase was accomplished, the level of pay was generally set at DM 1,000 to DM 1,200 net,[3] a sum surprisingly similar in most Berlin collectives in 1983. This was little more than students with state grants had at their disposal (the maximum rate in 1983 being DM 750) and was certainly less than a qualified worker with a previous income of DM 2,200 net would have received in his first year of unemployment, when his benefits would have amounted to between DM 1,500 and DM 1,700. Most established collectives paid social and pension insurance for their members and made allowances of between DM 100 and DM 400 for childcare.

In spite of their comparatively low incomes, most collectivists were able to live quite comfortably. When they joined, they were often at the beginning of a settled professional and private life and had few obligations and low demands as consumers. Most were content to own a high-quality stereo system, a secondhand television, and an old washing machine. A few had a secondhand car, the cost of which they sometimes shared with another person. They liked to travel far but without spending a great deal on comfort. In the early years, many members lived in communal households with four or five other people. In the last couple of years, however, this tendency has started to reverse. Collectivists now tend to live alone or with one other person. But even in these smaller setups the costs of housing can still be comparatively low because many large low-standard apartments in old buildings still exist in West Berlin. A three-room apartment with coal heating costs between DM 280 and DM 350 per month.

For most of the founding members, work in the collective has been an intermediary phase between youth and adulthood. As their lifestyle has changed over the last few years, as they became engaged in stable relationships, had children, and developed higher consumption needs, they have turned to more financially rewarding occupations.

Contrary to the public image, which often conveys the impression of asceticism, members of Berlin collectives enjoy living well and surround themselves from time to time with an aura of extravagance. During my fieldwork with *Oktoberdruck* in the summer of 1983, all the members appeared one evening dressed up in tango dresses and evening suits to sip cocktails and celebrate the completion of a large order that had demanded a good deal of overtime. The national congresses in Berlin, *Wintertage*, have featured an exquisite cocktail bar; however, a certain distance became obvious between the personal style of the "decadent" Berliners and their West German colleagues, who are not on the same level of fashion.

Collectives attempt to satisfy consumption needs collectively rather than paying out a little more extra money to members individually. *Wuseltronick*, for instance, bought a sailboat on the Wannsee that can be used by members or friends. *Oktoberdruck* discussed repeatedly whether they should buy or rent a weekend house in West Germany. To renew energy after a long period of hard work, the construction engineers' collective, *Baubüro*, gave each of its members half an hour's massage per week and increased the budget for collective lunches instead of paying out this money to the members individually.

Contrary to the Kibbutz analysed by Talmon (1972:211), where ascetic ideals were emphasized to justify the reinvestment of resources into the community and where "the ultimate disintegration of the ascetic ideal... deals a death blow to the principle of collective consumption" (Talmon 1972:208), asceticism is a value no collectivist would support. *Lust* (pleasure), *Lustprinzip* (pleasure principle), and *Bock haben* (being keen on something) are frequently used expressions. Consumption should be one of the pleasures of life and should become neither a compulsive behaviour nor a prohibited one. No member is ridiculed or criticised if she or he puts all her or his money into buying an expensive motorcycle or photographic equipment. Even those members who eventually leave because they cannot satisfy their wants on the collective salary are treated with understanding, provided they do not claim part of the collective property as their own.

Readiness to Invest

When they engage in a new investment, members of collectives have different criteria than those of the managers or shareholders of a limited company. Their shares in the enterprise do not appear on the stock exchange. It is not the increase in market value that concerns members of collectives, as the shares they hold in the firm generally do not grow with the firm's capital. Their decisions are determined by the amount of time they expect to stay with the collective and the amount of money they must forego as far as immediate spending is concerned. The economist Gui (1981:46) compared investment decisions in worker-managed firms in general with those in business enterprises: "A profitable calculation for the (labour managed) firm as such, based on the comparison between the rate of return and the cost of capital, is inadequate... The flow of per capita distributable income must be considered instead of the cash flow of the firm." The degree to which members can live on low pay differs widely, depending on family obligations and consumption habits, but the willingness to invest does not depend on material reasons alone. It is closely linked to the ideological outlook of the member.

Members who are more ideologically motivated are either in favour of saving capital for the enterprise or, conversely, they want their collective to avoid entirely the "capitalistic logic of accumulation" and refuse to follow any systematic investment strategy. The willingness to invest is loaded with different moral significance according to the overall ideological line the collective is following. As I pointed out in the previous chapter, collectives and their members can be divided into two groups in terms of the political role they see for themselves in the capitalist system they all reject. The first is not to engage in any compromise with the "system" in order not to be corrupted by it, which means not following its logic of capital accumulation and investment. The second is to expand collective enterprises into the "system," thus undermining it and transforming it through a "mushroom effect." The moral value attributed to the foregoing of immediate spending in favour of accumulation is different in the two cases. A member advocating investments in the first type of collective may be accused of behaving like a small-time entrepreneur, whereas, in the second type, an enterprising collectivist with a "Protestant Ethic" has a much more positive image. He is considered an idealistic member who has the collective interests at heart.

Members who are in favour of accumulation often set the economic interests of the firm before their private interests. Significantly, they are generally also the ones who have very few private commitments. They hardly ever complain about the level of their individual income. These members contradict all theories about investment behaviour in labour-managed firms as they are willing to forego immediate consumption in favour of building up the enterprise, even if they only expect to be there for a short time. In 1984, Fritz of *KoMet*, for instance, actively supported further investments, although it was clear he was going to leave in a few months. He did not profit in any sense, either through a higher income or through a share in property paid out when he left. The idealistic members are inspired by the conviction that it is morally and politically right to promote collective enterprises. The only return they may receive in the long run is that their economic behaviour has contributed to giving future generations of collectivists the chance to work in a self-determined way.

Their strategy, though, is not always in favour of new investment, as the conflict between Fritz and Noppe of *KoMet* shows. Fritz continued to argue in favour of new investments, even when he was sure that he would be leaving nine months later; whereas, Noppe wanted the collective to handle its money very carefully, payback its debts, and not acquire new ones. Both were equally dedicated to their collective but not equally disposed to take risks. As their colleague Hanne put it:

> Fritz thinks that a sort of pioneer spirit and attraction to risks is necessary for collective work. Noppe, on the contrary, seems to regard the collective rather as a friendly society that gets money from somewhere and is muddling along by keeping costs low. He prefers to solve problems with discipline rather than by a courageous decision that implies the risk of falling flat on one's face. (Hanne, *KoMet*, 8.8.1984)

The hesitation to take risks with investments is a theme that appears repeatedly in almost every collective. The members are often called upon to sign personal guarantees for the purchase of a new machine when the sum involved far exceeds anything they have ever handled or possessed before. New members, especially, fear the financial obligations that could result from a wrong investment. Some members of longer standing, however, react much more cold bloodedly. They maintain that they own little private property of any importance that could be seized in the event of a financial disaster. Nevertheless, their readiness to invest is hindered by those of their fellow members who have more interest in immediate spending.

The departure of the printer Thomas from *Oktoberdruck* in August 1984 was clearly motivated by immediate financial interests. When he returned from holidays in July, he discovered that the rest of the collective had abolished the recently introduced holiday payment and was considering the purchase of a typesetting computer instead. Some members calculated that this investment would mean roughly DM 120 less per month for each worker. Thomas felt cheated and decided to take a better paying job in a business enterprise. He had acquired enough experience to work as a skilled printer and to earn twice the income *Oktoberdruck* could offer; his new job paid DM 2,800 gross plus holiday pay and a thirteenth month's salary.

His departure was felt as a great loss. When he announced that he was going to leave the collective for a well-paid job, the group was assembled for lunch in the large kitchen. The first reaction was oppressive silence. Then Moni, the woman printer, started crying and her colleague, Donald, declared that no more notices would be accepted. He was desperate because he had become well-adapted to Thomas, working with him in alternating shifts on the large *Miller* press, and he could not stand the idea of getting used to a new colleague. The other members complained bitterly, saying that Thomas's leaving would shake the group, when it had just been consolidated.

Thomas's dilemma corresponds to what Nutzinger (1975:188) analysed as the distinction between individually owned and non-owned assets by members of labour-managed enterprises. From an individual's point of view, there is a choice between individual savings (in owned assets) and the giving of part of his or her current income for the firm's investment. "The latter, however, is collectively owned and since it is irreversible for various reasons, only the future returns accrue to the workers while the initial outlay and hence the individual's share of it gets lost" (Nutzinger 1975:188). In the Berlin collectives, the transfer of individually owned assets to collective property passes through a reduction of the individual salaries decided by a majority at the plenary meeting of members. The self-financed investment affects the different groups in different ways, according to their consumption needs and their expected stay in the enterprise. The financing of investments through credits can alleviate some of the conflicts involved in creating reserves (Eger and Weise 1978:162). The credit makes it possible for those members who pay back the credit also to profit from improved working conditions, and perhaps shorter working hours, or from higher incomes. The ideal case however, that investment returns increase so fast workers do not have to forego some of their immediate spendings, only occurs in a very favourable market situation.

Most *Oktoberdruck* members are closely involved in the investments they make. They sign personal securities to guarantee the enterprise's credits and renounce part of their income when important investments are made. Some of the skilled printers, especially, seem to enjoy the acquisition of new machines. They identify closely with the machine on which they work, and it is part of their professional pride to work on a printingpress that is technologically up to date. When the collective decided, in the summer of 1984, to replace the A3 *GTO* printingpress with a new machine, the printers studied catalogues for weeks, visited the manufacturers, and discussed at length the technological advantages the new machine would be able to offer.

The new technology often makes production less timeconsuming and the collective more competitive with other firms. According to Nutzinger (1975:187), labour-managed enterprises follow a different investment logic than capitalist ones. While the latter invest according to expected profit, the former take the expected increase of their income per working unit as the main decision criterion. As a consequence, the labour-managed firms show a tendency toward lavour-saving devices and might even omit profit-increasing decisions if they also mean an increase in the number of workers beyond a certain point.

In *Oktoberdruck*, the lavour-saving effect of new investments was heatedly debated. In 1984, the majority of members reached the conclusion that they would prefer to reduce their working hours, rather than refrain from employing new members. For others, however, needing a higher income, this was a reason to leave the collective. As Herbie, the father of a young daughter, put it:

> If I am putting money aside from my income to invest in a machine, I want to see the benefit of it one day. I don't have this printing job as a hobby. The work here isn't really that exciting, and one can't find such complete satisfaction in it that money loses its importance. (Herbie, *Oktoberdruck*, 19.4.1984).

In the final months of his membership, he wanted tighter controls on efficiency and the introduction of compensation for people who leave according to the number of years worked in the collective. He finally left for a job that would pay him twice as much. Nevertheless, he continued to keep in close contact with the group, came to lunch regularly, and seemed to miss the work atmosphere.

The two service collectives, *FahrradBüro* and *Wuseltronick*, do not have the same problems concerning investments in expensive machinery as the production collectives, *KoMet* and *Oktoberdruck*. For the engineers' collective, *Wuseltronick*, their "capital" consists of scientific and technological know-how, which they have slowly accumulated with the help of several research grants from the Technical University and the Senate of Berlin. They developed an original electronic measurement technology and, without any financial aid, produced the prototype of a small windmill. The departure of any member who participated in important research work and acquired insights other members did not share meant a substantial loss for the enterprise.

The investments of the bicycle collective, *FahrradBüro*, consisted mainly in the slow accumulation of stocks of merchandise and of a few specialised tools for repairs. The collectivists attempted to balance their accounts of profit and loss in such a way that the result was zero at the end of the year, so that they did not have to pay any profit tax. They tried to adjust the wages paid throughout the year to the presumed profit or loss; but in most years, the profits exceeded the losses so they either had to invest in some new item of equipment, such as a new carpet for the shop, or else pay tax.

High Demands on Idealism

As members of collectives have to forego voluntarily part of their individual income to finance investments from which they can only profit collectively if they stay long enough, the temptation is great to consume the firm's capital instead of investing it or to try to reappropriate part of it privately when leaving. Only a strong commitment to the collective can make members go beyond the realisation of these immediate individual interests.

Private Appropriation

Leaving the collective without a penny, thankful for the pleasant time they were allowed to spend with their fellow members, impressed by the important experiences they were able to enjoy by managing their works themselves: this is the correct attitude expected from a leaving member. In fact, most do leave like that and continue to feel attached to "their" collective, which they have helped to build up. Even if they do decide to take a job with an ordinary enterprise, they continue to uphold the ideals they shared with their collective. Sometimes they even become the fiercest defenders of the collective cause, more radical in their views than their former colleagues who still work in collectives. In 1984, for instance, most of the activists of the *Lundkreis* were ex-collectivists, living on unemployment benefits or doing casual work. It seems that bonds of friendship and the feeling of doing something politically sensible hold them together.

However, there are also those members who have left after a row, disillusioned about the ideals with which they started. They feel, like Hans-Christian of *KoMet*, that the collective exploited their labour power by making them work harder than they had ever done before, and for a pittance. Like Helmut of *Oktoberdruck*, they despise the chaos and lack of organisation of their fellow members and accuse them of irresponsibility. They feel, like Michael of the *FahrradBüro*, that their colleagues prevented them from building up a dynamic and successful enterprise. As they stopped identifying with the collective, they wanted their sacrifice of time and money to be repaid. Their previous idealism can easily turn into the most complete egoism once they decide to break with the collective. Some of them claim, like Michael of the *FahrradBüro*, "We have never been a collective," and ask to be paid their nominal share.

When these members prepare to leave, they turn from the logic of collective sharing to that of individual appropriation. They often feel acutely disappointed by the collective lifestyle and claim that the idea of mutual support was only an illusion. Their interests turn to assuring their own material future. Often without a secure job to go to, or intending to build up their own enterprise, they are tempted to claim part of the capital they have helped to accumulate. Members who were associates of a society of common law, and agreed to guarantee the enterprise with their personal property without even the cover of social insurance, feel particularly deprived.

In the first year, the founders of the *FahrradBüro* could not take any income out of the shop, and in the second year a research grant for a project on traffic politics started to split the group. A conflict with external members of the research group caused one collectivist to leave entirely and another,

Klaus, to retreat into the shop. New members joined the bicycle business, and Michael was the only collectivist to continue with the research project. He increasingly withdrew from the daily tasks of the shop. A conflict broke out when he proposed to separate the office completely from the shop and claimed a higher income corresponding to his academic degree. When the others refused, he decided to leave, demanding compensation for the first years when he had helped build up the collective without earning anything. Klaus then claimed even higher compensation, as he had worked for most of the time in the shop.

As the conflict appeared insoluble, they agreed to call in an arbitrator instead of taking the matter to court. They chose Gerd Behrens, the tax advisor for most collectives at that time. Behrens counselled them to pay compensation to Klaus and Michael in small installments and to change the legal form of the collective to a company of limited liability (*GmbH*). Michael left, followed a few months later by Klaus, to take up jobs in the professions they had studied. About a year later, they ceased to claim their monthly compensation installments.

The official legislation — as stated above — supports the claims of departing members against the collective so it is not infrequent that formerly united collectivists, with radical views about "corrupt bourgeois society," find themselves opposing each other in "bourgeois" courts, each party defended by a well-known, left-wing lawyer. However, attempts are made to replace law courts with arbitration committees composed of members of other collectives chosen by both litigant parties. The arbitrators are generally committed to the collective ideals and attempt to find solutions that will satisfy both parties.

As we saw earlier, in 1981 an arbitration committee composed of four members of collectives awarded Hans-Christian compensation of DM 10,000 upon leaving *KoMet*, conditional on his building up another collective enterprise. This sum represented a considerable loss for the young collective, but it was less than Hans-Christian could have obtained in a court of law. Although strained for a couple of years, his relationship with *KoMet* was not entirely severed, and later the two enterprises even cooperated occasionally.

The setting up of arbitration committees in West Germany is done on the private initiative of the collectivists. In cases of conflict, a body not previously involved, possibly composed of members of another collective, is normally called in. Arbitration committees can only be effective if both liti-

gant parties recognise their authority. The solution the committee attempts
to find does not always have legal backing under West German law but is
based on the assumption that the members still share the same basic set of values. Once agreed upon, the committee has legal authority.

The ultimate sanction that remains is to expose the member not adhering
to the collective values to the gossip of the "scene." As E. L. Peters
(1972:157) has pointed out, gossip as a means of upholding a system of moral
values can only be effective if there is a certain density of relationships. In his
example, this was found in a Lebanese village — a small locality — and
among people who were social equals. In the present case, the place where
gossip circulates and reflects a certain set of values is the Berlin collective
"scene." Members who work or once worked in collectives, as well as some
of their customers, are often more or less acquainted. They go to the same
parties and share certain leisure activities in common. Sometimes close
friendships develop, sometimes deep hostilities.

In the "scene," people gossip about Constantin still owning most of *Oktoberdruck*'s machines, about tensions between old and new members of *Wuseltronick*, about *agitdruck* going bankrupt and about Gisela of *KoMet* having a baby. Sometimes the information transmitted concerns serious matters, sometimes it is very vague or even false, but it mirrors a certain common
concern. If a collectivist suddenly breaks with the shared values of the
"scene," he often loses not only his job but also more important components
of his social environment as well.

The latter happened to Helmut, an influential member of *Oktoberdruck*,
when he attempted to persuade his colleagues to sell the enterprise. At a
meeting of the collective, when he was asked to justify his idea, he admitted
that he wanted the proceeds from the sale of *Oktoberdruck* to be distributed
among the members. He argued that most members intended to leave sooner
or later and would not then be able to take anything with them. All the machines, for which they had worked for years, would either fall into the hands of
Constantin, who they suspected of having the greatest staying power of them
all, or would become the property of new people, who would be able to sell
them at their leisure. In order to prevent this, the collectivists should change
the charter of the enterprise and either allow for the existence of sleeping
partners or facilitate the sale of the printing shop by abolishing the clause sti-
pulating that the veto of a single associate is sufficient to prevent the dissolu-
tion of the limited company. Helmut was supported by two members, Udo
and Amrai, who were working with him in the montage section — his "dis-

ciples, " as the others called them. For the rest, however, he had become an enemy who they had to rid themselves of.

Division of Collective Property

While individual attempts to appropriate privately part of the collective property are generally fought off by the majority of the members, a division of the collective becomes almost inevitable if a large proportion of the members becomes dissatisfied with the level of income and the performance of the group and strives toward higher investments. Payment according to performance and private shares in the enterprise are generally the claims put forward by the group wanting to split off from the main collective.

In a conflict in 1985 that opposed Hans and Bernhard of the *FahrradBüro* to the rest of the collective, even an arbitration committee was unable to reach a compromise. Hans had become increasingly dissatisfied with his low income and the unwillingness of his colleagues to expand the enterprise into a wholesale business. He wanted the collective to be organised according to the criteria of modern management; this led him to despise the democratic spirit of his fellow members and, together with his colleague Bernhard, he increasingly jeopardized all collective decision-making. In the end, he claimed that the enterprise should be split. At the same time, however, he tried to maintain his image as a dedicated collectivist in front of the other collectives organised in the union of bicycle collectives. Only when he did not turn up at the meeting of the arbitration committee, composed of members of bicycle collectives, did it become clear to them that Hans no longer respected the basic principles. He and Bernhard employed a lawyer and claimed 50 percent of the stock of merchandise plus 10 percent of the annual turnover of the enterprise, which amounted to DM 110,000. Although the driving force behind the conflict was obviously Hans, Bernhard willingly agreed with his arguments as he was in desperate need of money. Together with friends, he had bought a run-down house in Kreuzberg, which he was renovating himself with the partial help of Senate subsidies. The income from the collective was insufficient to support himself, his child, and his girlfriend, a student who received only a small contribution from her parents toward her expenses.

The other members reacted only hesitantly to this development. Although the tensions with Hans slowly increased, each time they were taken by surprise when the conflict reached the next stage. Accepting the logic of collective cooperation and reluctant to fall back upon legal means, they realized only very late that Hans had begun to think in different terms and was not prepared to listen to any argument that appealed to his commitment to the group. They offered Hans and Bernhard DM 55,000 if they would leave, but the two continued to claim DM 110,000, a sum which the others felt would ruin the enterprise. To show Hans and Bernhard how ridiculously high they felt their claims to be, they offered to leave themselves, leaving the enterprise to Hans and Bernhard, if the latter would pay them such a sum. To their surprise, Hans and Bernhard agreed to this deal and offered to pay the other members off with DM 90,000. Tired of the arguments and squabbles, the collectivists accepted. They then opened a new bicycle collective, *velophil*, in the part of the town where they lived, which proved very successful.

Since 1985, Hans and Bernhard have continued to run the *FahrradBüro*, trying very hard to polish up their image as an alternative bicycle shop, which was seriously tarnished as a result of several articles in *die tageszeitung* and in the collective newspaper *contraste*, which criticised their role in the conflict. Hans wanted to found a *FahrradBüro* association that would become a forum for discussions about traffic politics. As Norbert, a critical former member, put it: "This would give an ideological gloss to Hans's noncollective in order not to put off customers from the alternative scene."

Another conflict over property in a collective, which I witnessed, happened along similar lines. In May 1988, the toolmaking collective *KoMet* was divided into two camps after years of conflict about low collective performance, minimal income, and insufficient financial reserves for renovating the capital in machinery. The division followed the lines of social origin and educational standard of the members. Those eager to introduce a "noticeable connection between work-effort and pay or working time" were the most dynamic elements of the enterprise; most had a high school education and were self-confident enough to take on difficult orders and improve their technical skills. By the spring of 1988, all of them were preparing for the master's diploma (*Meisterprüfung*) and had already passed the oral examination. The other group consisted of skilled workers who had come from ordinary toolmaking firms to join *KoMet* and were not attempting to achieve a higher standard of professional qualification by passing the master's diploma. Strongly opposed to the principle of performance and to private shares in the enterprise, they affirmed that *KoMet* was "a collective of workers and not a team of entrepreneurs."

The more enterprising members criticised the fact that large parts of the work results "disappeared into a big black hole" instead of being available for investments and salaries. Long hours were spent in the enterprise without increasing the overall result: in 1986, 42 percent of all working hours had been unproductive. In order to achieve a transparence between work-effort and pay, they claimed that the work groups cooperating on one order should be paid according to the result of that order, or rather, according to their performance as a group, and that members should be given the possibility of acquiring personal shares in the capital of the enterprise in order to encourage their willingness to invest. Justifying their deviance from the collective principles, they wrote in 1988:

> The perseverance of a concept which evolved out of a political euphoria means economically for the enterprise and personally for the members a standstill of the project *KoMet*.... We have to become able to work under self-managed structures and earn an appropriate income.

The members of the other group claimed the protection of the collective principles. They insisted that unequal capacities should not lead to internal hierarchies, and even less to different salaries. Strongly committed to the idea of the collective as a refuge from the capitalist logic of production, they maintained in 1988:

> *KoMet* and its structure offers one of the few possibilities for workers to break out of their social role in the process of production and to work in a self-determined way. For this purpose *KoMet* put machines at their disposal that are not in the hands of entrepreneurs. They are not the private property of anybody and therefore de facto expropriated. This is the primary condition for offering to the worker the possibility of self-determined work in a collective.... He or she just does not have DM 20, 000 in his or her pocket to buy a stake in somewhere.

The separation of the two groups within *KoMet* — the "old concept" group and the "new concept" group as they called themselves — raised great interest in Berlin alternative circles. In January 1988, a public discussion was held in the *KoMet* workshop where the two disputing parties expounded their different views. The case was followed by the alternative newspapers *die tageszeitung, contraste,* and *Netzwerkrundbrief.* The "old concept" group hoped to win public support for their defense of the initial ideals of an alternative work-style and applied to the arbitration committee to be accepted as the only ones to have legitimate control over the collective property.

After years of debate in alternative circles about efficiency, collective financing, and investment, however, public opinion was no longer unanimously in favour of the initial "pure" collective concept. It was starting to admit that it was difficult to live on DM 1,000 per month and that collectivists wanted to see financial returns for years of work-effort. The arbitration committee decided accordingly and divided the collective property into two equal halves.

Compensation

Granting compensation to departing members has been a hotly debated issue in almost all the collectives I know — as a possible solution to ease the tensions when members leave and to give them greater material security in the transition period. Some members believe that if members know they will receive a proportion of the accumulated capital when they leave, they will be more willing to invest. Compensation for the number of years worked may also induce members to stay longer.

Labour-managed enterprises, especially in Yugoslavia, have acquired experience in granting compensation according to years worked. This compensation, if substantial, often led to a depletion in liquid assets if the mobility of members was great. As Vanek (1977:176) has pointed out, the current practice of granting shares in proportion to the contribution to the firm counted in years worked could also seriously undermine the equality between old members and newcomers. In labour-managed enterprises where members acquired private shares in the firm's property, shares tended to increase in value until they became so expensive that it was almost impossible for new members to join the enterprise. The members of the Plywood Cooperative in the United States (Gunn 1980:397), for instance — adopting a system of private shares — invested large parts of their income but also increasingly employed wage-labourers — the development denounced by Oppenheimer as the "iron law of transformation" of a cooperative into a capitalist enterprise, as discussed earlier (Oppenheimer 1922:64).

The form of compensation Berlin collectives choose to pay out, and the amount they are willing to give, depends upon the form of property and on the financial situation of the enterprise. The printing collective *Bloch und Partner* allocated shares in the property to each member according to the number of years worked and the amount of personal capital invested. In September 1983, Peter, who had worked in the enterprise for two years and had made the initial investment, owned 35 percent; Andreas, who joined a few months later, 30 percent; his mother, who worked there for six months and had brought in some capital, 25 percent; and Dagmar, who had worked for six months, 10 percent. The proportions change with new members joining and the number of years worked so that, provided no outside capital is introduced, after ten years the amount Dagmar will own will not differ greatly from the amount Peter will then hold. Each owner can take out his share in the property when he leaves, and Andreas hopes that he will even have accumulated enough capital by the age of thirty-five to be able to stop working entirely.

Collectives that have already experienced the comings and goings of many members and have fought to keep the enterprise's capital out of grasping hands, find *Bloch und Partner*'s attitude toward property deceptive and dangerous. For not only would the enterprise collapse entirely if Peter and Andreas left with their shares but the attitude toward work changes because of the individual interest of members in accumulation. As one of *Bloch und Partner*'s new members, Sabine, put it: "In the collective, the spirit of the young entrepreneur is dominant. Everybody works as well and as fast as possible on good new machines." Other printing collectives admire *Bloch und Partner* for their work efficiency but criticise them for their speculation on increasing private shares in capital, regarding them as having taken the first step toward becoming an ordinary enterprise. The founders of *Bloch und Partner* agree with this assessment. They do not regard work in a collective as a political action but simply as a profitable business that is not exploiting anybody and is "the fruit of our own hands' labour."

Contrary to *Bloch und Partner*, which started off with a strong sense of personal property, *Wuseltronick* was initially based on an equally strong idea of collective property, and only gradually developed an awareness of the fact that not all its members were inclined to give up the notion of private property. From 1977 to 1981, the group had five members who pooled all their private savings and revenues and invested this in the enterprise, taking out of the collective money-chest whatever they needed for consumption. From 1981 to 1983, the situation changed when new members joined. To close the gap in financial commitment and status between old members and newcomers, it was suggested that the new members should also put their private savings into the collective fund.

Differences arose between new members like Alex, who had savings of DM 30,000 but was afraid to invest them as they would be lost to him and to the collective in the event of mismanagement, and those who had nothing and were in favour of the neutralisation of the capital. At a full meeting in March

1983, members discussed how to compensate the contributors of private capital by allowing members to take out money when leaving. They considered the introduction of compensation depending on the years of membership, the amount of capital put in, and the current value of the enterprise. The private elements in the company's capital, contributed by individual members, were to be slowly reduced by deducting a negative interest from them until only the collective property remained. The compensation members received would then depend exclusively on the years worked and the financial situation of the enterprise.

However, members like Alex claimed they did not have sufficient confidence in the work-style of their colleagues to be certain their money would not be squandered. Handing over his private capital to the collective might in the end mean that, due to inefficiency or financial catastrophe, he would find himself with a low income and no property. He therefore insisted on giving his money as a loan. The idealistically minded Reiner, on the contrary, contributed all his private property at the foundation of the collective and intended to add a recent inheritance as well. He thought it natural that in difficult times individual interests should take second place, that members should take smaller incomes and receive lower compensation. He maintained that the main aim was to establish an original work environment, not to increase the amount of capital members could individually appropriate.

The issue of compensation remained purely hypothetical until the spring of 1984, when Hansi decided to set up an independent research unit in his house in West Germany. When he left, he took with him part of the electronic equipment, together with compensation in cash for the number of years worked. It became obvious, however, that if every member was to be compensated so generously and was to have the right to take away the project he or she was working on, the collective would collapse after the departure of only a few more members. As a matter of fact, *Wuseltronick*'s prosperity depended less on financial reserves than on the maintenance of the intellectual capital and therefore on keeping membership stable.

To inhibit private appropriation of expertise and capital in equipment, *Wuseltronick* has since founded a *Genossenschaft*, together with two other collectives, that holds the property of all equipment needed for production. Each member of *Wuseltronick* had to become an associate of the *Genossenschaft* and had to sign a restraint clause prohibiting the private use of collective expertise.

Responding to the preoccupations of a growing number of members, the issue of providing security for old age and of raising children began to be taken seriously after having been merely hypothetical for years. The members of *Wuseltronick* renounced their idealistic model of collective property, of income according to need, and admitted the possibility of private accumulation. A private life assurance, held by the collective, was opened for each member, the money to be paid out when a member left and in the meantime serving the enterprise as a security.

Wuseltronick is the first West Berlin collective to plan a collective pension fund. It is planning to invest the money accumulated in fixed property, that is, in housing and production space. Other collectives such as *Oktoberdruck* became interested in the model, as the pensions they can expect will be a small percentage of their present income and would be below the minimum subsistence level. In the last two or three years, more influence has been acquired by members advocating the granting of compensation and emphasizing the importance of providing greater financial security.

Conclusion

The form of property is what distinguishes collectives from business enterprises. However, the answer to the question "To whom does the collective belong?" is contradictory. Formally and legally, the enterprise is the property of the working members. In practice, they are not allowed to sell it; they increase the capital but should not decrease it. It is not a capitalist owner of the enterprise who extracts the surplus produced by the collectivist, but it is the enterprise itself that builds up its capital from the supplementary unpaid effort expended by the members. Investment is only profitable for members as long as membership is stable and if they have a long-term expectancy to work in the enterprise. As they forego any right of ownership when leaving, they have little interest in financing the creation of new workplaces.

The initial idea — that collective property would be at the equal disposal of all and that everybody would feel similarly inclined to invest his or her working power to maintain and increase it — was based on the assumption that membership would be stable. It did not give consideration to changes in personal situation nor to the actuality of members leaving. After a couple of years, almost all collectives had experienced enormous changes in membership and most had to realize that the priority of their members had shifted toward private and individual interests. Idealistic sacrifice of time and money became rare, especially when members were faced with family obligations, with growing older, or with a return to the dominant labour market. Collectives have only recently started to adapt to these changes by accounting financially for the contributions made by members.

Notes

1. The corresponding legal form in Britain is the partnership.

2. In the following section, I am referring to *Genossenschaften* when I talk about German cooperatives which have the legal form of an e. G. (*eingetragene Genossenschaft*). The term "cooperatives" refers to the British example.

3. "Net" means that taxes and insurance are already deducted.

6

Self-Management

Because of their complexity, planning and decision-making are the central problems of collective organisations. Collective decisions should be made by consensus, and ideally require the active participation of all members, who are expected to readily assume responsibility for a large number of decisions that may go beyond the range of their professional experience.

The structures of decision-making and planning developed by different collectives are experimental and constantly changing. As with the entire collective organisation, these structures must be regarded as part of a dynamic process that displays a certain pattern but little predictability. The decision-makers, the criteria of decisions, and the topics to be decided upon change constantly with the coming and going of members and with changes in the political outlook of the enterprise.

Collectivists maintain that their primary objective is not to provide for maximal profitability within the enterprise but to develop an anti-authoritarian, nonhierarchical framework for the realization of their ideals. The "traditional" separation between administrators, planners, and coordinators on the one hand and executors on the other must be replaced by "the collective," which both takes the decisions and executes them. However, they are aware that the effort to realize this ideal can only be a compromise within the surrounding economic constraints, as their informal spontaneous structures of decision-making are confronted with the strictly hierarchical business organisations of their competitors.

Non-Directive Planning

In business enterprises, the manager mediates between the pressures of the market, the demands of the capital owners, and the requirements of the actual producers. To those inside the firm, he transmits external pressures in the form of instructions and advice, and he camouflages internal inadequacies from the external observer or customer through negotiation and diplomacy. The workers are expected to execute his instructions to the letter but in return are not held responsible for any mistake in his planning. The manager in turn has to act in accordance with the ultimate interests of the capital holders and has to justify the success or failure of his decisions to the owner — if he is not himself the owner — or to the board of shareholders. His role is to balance the pressures from market and capital holders against the needs and satisfaction of the workers in order to keep the level of profit and capital to be reinvested as high as possible.

In West German industry, the tensions between capital holders and workers have been attenuated through the institution of workers' codetermination. On the supervisory boards of the steel and mining industries, half the delegates, and on the boards of all other joint stock companies, one-third of the delegates, are workers' representatives.[1] This, however, does not mean direct participation by ordinary workers in the company's decisions. As the representatives, once elected, are no longer formally accountable to the workers, a de facto separation occurs between the professional workers' representatives and the workers themselves (Heinrich 1981:83). In practice, the ordinary workers are badly informed concerning the politics of the board, and their representatives, on becoming board members, must respect the company's trade secrets.

In the labour-managed economy of Yugoslavia, where in theory the workers' council determined the politics of their enterprise, it was in practice controlled by the organisational pyramid; workers had little influence on the management decisions. Since 1965, three parallel institutional structures have coexisted. First, was the structure of self-management represented by an elected workers' council. All workers could in theory be elected to the council, though in practice the highly skilled and skilled workers were over-represented (Comisso 1979:56). Second, was the type of organisation that was strictly hierarchical and headed by an elected director. Third, was the enterprise branches of the socio-political organisations, which represented larger social interests as opposed to those of the enterprise (Comisso 1979:146). These three parallel structures interacted. The workers' council, together with the socio-political organisations, appointed the director, who then had ultimate authority over the organisation of work. The management, on the other hand, used the political influence of the workers' council and actually led it in pressuring government authorities when the enterprise found market conditions unfavourable (Comisso 1979:182).

Workers' councils and the elected or appointed hierarchy of management often stand in a contradictory relationship toward one another. While the elected director must justify the success or failure of his business politics to the working members, the workers in turn are expected to obey his instructions regarding the organisation of their work. Nevertheless, if his business politics fail, the workers may drive him out.

The nineteenth century *Genossenschaft*, described by Oppenheimer (1922:61), employed a director who was more highly paid than the other workers and who formally managed the enterprise. The full members of the *Genossenschaft* controlled him through their vote on the board of cooperants. His position was often not very strong, as he could be dismissed at any moment and often served as scapegoat for all the external pressures.

Gunn describes a similar contradiction between directory authority and democratic self-management structures in the case of the Plywood cooperatives in the United States. The director was "hired and fired" by the people he had to coordinate and could not become a member. He was employed for the task without being granted real power (Gunn 1980:395). A director from outside often does not identify sufficiently with the firm. The workers, having delegated their administrative tasks to him or her, lose effective control over the enterprise, as happened in the case of the Fakenham cooperative in Britain. There, a director, appointed by the creditor Scott Barber Association, mismanaged the enterprise while the women members were left uninformed of the financial situation (Wajcman 1983:64-67).

The particularity of the Berlin collectives lies in the fact that they do not possess a manager or director who fulfills the functions of mediator or coordinator. In the collective, the members themselves must execute the decisions they make and must bear the consequences of their own management. As they are themselves the owners, they do not have to justify the profitability of their self-management, but they experience its consequences in the amount of income they receive at the end of the month and the number of hours they must work per day. Pressures from the surrounding economy impinge directly on the individual collectivist, as each should take equal part in representing the enterprise externally and in the internal organising of tasks.

Like ordinary business enterprises, the collective has to maintain good public relations and present a favourable image of itself to its circles of prospective customers in order to guarantee an adequate flow of orders. Customers from the alternative scene also need to be catered to. Customers from business enterprises need extra reassurance that collectives produce like ordinary firms, respecting time limits and producing good quality work. Therefore, toward the outside world, the collective planners have to perform the role of an ordinary business partner who creates a feeling of security for the customer. Even if members reject the principles of competition from an ideological standpoint, the collective as an enterprise operating in the market must react to competitors, adjust its prices, and offer special services if it wants to keep ordinary customers as well as those from the alternative scene.

Internally, collectivists must plan the time needed for the completion of orders, distribute the tasks among members, purchase materials, and calculate prices. They have to discover who among them is able and ready to complete which task and to redistribute tasks if any member proves incapable of finishing on time. The structures of planning are variable and flexible. Planning is done at meetings, as a routine job in the office, at coffee breaks by members who cooperate closely, and by individual members who find themselves, deliberately or not, in a situation where they have to decide alone whether to accept an order, lower the usual price, and the like.

The two tools of collective planning are the weekly meeting and the office. To schematise these two institutions, one could designate the meeting as the "legislature," which determines the rules and principles of organisation and makes the political decisions that may effect even as small a detail as the purchase of Nicaraguan coffee for the kitchen. The office could be designated the "administration," which makes the routine decisions within the norms set by the meeting and sees that the running of the collective respects the laws and rules set out for enterprises operating under West German legislation.

Most collectives meet once a week outside of working hours to discuss the events of the past week and to plan the tasks for the coming one. The *Oktober-druck* collectivists assembled on Monday evenings from 6 p.m. to about 10 p.m. around a few bottles of wine in the large kitchen or, in summer, on the lawn of a nearby park. At one meeting, topics as diverse as the organisation of holidays, job rotation, reduction of working hours, level of income, and the employment of cleaning women were discussed. The members of the *FahrradBüro* closed their shop on Tuesdays and met for breakfast from 10 a.m. to 2 p.m. in the small office. They discussed the ordering of stock, the financial situation, and the integration of new members; one member kept a record of the topics discussed. *KoMet* and *Wuseltronick* members met twice a week, once formally in the collective kitchen to discuss business and a second time in the flat of one of the members to talk more informally about personal matters. Depending on the problems at stake, the mood of the members, and the weather outside meetings can be very informal and relaxed, or strictly organised with lists of topics to be discussed.

The Office

While the role of the meeting is equally central in all the collectives I know, the position of the office varies considerably, according to size, age, and organisational structure. *Oktoberdruck*, for instance, started off with an office space separated from the printing presses by two book shelves, and today has a separate office, where two people work permanently, and a room to receive customers. *Oktoberdruck* and the other three examples are larger collectives with a more crucial administrative section and a separate office, whereas the smaller collectives with only four to six members tend to carry out the administrative tasks in the midst of the production space. It is the belief of most collectivists that the office should not take a central and dominant position. Their ideal is that all the members should become capable of replacing each other in the office. How this ideal is realized in practice varies considerably, though, from one collective to another. *Oktoberdruck* and *Wuseltronick* had full-time office jobs, which were hardly ever rotated. In the *KoMet* collective, the office job was part-time and rotated half yearly; while the *Fahrrad-Büro* rotated the task daily — but at the time of my fieldwork was employing a specialist to bring the books back into order.

Most of the orders are accepted by the members who work in the office. Only for the more important orders are they supposed to consult the whole collective, the smaller ones being decided without further consultation. Some collectives, like *KoMet*, try to locate the task of caring for customers away from the office, in the hands of the producing members who are each then permanently responsible for a certain number of customers. But as the responsible members cannot themselves execute all the orders they take in, they are therefore only replacing the office in its mediatory function. *KoMet* members who had spent years as skilled workers in business industry were much less at ease in taking part in the management tasks and in representing the enterprise ontside than were their colleagues who had a university education and were trained to represent themselves and others.

When customers are dealt with by the members working in the office, the office plays the role of mediator between the producing members and market pressures. Complaints about mistakes made by the printers and repro-monteurs of *Oktoberdruck*, for instance, first pass through the office and are then transmitted to the members concerned. Members working in the office often complain about the strain involved in calming down the customers on the one hand and criticising their reluctant colleagues on the other. The relationship of the other *Oktoberdruck* members toward those in the office is ambiguous. Although the printers claim that they feel much greater responsibility for their work in the collective than they did in their previous employment, they still do not like to negotiate with a customer about a misprinted order. They can go into fits of despair, refuse to eat lunch, and work until late at night if they make a mistake, but they will not accept criticism from the office.

In one instance, the office put the wrong paper size for the reprint of a song book onto the printers' worksheet. The printers ordered the paper, and, working the evening shift, Thomas started to print the order. He only realized later, when he folded the printed sheet to check the print, that it was some millimeters too small. He left a note warning Donald, who was to continue the task in the morning. Donald measured the paper again, decided that it was big enough, and continued the printing. When Thomas arrived at lunch time, the whole series had by then been misprinted and had to be thrown away.

In the conflict that followed, Marita and Helmut, who worked in the office, criticised the printers for not consulting them if there was any doubt about the paper size. The printers in turn accused the office of carelessness in the taking of new orders; they were supposed to know, or to look up, what sort of paper was required for the reprint. Neither side was willing to accept responsibility for the mistake. The printers argued as if the members in the office were their instructors, whose advice they were executing to the letter, although in fact they had acted independently, Thomas deciding of his own accord to stop production and Donald to continue it. Marita and Helmut, on the other hand, refused to accept responsibility for something about which they had not been consulted.

As the customers feel personally at ease with the collectivists, they are tolerant of minor shortcomings in planning and small delays in the execution of their orders. However, more serious mistakes and longer delays are treated more and more severely. Customers from the "Alternative Scene" also increasingly expect a higher professional standard in the execution of their orders and threaten collectives with claims for damages. As a necessary consequence, collective planning now shows signs of increased professionalisation and greater routine. All collectives I know have introduced an increasing number of more elaborate work-plans. These are large charts, on which the distribution of tasks to machinery and people is marked by means of small coloured cards. In this way, each collectivist can see the results of the planning. Short-term planning has become a routine occupation, even if the realisation of the plan is not always perfect.

Much more time consuming are the discussions that involve long-term planning for economic development. Discussions about a new investment often continue for months and may only be brought to a conclusion because a "lobby" raises the topic time and again, eventually wearing down its opponents. Making new investments, lowering or increasing income, limiting working hours – these pose considerable difficulties because most collectivists either have problems understanding business accountancy or do not want to become involved in something the logic of which contradicts their own principles. As mentioned earlier, collectivists claim to want to abolish the economic category of pure economic performance expressed in the maximisation of profit. Classic accountancy would be opposed to what they wish to achieve. According to Weber's classic definition, "accounting in terms of money... is the specific means of rational, economic provision." It allows for the valuation of all the means of achieving a productive purpose, an estimation of net profits to be gained from alternative lines of economic action, a periodic comparison of all the goods and other assets controlled by an economic unit, an estimate and the verification of receipts and expenditure, and the orientation of provision for consumption (Weber 1964:186-7).

Collectivists often feel ambiguous towards if not bored by, accountancy. They refuse to argue from the point of view of the economic logic of the enterprise alone. In the early phases of collectives, members' reactions to accounting were similar to that toward legal forms. They did not take it seriously and therefore did not keep the accounts correctly, considering them merely a chicanery of the capitalist economy.

However, one or two years, at the latest, after the collective enterprises were established, they had to deliver detailed tax declarations. Some had to cope with temporary insolvencies, which meant that members received their pay weeks or months late, or not at all. Members realised that they must update the accounts of the past years and maintain them more or less in order if they wanted the enterprise to survive. However, they were still far from doing this in order to maximise their economic performance.

In an economic unit that is explicitly not performance oriented, where work-effort plays no role and time spent a minor one, accountancy is quite a paradox. On the one hand, members of collectives claim that they refuse to have their economic actions determined by the net profit that could be gained; on the other hand, they want to maintain a stable level of income — and possibly raise it — and form reserves for investments. Like every other enterprise, they have to pay taxes regularly and, of course, have a strong interest in paying as little tax as possible. For this purpose, skilled accountancy is necessary; expert bookkeeping has an undeniable advantage and is even a good defense against external economic pressures.

Most collectivists, like Bolle, who was for years the accountant for the newspaper *die tageszeitung*, have come to regard as a political necessity the possession of bookkeeping skills by each collectivist. In a paper he presented to the collective at a meeting, he advocated the "anarchist accountant":

> Since time immemorial accountants have been regarded with suspicion by those for whom they sorted out reality. Nevertheless, they received gratitude for their efforts as long as they did not distribute the material reality too much to their own advantage. People were willing to pay them tribute in order not to take responsibility for reality themselves — just as one treats one's mother and father with respect because they try to take care of the insecurities of life for the young person.... Occasionally accountants were chased away... because they had reserved the most agreeable part of reality for themselves and had unlearned to estimate the disagreeable part they distributed.... However, ever new generations of bookkeepers took material reality — and thereby freedom — out of the hands of their fellow-men ... Anarchy is the only possibility to make sure that we all become bookkeepers who prevent material reality from being divided and rule of one over others from emerging. (*Unter Geiern* 1982:88).

A computer printout from the tax advisor once monthly, with all the figures neatly lined up, is not sufficient to clarify the connection between work performance and results achieved. Older members, especially those working in the office, are in a more informed position and may have considerable influence on planning, using the knowledge they have acquired. Most members are conscious of this problem and try at least to prevent those colleagues who are in conflict with the majority from taking over the office job. When Helmut in the *Oktoberdruck* office was opposed to most of his colleagues, they objected to a friend of his taking over the second office job because they felt threatened by this accumulation of power.

Other collectives such as *KoMet* tried to rotate the office job every six to twelve months, to give every member the chance to understand the administrative proceedings. For many *KoMet* members, this meant obtaining an insight into mechanisms from which they had been excluded while working as dependent workers in ordinary industry. As Noppe put it:

> For the first time I was able to realize how capitalists deal with one another, how their personal and business quarrels have to take second place to their common interest in money. (Noppe, *KoMet*, 8.8.1984)

However, the high turnover in membership made it impossible to generalise the administrative expertise. In 1984, only two of the eleven *KoMet* members had actually worked in the office, and the principle of rotation was beginning to be questioned. Members complained of the waste of time and money involved in introducing yet another member to the workings of the office.

Even those members who have worked in the office are not always clear about how the accounts operate, and if they do understand they are usually incapable of passing on their understanding to the others. In the autumn of 1984, *KoMet* was considering the question of looking for a professional accountant who would be able to make the books more comprehensible for all members and relate the income received each month more closely to the results. The members hoped that they would then be able to participate more equally in the process of planning.

Some collectives, like *Oktoberdruck* and the *Baubüro*, have introduced microcomputers to facilitate accounting and the writing of standard letters. Others, like *Wuseltronick*, which makes extensive use of computers in its engineering projects, rejects their use for administrative purposes. *Wuseltronick* members maintain that the use of computers for accounting and business correspondence detaches the members from the intrinsic content of these activities and restricts their overview (*Wuseltronick-Kollektiv* 1984:34). The general tendency among collectives, however, seems to be toward favouring computers as a means of presenting clearly outlined balance sheets to the collective and increasing the clarity of the accounts.

Even clear accounts, those that go a long way toward putting the results within everybody's grasp, do not necessarily succeed. The accountant for the largest collective in Berlin, the newspaper *die tageszeitung*, which had

120 members in 1984, said that he spent most of his time trying to develop new ways of making the accounts more intelligible to everyone. He drew diagrams and wrote page after page about the financial situation and the measures needing to be taken. But although his colleagues are now capable of understanding his financial statements, they often still do not bother to read them. The only time when he can be sure of making his financial concerns understood is in a state of emergency and imminent financial crisis. Even if the basic political decisions of the enterprise are made in the meeting, the de facto economic development is for a large part influenced by the office administrating the finances.

The lack of involvement in administrative matters and the reluctance to assume responsibility for difficult negotiations cannot be explained simply by a lack of personal commitment to the collective experiment. Newcomers and younger members often feel overwhelmed by the double obligation of administration and execution. They are not sufficiently secure to make decisions that could decide the destiny of the entire enterprise, especially if they are still struggling with the basic requirements of production. Work planning not infrequently becomes a problem of competence. As in theory all the members should feel responsible for all the tasks, the dilemma arises that sometimes nobody feels responsible at all. The desire to take into consideration the opinions of all members, in view of their different levels of experience and willingness to take risks, becomes an important cost factor for the enterprise.

Discipline

Work planning in the collective is based on a high level of mutual understanding among all its members and can only be efficient if everybody feels responsible for the enterprise and if the common decisions are executed voluntarily. External pressure is replaced by self-discipline. Usually it is assumed that everybody gives his or her best, according to his or her individual capabilities. This type of relationship comes close to what Fox calls "high trust relations," based on the "assumption that commitment includes effort and application being freely offered rather than measured calculatively against a specific return." Fox found that where relationships of this kind were prevalent in an enterprise they included freedom from close supervision, open networks of interaction and communication, emphasis on problem solving through mutual adjustment, and the handling of disagreements on the basis of "working through" in the light of shared goals (Fox 1974:77). The opposites on the scale are low trust relations, characterised by closely checked and monitored work where small indulgencies are eliminated (Fox 1974:107). Control mechanisms and sanctions are used to enforce conformity.

Working as a repro-monteur with *Oktoberdruck*, Herbie moved from the usual relationship of high trust vis-à-vis colleagues to one of low trust when, in a personal conflict, he was accused by the other members in his section of being careless and of wasting a great deal of material by making unnecessary mistakes. As he felt wrongly accused, he collected all the material wasted in the section over a five-week period and presented the full meeting with an analysis proving he was responsible for the waste to no greater degree than were any of his colleagues.

Criticisms of work-style are often formulated in terms of "commitment," rather than in terms of performance or efficiency. The judgement of work-style and personal relations are closely intertwined, as a single member's lack of goodwill may cause the entire system to crumble. If a member frequently arrives late or spoils materials, he or she is accused of exploiting fellow members and of lacking commitment to the collective. If members have serious personal problems with colleagues, they often express their hostility through criticism of other members' work-styles. Members responsible for delays or shortcomings in production are expected to admit to their mistakes informally and to show concern. The other members then generally will not criticize them but, instead, may pity their misfortune or joke about their clumsiness.

Only in very serious cases, and when the same mistake occurs repeatedly, will the member be criticised for his lack of responsibility. According to Jarchow and Klugmann (1980:118), collectives have a strong belief in the power of self-regulation that can, however, turn into open aggression if it is disappointed. The absence of formal obligations makes it difficult to tackle conflicts at an early stage.

A comparison between the attitudes toward conflicts in British communes and Berlin collectives leads to some interesting observations. As Abrams and McCullough (1976:200-201) explain, the members of British communes felt fundamentally threatened by disputes over tools, household tasks, and consumable objects. They point out that the more people relate to one another as "whole persons," the more at risk they are of endangering their personal relationships by conflicts over practical matters. The members of Berlin collectives also engage in their small and large conflicts in a very personal way, but they sometimes maintain that conflicts are a proof of creative and developing human relationships, that they are in a way inevitable and in their ultimate outcome often positive. Both attitudes toward conflicts seem extraordinary. Members of British communes overemphasize the need for harmony, the Berlin collectivists the need for open conflict. Neither seems yet to have found an equilibrium.

The forms of control and coercion frequently used in business enterprises — such as refusing a day off when an employee requests one, relegating him or her to a lower position, not granting an increase in salary — would contradict the collective principle of fundamental equality and are never used. Members who are dissatisfied with a colleague often feel they do not have any concrete means at hand to compel him or her to improve their work. The only form of punishment they use is as personal as the way in which criticisms are expressed. If a member does not submit to a minimum of collective discipline and constantly jeopardizes the production planning, his or her colleagues may start to ostracise the offender. They refuse to speak to him or ask his advice and will not help him in his tasks. If these measures are ineffective and the recalcitrant member continues to lead "a parasite's existence," the other members may resort to the ultimate means of punishment — exclusion from the collective.

Exclusion occurs extremely rarely and only if the member in conflict has obviously ceased to identify with the collective. Most collectives require a majority of three-quarters or a unanimous decision to exclude one of their members, a procedure I witnessed only once during my two years of field-work.

Compromise and No Decision

"The great disadvantage I see in collective work is that you have to talk about everything far too much all the time." This is how Friedel, a member of *Ko-Met*, sees the difficulties of collective decision making.

Trying to analyse the interminable discussions and the mechanisms of decision making I witnessed during innumerable collective meetings, I not only started to agree with Friedel, I also realised that the most frequent result of these discussions was the absence of decision. Are collectives so racked by conflict that they cannot reach any agreement? Do they consist of people without strong wills or opinions who are incapable of making up their minds? How then do they survive as a group?

Just as a political party or an academic department may have internal factions but must present a united front toward the outside world, so collectives are built on a basic personal consensus of all members. Most of the decision-making processes I witnessed were not long or complicated because of irreconcilable conflicts; instead, the complication lay in the fact that maximum unity of opinion had to be reached. The ideas of the individualistic members had to be reconciled in order to guarantee their loyality to the whole. For this purpose, long debate and failure to decide may sometimes be more appropriate than a rapid, clear-cut decision. The decision-making processes of collective meetings fit into the three categories of unauthoritative decision-making distinguished by Kuper (1971:21) in his studies of the political institutions of acephalous societies. His first category represents the complete failures debated at length without any resolution; the second, represents ceremonial decisions that in fact had already been taken beforehand; and the third, represents the ambiguous decisions that make action impossible until a further, more clear-cut decision is taken. As we shall see, collectives in fact practice all these three types.

Most controversial are those decisions that make obvious the contradictions between ideals and practice. Often the proposals of the more idealistically minded members are not rejected outright but, at the same time, are not supported if they go against the more pragmatic interests of the majority. Actual decisions, then, become very difficult, if not impossible, to make.

When Marita, *Oktoberdruck*'s bookkeeper, wanted to push through the decision that the collective should cease to employ women on a part-time basis to do the cooking and cleaning, she met the passive and silent resistence of the other, mostly male, members. Although she brought up this point at every meeting for weeks, no clear-cut decision was made. She boycotted the common hot lunches and spoke with each member individually in order to recruit supporters. Although most of the male members agreed in principle that each member should do all the tasks and that no wage-labour should be employed simply to free them from the more unpleasant chores, they did not relish the idea of cooking for twelve people once a fortnight or of working late on Friday evenings to clean the workshop.

At the first meeting I witnessed, Marita presented the group with a calculation proving that they were spending DM 1,200 per month on part-time female wage-labour, a sum that would allow them to integrate another full member into the collective and rotate the unpopular tasks among them all. She underlined her financial statement with the moral claim that these women were working under appalling "precapitalist" conditions, without social security and without the right to participate in the collective decision making. Her argument provoked interminable discussions. It was neither rejected outright nor fully accepted. Only Helmut, who for a long time had filled the role of opinion leader, objected openly to her proposal and accused her of being unrealistic and moralising. He claimed that nobody would carry out these tasks properly if he or she was not paid expressly to do so and therefore felt under an obligation. Only after weeks of discussion did a solution present itself, and it was from outside. Some of the women previously employed to do the cooking founded a mobile collective canteen that provided several collectives with hot lunches while having the status of an independent collective.

Decision-making processes rarely lead to clear-cut solutions but rather end in compromise. Hardly ever do the members actually vote on a decision, as they are conscious of the dangers of majority decisions in conflict situations. A majority decision leaves a minority of members dissatisfied and, therefore, threatens the unity of the collective. Repeated majority decisions with a stable minority lead, in the long run, to factions inside the group and hence to instability and fluctuating membership. Only unanimous decisions and unanimously accepted compromises are capable of maintaining the unity of the collective. Although differences of opinion among members are frequent, the general understanding is that compromise is always possible and that the points of view of all members must be respected.

This attitude appears very clearly in a conflict I witnessed in the summer of 1984. *KoMet* was divided over the question of whether a former member, Michael, a friend of Noppe and the declared enemy of Fritz, should be allowed to use the collective's machinery for a few days to prepare some tools for a development project in Nicaragua.

During the lunch to which Michael was invited to discuss the question, Gisela and Noppe did most of the talking. Gisela shared Fritz's hostility toward Michael because he had once offended her during her apprenticeship with *KoMet* by accusing her of being an unproductive parasite within the collective. She accused Noppe of having suggested that Michael should use the *KoMet* machinery deliberately in order to provoke Fritz and herself. Instead, she offered to find another workshop for Michael. Noppe countered that he considered Michael's unpaid work for the Nicaragua project very useful and that he had been sure the others would have wanted to support it. He proposed that Michael could use the machines in the early hours of the morning at a time when Fritz and Gisela were not working.

The discussion continued to oscillate between the two poles and no clear-cut decision was taken. Fritz and Michael, the actual opponents, did not participate in the discussion at all. Gisela claimed that she did not wish to impose her personal view of Michael on the others but wanted Noppe to show some understanding of her point of view, otherwise she would not "grow old in this collective." Most of the other members had no particular sympathy nor dislike for Michael and wanted the conflict to be resolved peacefully. However, none of them was capable of proposing an acceptable compromise, and in the end Michael simply came to work in the early morning, leaving before Fritz and Gisela arrived.

In this conflict, only a small minority of members was involved: Noppe made the proposal, and Fritz and Gisela objected to it. But Fritz and Noppe were the members of longest standing and had considerable influence as opinion leaders, so their conflict could not be ignored by the other members. It developed into a power struggle between Fritz and Noppe, which went much further than the actual topic under discussion. A clear-cut decision by the other members in favour of one or the other would have split the collective by showing very clearly the allegiances to Fritz or to Noppe. By stressing that she did not wish to push through a decision but wanted to see signs of understanding on both sides, Gisela tried to disarm the two factions and show willingness to compromise. In fact, by the time Fritz left the collective a few months later, Gisela had managed to change positions from that of an ally of Fritz to a figure of reconciliation.

Dealing with one another in an egalitarian context is a social skill that must be learned, and members possess it in differing degrees when they join. The members who have a greater say in the enterprise and are most listened to are not necessarily those with the most developed manual skills and the greatest work experience; sometimes those with greater say have more social skills and are accustomed, from their previous work and living situations, to dealing with problems and conflicts in larger groups. Gisela, for instance, had only six months' work experience as a toolmaker but had lived for years in communal households (*Wohngemeinschaften*) and had participated in group experiments. She was already much more at ease in fighting her points through at meetings than were Friedel and Noppe, who had worked for years as toolmakers in business industry.

Collectives abundantly use what Hirschman calls "the voice option."

Dissatisfied members are expected to discuss at length their problems in the group and to search for a solution that enforces their loyalty to the group (Hirschman 1970:77). However, those members, especially, who are not able to make their opinions heard or who have started to disagree profoundly with the very principles of collective organisation often quite suddenly choose the "exit option" – they leave the collective. The sudden departure of a fellow member often throws the group into greater confusion than months of heated debates, as there is "no talking back to those who have exited" (Hirschman 1970:126). The group remains behind with its contradictions and often only then is it able to make the decisions it has delayed for so long. As we saw in the preceeding chapter, it was the "exit" of Hansi that pushed *Wuseltronick* into allowing for the possibility of private accumulation.

The outcome of a decision-making process often depends on the presence or absence of reconciliatory figures; the ability of one member to formulate generally acceptable compromises proves as important as efficient production planning. As the chairman of a large German firm pointed out to me, the avoidance of majority decisions is also characteristic of decision-making processes on the managerial boards of business enterprises. Disagreements between managing directors are frequent, but actual voting on a controversial issue occurred on the board of this particular firm as rarely as two or three times a year. Decisions were rarely made on the board itself; agreements were reached through a slow process of finding a generally acceptable solution. The role of the chairman was to pose the problem and to listen to the solutions suggested at the meeting, discuss these with the opposing factions individually then, at a further meeting, formulate a generally acceptable compromise.

According to Bales, most successful groups first assemble information, then from this make inferences to try and form common opinions. Only after such groundwork of accepted facts, common inferences, and sentiments do they come to more specific suggestions (Bales quoted in Sofer 1972:171). As the example of the chairman given above shows, this can be done more efficiently if somebody is allocated the task of summing up and formulating compromises. Kuper (1971:18) makes a similar analytical point referring to decision-making processes among the *Kalagari*. He writes that, especially when a chairman with an external power base is introduced, decision-making becomes more efficient.

The "Boss"

All the collectives I analysed once had, or still have, one or two members who stand out clearly from the rest. The collectivists themselves jokingly call them "our bosses." At different periods in the history of their respective collectives, Hans-Christian and Fritz of *KoMet*, Reiner, Hansi, and Eberhard of *Wuseltronick*, Helmut and Constantin of *Oktoberdruck*, and Klaus of the *FahrradBüro* have occupied this position. These strongly motivated members imposed themselves on the others by their determination to realize their ideals and to take action where others were hesitating.

Characteristics of the "Boss"

Of the eight "bosses" listed above, Fritz of *KoMet* is a classic example. He took part in the founding of the collective in 1979 and was an enthusiastic propagator of the idea of workers' self-management. He strongly believed in emancipated structures of production in which everybody would voluntarily contribute his best to the running of the enterprise. Relatively inexperienced when he began work with *KoMet*, he invested a great deal of energy in acquiring the skills of a professional toolmaker and in building up the enterprise.

When the old founders — who had initially shared his enthusiasm — left, Fritz found himself the most experienced and enterprising member, surrounded by inexperienced newcomers. He dealt with the customers, who became used to asking for him if they wanted to negotiate an order or required a special service. To complete orders he had personally promised to customers, Fritz sometimes worked late into the night. At meetings, the other members became accustomed to waiting for him before starting to discuss business matters. His burden of responsibilities constantly increased. He not only had to excuse the other members' shortcomings to the customers but was also asked by the other members to check their products before they were sent out. But his criticisms were not always well received and were sometimes rejected as displaying a bosslike attitude.

Informally, Fritz acquired the roles that are attributed formally to a manager in business. To maintain the continuity of the collective's production, he became the mediator between collective and customers, feeling personally

"Hey boss, could you come here! There's someone here who wants to know about our collective."

responsible for any shortcomings that affected the orders. He felt that he had been pushed into this role, despite his own political convictions, by pressure of circumstances and was now unable to escape from it. Although the problem was discussed in the collective, it appeared difficult to redistribute the burden Fritz was bearing. He had grown into this role and was now kept in it not only by his colleagues but also by the customers, who addressed themselves to him because they knew him best. To escape this contradictory situation, Fritz finally left the collective.

The comparison with Fritz's colleague and co-founder, Noppe, shows that stepping into the role of "boss" when the more experienced and qualified members leave is not an entirely automatic development. Noppe never tried to take on more responsibilities than were necessary to sustain the tasks he undertook. Although he had a great deal of work experience, he did not feel at ease in dealing with customers, nor did he enjoy training newcomers. Gisela, the trained pedagogue, explained the reluctance of her colleague to represent *KoMet* to the outside world in terms of education. While Fritz had spent several years at university and in political groups mainly composed of students, Noppe had left school at fourteen and had been employed as a qualified worker ever since. He had not had the opportunity to acquire the same self-confidence in presentation as a university student.

Fritz's position with *KoMet* was characterised by aspects he shares with other informal leaders. Of the eight "bosses" mentioned above, all had received some university education; six had been, like Fritz, founders of their collectives; five were the most-qualified members; seven had the most intense contact with customers; four had a strong influence within the collective; four were or still are the formal owners of the machinery; and all are men. Six of the leaders were virtually living for their collective. During the period of their leadership, their energies were concentrated on the enterprise. Their allegiance showed symptoms similar to those described by Coser as typical for members of "greedy orgainsations" such as utopian communities. "The good communitarian had no private self. The greedy community had succeeded in sucking up his substance, leaving only a shell" (Coser 1967:215). Typically, emotional energies were also transferred from the dyad to the community (Coser 1967:212). For years, the informal leaders had no strong love-relationships, and not uncommonly their departure from the "boss" role coincided with them having children and entering into a more demanding domestic relationship.

To become a "boss," a member must be prepared to assume increased responsibility, besides the additional tasks that any organisational mistake may require; he must also enjoy this exposed position. Not all members would do this, and some are even glad when certain tasks are taken from them. Analysing decision-making in business enterprises, Barnard points out that the making of decisions was generally felt to be burdensome by managers. He concluded that people tend to avert decisions if possible, rather than feel pleasure by imposing them on others (Barnard quoted in Sofer 1972:164). To alleviate the tasks of decision-making and representation, some members of collectives would gladly tolerate an informal leader for a time and then reject him if he becomes too powerful.

Sex Bias

In none of the four collectives analysed was a woman in the position of "boss," but women were often active in overthrowing the male "bosses" if such a situation presented itself. In this way, women were the vanguard for an alternative style of leadership. In my research among other Berlin collectives, I came across only one woman who was clearly the informal leader. Marlene, a founding member of the consulting office *STATTwerke*, had the same characteristics as those listed for the eight male "bosses." She was the most qualified member, writing a doctoral thesis on the means of financing collective enterprises. She played the role of ideological leader and had taken an important part in developing contacts with customers.

Comparing the five most influential women in the four collectives — Marita, Gisela, Ulrike, Brigitte, and Veronika — with the eight male "bosses," it is seen that most had a university education, like the males they kept close contact with the customers, and they had some influence in ideological issues. But most of the women lacked higher working skills, none were among the founders of their collective, and none were in the position of being the formal owner of the enterprise.

It is still the exception for women to be among the founders of collectives. The only woman who participated in the setting up of any of the four collectives studied was Marlis, Constantin's girlfriend. Although she helped found *agitdruck* and later *Oktoberdruck*, she never became one of the formal co-owners of either enterprise. With both collectives, it was Constantin, alone or with a male friend, who was registered as the owner. In most metal and printing collectives, women play a much more important part than they do in the general labour market. However, men are still in the majority and tend to be better qualified. In the bicycle collectives, the sex ratio is more balanced. For instance, in the *FahrradBüro* Ulrike, the first woman member, advanced after years of membership to become one of the most experienced bicycle mechanics, but she did not become a leader, although the women outnumbered the men four to three. Instead of becoming a leader herself, she actively participated in removing Klaus, who occupied the role of "boss." She even consulted a lawyer in order to take legal action against Klaus. Together with other women fiercely opposed to the emergence of leadership-roles, she then tried to inhibit the emergence of replacement "bosses."

Hans, who is now the owner of the *FahrradBüro*, tried to assume the role of leader but without success. When he left the *FahrradBüro* in the autumn of 1983 to take a temporary post as a trainee teacher (which he later abandoned), he tried to install a successor who some of the women rejected. Apart from his personal desire for greater influence, Hans had the conviction that an enterprise like the *FahrradBüro* had to expand if it was to survive in the market and offer its members a reasonable income. To achieve this goal and give the collective a more dynamic structure, he was convinced that strong leaders like himself were necessary.

The other members did not allow him to assume this role. Veronika, a feminist, was strongly opposed to his choice of successor because she did not want another pretender to the "boss-role." When she vetoed the integration of Rolf, Hans's candidate, Hans in turn vetoed the continued employment of

Mathias, a member dear to the women's faction, who was still in his probationary period.

Veronika, the leader of the female faction, explained the conflict in terms of sex roles. According to her, Mathias was rejected by the male faction because he was not fulfilling the expected male role of a "macho" comrade. He was a quiet man, calmly going about his work without trying to appropriate the most interesting tasks for himself. For the women, he was a competent person who had the needs of the entire collective at heart and was fulfilling his tasks wherever necessary. They considered him ideal as a colleague, in contrast to Hans, who in their eyes was a progressive collective manager interested in developing profitable structures without caring greatly for the people involved. They insisted that good personal relationships and a friendly atmosphere were more important to them than a profitable organisation that would earn them a fortune. The collective achieved a compromise by employing both Rolf and Mathias in February 1984, but a year later Hans sent Rolf, who was not yet a full associate, a letter of dismissal in order to show him who was boss. The resistance of the female members, however, made it impossible for this to be implemented.

Hans was unable to become the "boss" because the other members denied him access to this role. The innovations he wanted to introduce were considered unsuitable, even objectionable, and the other members refused to surrender their responsibilities into the hands of a leader.

Education and class background seem to be important elements in determining how women react to the male appropriation of power. The twelve women workers of the Fakenham cooperative discussed by Wajcman felt in a much weaker position toward male managers seizing power than do the women in the Berlin collectives. The Fakenham women had occupied their small shoe factory when it was to be closed down in 1972 and attempted to continue it as a workers' cooperative. All the women except the workers' director, Nancy, had no higher education and no experience in dealing with administration and male authority (Wajcman 1983:85). The cooperative was at first sponsored through loans from Scott Bader, who introduced a managerial system of work-control and a male director. The new director removed the responsibility of bookkeeping from the women, who thereby lost the possibility of participating effectively in the management of the factory, but was himself unable to accomplish the managerial tasks. After months of mismanagement, the women passed a motion of no confidence and dismissed the director (Wajcman 1983:78). They did not feel sufficiently self-confident and skilled, however, to continue without a manager and were seeking a male replacement. "As far as the Fakenham women were concerned, their knowledge that Hicks (the manager) had been incompetent did not disturb their belief that, in general, men made the best managers" (Wajcman 1983:178).

The Fakenham women were not motivated by broad political considerations when they occupied their factory but by the imminent need to preserve their jobs. They only slowly acquired more self-confidence and a certain pride in running their own enterprise, although their general attitude toward men and society remained profoundly conservative. The women in the Berlin collectives, on the contrary, choose to work in collectives because they are strongly influenced by feminist ideas and are determined to make a stand against male dominance.

Keeping the "Boss" Under Control

The source of the informal leader's power arises out of the inherent contradiction that all the members are expected to take an equal share of the responsibilities but are often incapable of doing so, and out of the fact that decisions made in the meeting are often so ambiguous that they cannot be directly implemented. Recognising a similar dilemma on a large variety of councils, Kuper (1971b:23) maintained that "ambiguous decisions suppose an effective decision-making institution outside the council." He quoted the example of the Secretary General of the United Nations, whose status and authority arose from the fact that decisions taken by the United Nations council were ambiguous, leaving him free to interpret them. Collectives do not have a formal head, so any member can assume the role of de facto decision-maker, a fact which contributes to some extent to the chaos of collective organisation. The question that arises here is: are informal leaders more easily controlled than those to whom power is formally assigned?

No structures are developed to account for differences in qualifications, work experience, and length of membership, which therefore manifest themselves unpredictably. Members with work experience have greater influence in matters of production, those who have known customers for years continue to negotiate with them. In periods of strong fluctuation, these members represent continuity and stability for the customers and the creditors. Enterprising leaders often acquire their position by opening up new markets or promoting new products.

In the *Wuseltronick* collective, for instance, Hansi — the first "boss" —

provided the initial impetus to found the collective by virtue of his connections with research funding. Reiner, the second "boss," brought in one of the most important research projects; and Eberhard, the most recent "boss," travelled to the United States to assess the market for their new product, the large windmill.

Hansi lost his position as the founding "boss" in 1981, when he was accused of monopolising both contacts and the most interesting tasks. Reiner was accused with him, but nobody took him seriously because of his dreamy and unpractical attitude. Hansi agreed to withdraw from part of his activities and recommended that everybody should take on more responsibility for the collective. Reiner feared this solution, in case it resulted in his having to carry the entire responsibility alone. He put moral pressure on Hansi to resume his activities, but as he continued to refuse, the two old friends soon became declared enemies.

The collectivists explained this conflict in terms of "the chiefs" versus "the workers." The structure of the collective was centred around the planners, who organised the projects the others were executing. The simple withdrawal of Hansi did not solve this more profound structural problem, as no alternative was in sight to replace him in his role. Two of the "workers," Matze and Brigitte, tried the individualistic solution of leaving the collective for a couple of months to find out for themselves what job they really wanted. Both have since returned, and Matze, especially, has built up a work domain for himself in which the others interfere as little as possible.

Hansi's central position in the collective has since been taken over by a fairly recent member, Eberhard. He became a close friend of Reiner, cooperated on the collective's three most important projects, and intensified external contacts. According to him, a collective involved in such complicated work processes cannot manage without a chief, and a person capable of understanding complex contexts can very easily slip into this role.

By 1988, the responsibility for external contacts was clearly divided among the members, according to the products they produced. Brigitte, for instance, became responsible for the wind-measuring section. Eberhard, however, well known to all the customers, continued to be addressed by them.

The shyness and inexperience of some members reinforces the position of the "boss," as these members often turn to him for help and advice. As new members are often not systematically introduced into the collective organisation, most are only too glad to find somebody who will take charge of them.

However, more experienced members strongly resent a fellow member giving them advice without being asked to do so. One of the usual reproaches made to an informal leader is that he walks through the workshop surveying his colleagues' work just like a foreman.

"Bosses" in collectives are in a precarious situation, as no special position is assigned to them, and the mere recognition of their existence would contradict the collective principles. A master artisan working in the crafts' collective *Handwerker Genossenschaft Mannheim*, compared his present ambiguous role in the collective with his previous work experiences in a business enterprise. In the latter, his functions as a master were clearly defined and his relationships to his colleagues determined by them. He was the mouthpiece for the boss. He made out the lists of tasks to be done, acted as mediator between customers and journeymen, and organised the training of apprentices. In the collective, he was formally on an equal footing with his colleagues, but it was still he who gave the technical advice. When customers complained about the completion of an order, he felt entirely responsible for the professional performance of his colleagues, an attitude that was incompatible with the principles of self-management (Flieger 1984:219).

Faced with a similar problem of unauthoritative leadership, the contemporary commune *Twin Oaks*, in the United States, attempted to solve it by appointing three planners who would serve eighteen month terms. These rotating planners did not develop any long-term plans, however, but tried to serve the immediate wants of the commune. As they were nevertheless constantly subjected to heavy criticism from the other members, their role soon became so dreaded that nobody was willing to take it on (Kanter 1972:18-21).

An informal leader must keep a low profile in order to survive. Only if he manages to convince the other members by his arguments and commitment to the collective may he keep his position for some time. Leaders in collectives tend to be "expressive" rather than "instrumental," to use the distinction made by Parsons and Bales (1956:318). They are mediators; they defuse disputes, and they can only be permissive as they lack the possibility of punishing their fellow members. If they attempt to take on the role of "instrumental leader" — that is to say, if they try to impose discipline and give instructions — they are generally discarded rapidly. Leaders who try to impose their point of view by manipulation or conspiracy, and those who no longer make special contribution to the collective, are generally excluded from the group with great rapidity. Having occupied the position of leader, they can rarely be reintegrated as ordinary members.

Since 1981, of the eight "bosses" I have mentioned, three (Hans-Christian, Klaus and Helmut) have been more or less forcefully evicted, two (Hansi and Fritz) have left voluntarily, and one (Constantin) was sent on holiday for a year and then became an ordinary member. Only Eberhard and Reiner are still recognized as the informal leaders of *Wuseltronick.*

Helmut of *Oktoberdruck* is a typical example of an unloved "boss" who his fellow members finally evicted. He had managed to make the collective dependent upon him in a situation of flux and friction. As he had been responsible for the office for some years, he was able to use his knowledge of the financial situation to influence others at meetings. For instance, he decided almost entirely on his own initiative to allow the typesetter to set up his business in one of *Oktoberdruck'*s rooms. As he was working not only in the office but also in the repro-mounting department, his influence was felt everywhere. His excellent contacts with customers and suppliers were considered very valuable for the enterprise. It was also generally admitted that a proportion of the orders depended directly on him. Helmut did nothing to dissipate this impression, nor did he try to make the others participate more; on the contrary, he enjoyed being the "boss." At lunches and meetings, he sat at the head of the table and, on one occasion, even chased away a visitor who had inadvertently taken his seat.

But while he occupied a position of power, he also became an outsider to the group. Most members disliked him personally, and he could only count two members among his friends. These two, Udo and Amrai, were so closely attached to him that they supported all his opinions and were nicknamed "Helmut's disciples." Although Helmut was disliked, he was also respected. This respect only ceased when it became obvious he was no longer identifying with the collective and that he intended to convince the others to sell the enterprise. Although most members disagreed entirely with his intentions, they still hesitated to force him to leave because they feared disastrous consequences. Cut off from direct relations with customers and administration, the other members had developed a certain awe of marketing. In this respect, they had become as "alienated" as their colleagues in business enterprises.

Helmut was well aware of this insecurity and stated publicly that his fellow members were dependent on him. He promised to create such a bad atmosphere that the others would leave before he did. However, after weeks of psychological warfare with silent communal lunches, he and his two supporters left of their own accord. Since then, the seat at the head of the table had usually remained unoccupied, and when one member sat there it was jokingly said that he would become the next "boss."

In the process of excluding an informal leader, the values of non-hierarchical organisation are again upheld and the leader becomes the scapegoat who is made responsible for failures. The collective can liberate itself from a negative self-image by sending a "boss" away, while it would have to struggle with all its contradictions by reintegrating him as an ordinary member. Berlin collectives seem to practise the periodic overthrow and exclusion of leaders to reestablish egalitarian structures similar to Barth's (1959) observations among the Swat Pathan. Meanwhile, members become increasingly conscious that the fact alone of sending a leader away does not solve the structural problems that made it possible for him to obtain his position in the first place.

Conclusion

The initial ideal of collective organisation was that every member should participate equally in internal decision making and external representation. In practice, however, differences in age and competence, self-confidence, and willingness to listen to others form a complex blend of human relations and informal power structures. Members have to acquire social skills to enable them to relate to one another, to limit the power of the few, and to overcome their fear of important decisions. Collective planning and decisionmaking are time consuming because of the high degree of participation and the reluctance to assume responsibilities. Skill in administrative tasks is constantly compromised by fluctuating membership.

In place of hierarchy in the organisation of production, the collectivists reintroduce the personal element. Group consensus and good personal relations between members are the fragile basis of collective self-management. Relations between members are not defined through formal social status but through the skills of convincing others and of reconciling differences. The power of the informal leaders who emerge is often more difficult to control than if they had a formal status.

The abolition of relations of power and dominion, which are at the basis of the idea of self-management, can only be realised if the collectivists admit that power relations play an important part in cooperation (Crozier and Friedberg 1984:336). Only if they are brought into the open can these relationships be effectively regulated. If they are covered up, new structures of dependencies will arise at the nodal points of the collective system, especially where informal "bosses" take over the roles of managers and mediators between the collective and the "system."

Notes

1. The Montan law of codetermination (*Montanmitbestimmungsgesetz*: 1951) determined that the supervisory boards of the mining and steel industries were to be 50 percent composed of representatives of workers and employees. In 1952, the constitutional law of enterprise (*Betriebsverfassungsgesetz*) decreed one-third parity codetermination for all other joint stock companies.

7

The Division of Labour in Collectives

Collectivists do not often refer explicitly to Marx, but implicitly many of their ideas about how a collective should function are strongly influenced by Marxist critical analysis of capitalist society. One of the key issues is the Marxist concept of alienation, in the sense of the estrangement of the worker in a capitalist enterprise from both the work process and the item he is producing. Marx writes about the division of labour in capitalist manufacture:

> It transforms the worker into a cripple, a monster, by forcing him to develop some highly specialised dexterity at the cost of a world of productive impulses and faculties. Not only are the various partial operations allotted to different individuals but the individual himself is split up, is transformed into the automatic motor of some partial operation. (Marx 1930 (1890), I:381)

The alienated worker is incorporated as a continuously replaceable part in a defined division of the production process, sometimes without knowing the finished form of what he is producing, or what purpose it will ultimately serve.

Marx did not attribute alienation to the division of labour as such but rather believed that in a higher phase of communism the enslaving character of alienation would disappear, and even the distinction between mental and physical work would vanish. The key to the exploitative nature of the division of labour lay in the property relations under capitalism as the division of tasks was decided upon by the capitalist owners of the means of production, who made use of the labour power purchased to its full advantage. Once the capitalists were overthrown, the division of labour would take on a different meaning and would be based on the workers' natural inclination to cooperate, each making full use of his or her abilities and carrying out the task to which he or she was best suited until "labour" entirely disappeared.

The collectivists, aware of the workers' position in the state industries in East Germany, no longer trust this vision of the remote future. Closer to Marcuse, they regard this type of work as being as alien to workers in the "real existing socialism" (the ironic phrase used by members of collectives to describe the East German economy) as it used to exist on the other side of the Berlin Wall, as it is to those in capitalist society. As Marcuse does, they maintain that it is the logic of industrial society, obeying the principle of increasing mechanisation, rationalisation, and efficiency, that imposes its laws on the worker and transforms him or her into an element of the work process. As a result of this, he or she has no individual influence but must continue to fill the world with useless objects, which the manipulated consumer is then called upon to acquire (Marcuse 1968).

In 1968, in a series of lectures at the Free University of Berlin, Marcuse (1970: 62 ff) emphasized that in a free society "freedom must appear in labour itself and not beyond labour." It should allow for a "creative experimentation with the productive forces." Calling upon students to take action, he said:

> In established societies there are still gaps and interstices in which heretical methods can be practised without meaningless sacrifice, and still help the cause.... The interstices within the established society are still open, and one of the most important tasks is to make use of them to the full. (Marcuse 1970:76-77)

Members of collectives define their work as breaking with the logic of industrial production and as practising complete control over the process of production in the small enclaves of the system they occupy. They emphasize that they are attempting to overcome the isolation of a highly divided and closely delimited workplace and that they want to restructure the organisation of production in such a way that any one worker may participate in an almost complete cycle of production in the workshop and perform a large variety of tasks. They try to acquire a broad range of skills, to rotate tasks among each other, and to follow up the making of the product from beginning to end, attempting to learn all the necessary worksteps.

Collectivists try to practise what Wallmann (1979:17) called work with a low degree of alienation:

> Degrees of alienation are greatest where the worker has negligible control over the value and the disposition of his product, least where he initiates the work-effort, organises time, place, person — all the elements of the work process — and can identify with the product and the values of the product.

A Working Day with *Oktoberdruck* — 18 February 1984

When I entered the kitchen of the *Oktoberdruck* collective at eleven in the morning, Ingrid was drinking coffee and skimming through a wholesale marketing catalogue. She had been at work since eight o'clock and had cleaned the montage room, together with her colleague Constantin, who was generally the first to arrive. Ingrid was one of the more recent members of *Oktoberdruck*, having joined after Helmut and his friends left in September 1983. She is a feminist who worked for many years free of charge as a paste-up artist with the feminist journal *Courage* before it went bankrupt, earning her living at the same time in an ordinary printing shop. She had now settled in with *Oktoberdruck* and felt at ease with her colleagues. She was respected professionally, although she had not yet acquired much experience in repro-photography.

As soon as I arrived, she returned with a cigarette and her cup of coffee to the light-table, where she was mounting a printing foil for a comic book. "People don't know how to read any more, so we have to do comics now," she commented jokingly on her order. When I explained to her that I intended to write down everything she did during the day and analyse it as an example of how she organised her work, she began to criticise the way many newcomers start work. "Some start by working fourteen hours in one go, and then sleep late for days". She was convinced that the irregular work patterns of one person could spoil all the other members' work rhythms and make for a very stressful situation. In her previous employment in an ordinary printing shop, she had felt much less tired, even though she had simultaneously been working ten hours per week with *Courage*. She considered the emotional, interpersonal discussions the most tiring aspect of her current work.

Ingrid then asked Constantin as a favour to redo one of the films she had made for her order, so that she could continue mounting the foils. She brought a new foil, mounted the marks for the print and the fold, checked the page numbers with the help of an imposition sheet (*Ausschießmuster*), and marked them with a blue pen on the eight fields of her plan of the layout (*Standbogen*). Then she fetched one film after another, checked them against the paper model where the proportions were marked, and glued them immediately to the foil, to avoid having to look them up again.

Klaus asked her where his ruler was, and she gave him hers. She put the finished foil on top of the others with a thin piece of paper in between. A temporary helper came from the office looking for an order sheet. These sheets were filled out in the mounting and print sections to allow the office to calculate prices corresponding to hours worked. The order sheets had only recently been introduced because the previous prices calculated by the office differed too considerably from the actual hours worked. Ingrid's search for the order sheet was interrupted by the telephone. She spoke for a while on the phone then went back to work until Helmut, the typesetter who ran his own small business next door to the mounting room, arrived for a chat. "If the customers aren't sloppy, for once, then we are," he said, then added jokingly, "I am in favour of the replacement of man by the machine!" Ingrid responded that this was not creative enough for her and drew Klaus into a discussion about the pressures under which they were working.

When she had finished her fourth sheet, Ingrid took new foils from the drawer punched them with a punching machine, which also served to punch the printing plates. These holes are used to fix the plates in the press, and also serve as an orientation for the mounting to keep the distance to the edges correct. Donald (the printer) came up searching for the printing plate for the "social help leaflet" envelope, and Ingrid showed him where it was.

She explained to me that she was checking black and white lay-sheets (*Montagen*) by placing two foils mirror inverted on top of each other. She then made carbon copies, which the customers had to check before the print run was started. For each alteration that was not due to an error on her part, she charged the customer a set amount: for instance, if she had to replace a drawing and this had not been indicated beforehand. If she made a mistake herself, for example mounting mirror inverted, she would make no charge. Carbon copies had only recently been introduced to avoid the customer not identifying a mistake until after the order had been printed and then claiming a reduction or refund.

At one o'clock, lunch was ready, cooked by a woman from the canteen collective. One after another, the members arrived, the last being the printers who worked the evening shift from 2 to 9 p.m. The conversation at the dining table revolved around a dispute between a member of the commune *UFA* and a member of *die tageszeitung* about whether the informal meeting of collectives, *Lundkreis*, had the right to organise the "congress" of West German and Berlin collectives in Berlin.

At two o'clock, Ingrid returned to her work. Jürgen, who had taken the order, came to explain to her that the paper for the order was to be 63 cm, not 61 cm as she had initially thought, so she could work more easily. A customer came to bring Constantin some models and fix a date for checking the carbon copies. Constantin went to look up on the printing plan when the order was scheduled for printing, and the customer commented, "My god, you're getting pretty precise around here!" In fact, the printing plan was also part of the recent innovations.

At half past four, Ingrid started the last foil of the order. The order had been a rather urgent one, which had put her under pressure. She had already worked on Saturday in order to be able to work at a more relaxed pace thereafter. She intended to take another day off during the week instead. She hoped to finish the rest of the carbon copies before leaving that night and to have enough time to make the corrections the next day and develop the last printing plates in the afternoon. The printing would then be finished on the following day. "Determining the working time myself is a pleasure, but not everybody has learnt to estimate how long the individual work-steps are going to take. With inexperienced newcomers this can be quite a strain."

Some films were missing for the last foil. Ingrid was running back and forth between the montage room and repro-camera. At the same time, she was chatting with Klaus and me about whether one should emigrate from Germany if F. J. Strauss came to power or the fundamentalist of the party *Die Grünen*, Rudolf Bahro. Ingrid seemed rather suspicious of Bahro's fundamentalism but had been determined since 1963 to emigrate if Strauss became the new chancellor.

Klaus, who had finished his own work, suggested that he might help Ingrid with the final repro-photography. She had to search for the copies (*Vorlagen*) on films from previous orders. She put the films under the repro-camera on one side, and Klaus took the picture on the other. She realized too late that the films were too large to fit her montage foil and would have to be reduced. It was five past five and Ingrid felt too tired to concentrate properly. Klaus too advised her to stop. But as she had set herself the goal of finishing, she made a final effort, stuck the films together, and made a reduction with trans-illumination. But this process was unable to reproduce the small-size lettering.

Just as she was deciding to give up and try again the next day, Constantin joined them and advised Ingrid to put the film on white paper and make a photograph with seven units. This was successful. Constantin was more experienced than any other member in the repro-montage department as he had worked for ten years an as autodidact in all parts of the enterprise.

The printer on the evening shift came with the first printed sheet of the comicbook, complaining that the drawing mark was in the wrong place. He showed Ingrid the correct place. Constantin intervened and remarked that it would have been better to mount it on a larger foil altogether, because the text was very close to the edge and difficult to copy onto the printing plate. Ingrid reacted calmly, explaining that she only received the correct paper size after lunch and was going to replace the drawing marks the next day. The last pages with the photographs of the authors were still missing and the pictures had to be screened. But Ingrid preferred to leave this until the next day as she was no longer working efficiently. She tidied up, threw the remains of the foils into the foil bin — *Oktoberdruck* collects leftover printing materials separately for recycling — covered the foils with tissue paper, and entered the hours worked on the order sheet. It was 6 o'clock.

During her work day, Ingrid had performed many tasks that in an ordinary printing shop would have been taken over by several different people. She carried out the repro-photography, mounted the foils, copied the printing plates, and made the carbon copies, and she also dealt directly with the customer. Although she was solely responsible for her product until it reached the printing stage, she constantly interacted with her colleagues. Unlike in a business enterprise, her colleagues participated in a sporadic and spontaneous way. When Constantin made a few repro-photographs for Ingrid's order, it was not because his assigned work was repro-photography but because he wanted to do her a favour, and anyway was doing a few for the order he was working on. When Klaus stepped in to help Ingrid, he did so without any obligation, simply to allow her the possibility of going home earlier; he might expect her to do the same for him another day.

The closest interaction going on during this working day concerned mutual problem solving. Members passed each other tools, discussed problems of production methods, and gave each other a hand with difficult tasks. To make the reduction with the repro-camera, Ingrid and Klaus used trial and error until Constantin contributed from his own experience. In an ordinary printing shop, this technical problem would have been solved by the foreman or master; the workers would not have been allowed to spend so much time in experimentation. In the montage section of *Oktoberdruck*, problems have to be solved in discussion with colleages, and mistakes are also discovered in that way. Unlike in an ordinary enterprise, the printer complained directly to the repro-monteur about an incorrect drawing mark and explained how he wanted the printing plate to look. No foreman existed who could have intervened.

The Non-Division of Labour...

Most collectives set themselves the aim of seeing that each member becomes familiar with the entire production process, participates in its coordination on an equal basis, and organises his or her own tasks at his or her own pace. Fritz, a skilled metalworker, emphasized the members' high level of individual autonomy:

> The great advantage of work in a collective is the completely free organisation of one's own workplace and together with the members of one's own enterprise, the possibility of acquiring experience which you can get nowhere else because elsewhere it is linked to formal qualifications. (Fritz, *Ko-Met*, 13.4.1984)

Collectivists believe that only if each of them has reached a high degree of individual autonomy will they then be able to replace a hierarchical organisation of production with a collective one. The ultimate practical aim is, therefore, to make each member replaceable by any of his colleagues, requiring an equal level of skill and knowledge for all members.

...Versus Scientific Management

When I discussed the organisation of work in collectives with Constantin of *Oktoberdruck*, one of the ideologists of the "movement," he advised me to read Braverman's *Labour and Monopoly Capital*, so that I would be able to appreciate the concept of work in collectives as a radical response to the Taylorist theories of "scientific management."

Braverman (1974) analysed the theories of management developed by Taylor at the end of the nineteenth century. Based on his own experiences as a

Alternative Technology

Foreman: "Hup! Hup!"
Worker: "No way!"

foreman and master in the metal industry, Taylor wanted to develop a system of work that made deliberate "go-slow" impossible and that forced workers employed on a piece rate basis to accelerate their pace. His central idea was that managers should also acquire all the practical knowledge possessed by the skilled workers and should start to plan and divide the production process into very minute detail. Braverman (1974:86,90) defined "scientific management" as

> an attempt to apply the methods of science to the increasingly complex problems of control of labour.... It starts, despite occasional protestations to the contrary, not from the human point of view but from the point of view of the management of a refractory work-force in a setting of antagonistic social relations.... Taylor was seeking ... but an answer to the specific problem of how best to control alienated labour — that is to say, labour power that is bought and sold.

The skilled worker of Taylor's day performed a large variety of tasks and possessed the actual intellectual and practical knowledge necessary for production, which the manager did not.

The machinist ... started with the shopdrawing, and turned, milled, bored, drilled, planed, shaped, ground, filed, and otherwise machine- and hand-processed the proper stock to the desired shape, as specified in the drawing. The range of decisions to be made in the course of the process is ... by its very nature enormous. (Braverman 1974:110)

The radical alterations proposed by Taylor to gain control over the labour power were directed toward deskilling the worker. His first principle was to render the labour process independent of craft, tradition, and the workers' knowledge. The second was to remove all possible mental labour from the shop and centre it in the planning or layout department. The third was to use this monopoly over knowledge to control each step of the labour process and its mode of execution (Braverman 1974:113-119).

The workers in the industries in which Taylor's methods were first applied strongly objected to this deskilling, combined with strict control, and mostly left to work in other traditional enterprises. Braverman (1974:149) quotes the example of the Ford workers:

So great was labour's distaste for the new machine system that towards the close of 1913 every time the company wanted to add 100 men to its factory personnel, it was necessary to hire 963.

However, soon the new style of organisation became so generalised that workers had no other alternative. Braverman (1974:151) concluded: "The apparent acclimatization of the worker to the new mode of production grows out of the destruction of all other ways of living."

Braverman's analysis of the labour process under modern capitalism is certainly very much to the point. It does not account, however, for the defense mechanisms, such as sabotage, practised especially by workers in Taylorised industries. Nor does he consider the much finer psychological measures with which enterprises experiment today to coerce employees to work hard and identify with the enterprise. As Goldthorpe (quoted in Beynon and Nichols 1977:xiii) wrote about new management techniques:

The second industrial revolution was sweeping aside the satanic mills of the first and creating new types of factory. Managements were becoming increasingly concerned with 'human relations,' while automated or process production systems gave rise to conditions of work which, from both a physical and a social point of view, differed markedly from those characteristic of an earlier age of industry.

Analysing the working conditions in a modern chemical factory with the reputation of being a vanguard for humane, automated production, Beynon and Nichols concluded that the setup in the factory did not return to the workers any of their original skills. Instead of re-establishing a direct link between the worker and his product, the "system" only became more contradictory:

> It wants to engage people as a commodity, as labour power, to be managed, directed, controlled; it also wants them to become engaged, to be involved — but not to control, not to manage for themselves. (Beynon and Nichols 1977:203)

While Braverman underlines the mechanisms of total control over the labour force and Beynon and Nichols analyse the manipulative mechanisms of modern management, Burawoy tries to resolve the paradox that workers still do actually identify with a labour process in which they have lost all control over the product. He attempts to explain why employees work as hard as they do. Analysing the piece rate system in a machine shop in the "Allied" corporation in South Chicago, he emphasizes the importance of competition between workers and of a certain amount of self-determination to motivate them (Burawoy 1979:94). Engaging in what Burawoy calls "the game of making out," trying to exceed the assigned production quota, the employees not only strive to make more money but also compete against each other to affirm their status in their own informal hierarchies (Burawoy 1979:64). The game is entered into for its relative satisfaction and ability to alleviate the monotony of repeated tasks and because it presents an individual challenge to achieve the best result inside the narrow limits of the piece rate system. It is the desire to see outstanding individual performance rewarded and singled out from that of fellow workers that motivates wage-labourers.

A "Network" Model of Production

Collectives wish to develop an alternative to the large scale industrial production with which some members are familiar from personal experience during their traineeship or previous employment. Instead of hierarchically organised units, where each worker has an insight into only a tiny aspect of the overall process, they try to conceive of the production of ecologically and socially useful goods through the cooperation of small independent units. They want to substitute for the hierarchical "military" model a "network" model of production. Uwe, a former member of *KoMet*, developed the initial ideas his collective held about the substitution of industrial production:

> It was not only our aim to produce under non-hierarchical relations ourselves but we also wanted to demonstrate a social principle. We wanted to show that a society which is organised on a small scale can nevertheless produce products like ballpens, spoons and tape-recorders. ... If you could prove that complicated final products, also mass products, can be produced on a small scale and in collective relations of production, then you could say to people: 'You don't need military hierarchical production to get a refrigerator or a washing machine.' Because this is their fear, that a revolution or other fundamental change would alter their standard of living and endanger the production of consumer goods. (Uwe, *KoMet*, 25.4.1984)

Uwe's view is not altogether representative of the majority of collectivists, but all of them would agree with his preference for small scale production. Most collectives maintain that their ideal for work organisation can only be realistically approached in small, easily managed structures, where communication between members is direct and the level of qualifications high. Size seems to be one of the decisive factors in determining whether a collective can manage without a formal division of labour. In fact, none of the forty-six production collectives in West Berlin has more than seventeen members (with the exception of the newspaper *die tageszeitung* with more than 200 members). They tend toward crafts, which can be practised in small units. None of the collectives have engaged in industrial production of mass items. They manufacture single parts and small series for which a fairly high level of skill and creativity is required. As Wallmann (1979:17) points out, the balance between identity and alienation is easier to maintain in a small-scale setting with "multiplex" relationships, where the workers "know all about each other and where they have more than a single work-role."

In an analysis of ninteenth century *Genossenschaften*, Franz Oppenheimer (1922:70) maintains than this appeared mainly in crafts that had not yet been "revolutionized by the machine," where the machine was still a tool of the worker, not the worker an auxiliary of the machine. It is striking that a large number of the crafts he lists as being practised by these *Genossenschaf-*

ten are the same as those undertaken by contemporary collectives, particularly woodworking, printing, baking, shoemaking, and pottery. They have remained occupations that can be performed on a small scale by one or two workers alone producing the whole item. Watchmaking, combmaking, and gilding, other nineteenth-century crafts, have since been replaced by large scale industrial production, which collectives have not taken up. In some crafts unknown in the last century — such as car, cycle and electrical repairs, electronics, alternative energy, and computing — contemporary collectives have found new fields of activity.

In recent years, there have been numerous attempts to undertake larger projects involving the cooperation of several collectives. Because it was featured several times in the media and is technologically very demanding, the most well known is the cooperative founded by *Wuseltronick* producing windmills and wind-measuring instruments. The cooperative of construction engineers, *Baubüro Schöneberg*, encouraged the cooperation of collectives in the building trades — plumbing, carpenting, building, and painting — to undertake the renovation of entire houses. The *Baubüro* also founded an association grouping architects, construction engineers, carpenters, and specialist woodworkers, which specialised in the hot-air treatment of woodwork infected by fungus. This joint activity has become a supplement to their regular incomes.

In both cases, the intention was that these associations should function on an egalitarian basis; however, they were initiated and coordinated by engineers who played the same leading role as individual engineers in business industry. Both engineers' collectives, *Baubüro* and *Wuseltronick*, had more direct access to larger orders and state funding than the craft collectives that participated. Their members were trained for coordinating and planning the tasks that others were going to execute, and this role was to some extent perpetuated in the relations between the autonomous collectives.

The counterpart to autonomous collectives undertaking joint activities is the subdivision into quasi-autonomous units of the larger collective. The newspaper *die tageszeitung*, for instance, is subdivided into units of from three to six members. In the initial conception of the newspaper, it was intended that the people working in the different sections would from time to time exchange work-places — a paste-up artist working in the office, for example, and an editor doing the typesetting. This idea has since been abandoned, and the division of labour between the sections has become fixed. Although members doing technical and administrative jobs may occasionally have the opportunity to publish an article, the editors no longer replace them in their work. Within the newspaper, editorial work has higher prestige than have technical or administrative jobs. Although the level of pay and the vote in meetings is the same for all, a certain hierarchy of prestige has slipped in through the backdoor, and the de facto equality is only maintained within the individual sections. Compared to other newspapers, however, where people doing technical jobs have no influence at all on the content of the paper or its political tendencies, in *die tageszeitung* they have both the right and the opportunity to make their opinions heard.

Collectives with more than five or six members tend to be subdivided into smaller units with clearly delimited functions. Among the six printing collectives in West Berlin, the five smaller ones with no more than five members each lack any formal division, but *Oktoberdruck*, with twelve members in 1984, introduced a formal division of the enterprise into three sections: office (two members); repro-montage (five members); and printing (five members).

Following the Entire Production Process

The division of *Oktoberdruck* was not intended to be rigid but to allow for the moving of members from one section to another. The idea was to equip everybody in the long run with all the skills necessary for printing. In fact, in 1983, three of the twelve members changed from one section to another: Jürgen, an unskilled printer, took over one of the office jobs; Marita, who for three years had been the bookkeeper, started training in the repro-montage section; and Constantin, a printer with experience in the repro-mounting department, took over a job there. Neither the rotation of Jürgen nor that of Constantin affected the smooth running of the enterprise. But the whole collective felt it a great disadvantage that Marita wanted to change. It meant that a new bookkeeper had to familiarise him or herself with the task and that Marita, who was not a trained repro-monteur, had to be trained from scratch. In discussions on the issue, the argument was raised repeatedly that it would mean a loss of income for the whole collective simply to satisfy Marita's individual wishes. It was only after she had raised the issue for a year and had threatened to leave that she finally had the opportunity to change. In fact, the rotation of tasks is practised only to a small extent and exclusively by long-term members. In 1983, only the founder, Constantin, was able to perform all the tasks, though not all of them equally well. The highly skilled members of one section tended not to move elsewhere because their skills were badly needed to make their own sections run smoothly.

The *Oktoberdruck* collectivists claimed that the real difference in the division of labour between their collective and a business enterprise showed itself within the sections. Herbie, a trained repro-photographer, maintained that, in the enterprise where he worked previously, all the tasks in the repro-mounting department were clearly divided. A repro-photographer would spend all day in the darkroom and would not take over any montage task. In the montage section, the tasks were divided between those done by unskilled workers, such as scratching and cutting films and developing the printing plate, and those done by a trained photomonteur, for instance mounting films on the foil. In the collective, this division did not exist: all tasks from repro-photography to the development of the plates were done one after the other by a single person. Only when larger books had to be prepared did several people cooperate.

In the printing section, the collectivists tried to train themselves to be able to carry out all the jobs, operate both printing machines and become entirely interchangeable. Donald, a skilled printer, maintained that he was performing the jobs that five different people would have carried out in the enterprise where he worked previously: ordering paper and colours; cutting paper; putting paper onto the printing press (*Vorstapeln*); printing; and machine maintenance. This firm — *Druckhaus Tempelhof* — was one of the largest printing shops in Berlin with no fewer than 150 employees and printing presses up to 15 m in length. But although *Oktoberdruck* was much smaller, the abolition of any division of labour was still not perfect. In the summer of 1984, only four of the five workers in the printing section were really skilled and the fifth member, the only woman, did mainly unskilled work such as transporting and cutting paper, although she was meant to be training as a printer. The running of the large *Miller* two-colour printing press could not be undertaken by all the printers — of the five, only three could do this.

The aim of many members was to perform all the steps in a job, from the acceptance of the order to the delivery to the customer, themselves. In the *KoMet* collective, the members tried to carry out all four steps involved in producing a machine-tool: design, production planning, execution of production, and quality control. The qualifications needed were therefore more diversified than those most skilled metalworkers acquire during their apprenticeship.

Designing a machine-tool is usually not part of the training of a qualified metalworker. Although a skilled toolmaker in a business enterprise constantly has to interpret designs, he normally could not have produced these himself. Only when qualifying for the higher stage of master of his craft are skills in design required. The design a worker in industry uses is drawn, in minutest detail, by an engineer or technician who usually has never actually worked with such a machine himself. Wolfgang, one of *KoMet*'s most experienced toolmakers, regarded the most serious disadvantage of his former job the fact that the masters and foremen did not take seriously his own suggestions for improving production and that he had to work with designs that did not provide what he considered to be the best possible solution.

In the collective *KoMet*, the designs the workers drew for themselves were less precise and elaborate than those produced by industrial designers. Very skilled members, like Fritz and Wolfgang, had in mind the functions their product had to fulfill and the problems involved in actually making it. Their designs were more adapted to the actual production than those of an industrial designer. They were often able to recognise small mistakes rapidly and to change their design accordingly, as the preliminary design was not intended as an exact specification but as an interpretation of the customer's requirements.

Fritz maintained that he would be able to produce a complicated tool more rapidly and efficiently than an enterprise with a high level of division of labour. But not all *KoMet* members were equally capable of both design and execution. For instance, despite having worked for years in business enterprises, Friedel still left the more difficult designs to Fritz, Noppe, or Wolfgang. The newcomers, Gisela, Thomas, Otto, and Peter – almost half the collective at the time of my fieldwork – did not know how to design at all, although they were gradually learning.

If all *KoMet* members had been as skilled as Fritz and Wolfgang, their method of producing highly specialised tools might have been more efficient than that of an enterprise with a high division of labour, as the problem of communication between technician and executing worker did not exist. However, only three of the ten members had achieved this level of skill. For the others, the collective way of producing meant slowly learning to take on more aspects of the production process. In the business enterprises where they had worked previously, the responsibilities of the workers and the technicians were clearly delimited, and the workers only had to execute a design to the specifications and tolerances supplied by the designer. Mistakes in the design were not their responsibility. Often they did not know for what type of production machine the parts were designed, nor the customer to whom they would be delivered. The members who had worked in small toolmaking shops had a better overview of the entire production process, but even so they had still been excluded from the administration and design aspects, which were reserved for the owner or master.

As we have seen, one ideal many founders of collectives believed in was that, if they owned and ran the enterprise, they would also be able to stipulate that only ecologically sound and socially useful products were to be manufactured. This, however, was in practice not always economically feasible. In order to compete on the open market, collectives had to transact with firms they might politically despise. The founders of *KoMet* had to revise their hopes since 1979. The tools and devices they were making in 1984 were the same as those made in any other toolmaking enterprise in West Berlin. Their customers were big business enterprises that ordered tools and devices for their large manufacturing plants. The social and ecological usefulness of the products manufactured in these plants was beyond their range of influence. As mentioned earlier, only once did *KoMet* refuse to make a tool, when they learned that it was destined for stamping the housing of a police walkie-talkie. This decision led to the loss of their most important customer and created considerable tension with those members who would have preferred to accept the order and thereby save the economic situation.

Their actual customers order tools for manufacturing plants that produce cars, dialysis machines, equipment for packaging, crown-corks, etc. – often products that determined ecologists would regard with horror. *KoMet* members regret their dependence upon their large customers as one of the most serious handicaps to the collective experiment. Wolfgang's view illustrates the dilemma:

> We are still the extended workbench for other firms. What we are doing here is still the lowest level of a self-reliant enterprise. We often receive orders with such detailed constructions that it almost feels as if one was still working in an ordinary enterprise. ... We have to start producing whole machines, develop our own product. (Wolfgang, *KoMet*, 15.8.1984)

The realisation of the dream of their "own product" seems far away. Production machines are expensive and their purchase is only profitable if there is a ready market for the products. The purchase of a small lathe and chainsaw for series production had already split the collective. Some members only agreed reluctantly to the "waste of money" involved in this attempt to build up machines for series production.

In order to show the world that a radical division between workers producing "monotonous" series and those creatively manufacturing special machine-tools can be overcome, Uwe, one of the founders, wanted the collective to integrate repetitive series into their work. He regarded it as a socio-political aim of work in a collective that members should share equally certain undesirable tasks in series production and dedicate the rest of their time to the more creative making of complicated tools. However, he admitted that this method of overcoming the division between repetitive and creative work could only function if the skilled toolmakers also performed the recurrent tasks, as it would be beyond the capacities of the collective to employ workers familiar with serial work and train them as skilled toolmakers. Most members were not enthusiastic about the idea of series production and were in favour of farming out uninteresting and disagreeable parts of orders to other firms, keeping the more stimulating ones for themselves. The "own product" they would like to produce would have to be complicated and specialised.

The wish to promote and produce a socially valuable product also inspired the service collectives *Wuseltronick* and *FahrradBüro*. Their aim was to overcome the limitations of providing services to an anonymous clientele and to engage in much broader relationships with customers and products than ordinary firms in the same field.

To enlarge the functions of a simple bicycle shop and to make it into a political forum were the aims of the intellectuals who started the *FahrradBüro*. The activities of the collective involved not only repairing and selling cycles but also writing and publishing books on traffic politics and about cycling holidays and producing a map of Berlin for cyclists. During the first few years, each member performed the job he or she liked best, but as the male members started to monopolise the work in the repair shop and leave the unpopular salesperson's job in the shop to the female members, a system of job rotation was introduced. At the meeting on Tuesday mornings, the tasks for the coming week were distributed. Every member had to work for two days per week in the shop, one in the office, and one in the repair shop. Work in the repair shop was regarded as the most attractive, especially by the female members. They stressed how important it was for them to learn a technologically useful skill and to work with metal, which had always been a male preserve. Most members enjoyed the alternation between manual and intellectual tasks. They found it stimulating to repair a bicycle one day and to run the publishing side and write an article on traffic politics the next. They appreciated the constant shifting between a hectic work-style serving people in the shop and working alone in the office or repair shop.

The usual task of an engineer in industry or university is to solve problems posed by others, to conceive products that are then produced by others, and, in the end, to lose all relationship with the product and the consumer it will serve. The engineers of *Wuseltronick* wanted to reverse this relationship and enlarge their control over the product they conceived. Their main idea was that the technology they developed was not neutral, that the decentralised, locally controllable, wind-power station they developed bore a different value than an atomic powerstation. They therefore intended to conceive and also to produce only products they considered useful. They received research grants from the Ministry of Research and Technology for some of their products, and as they paid themselves much less than the salary of an ordinary qualified engineer, they were able to finance the development of some prototypes that were not subsidized. One of these products was a small instrument for measuring wind strength, which they developed for determining the most suitable site for their wind-power plant. But having produced a small series of this instrument and displayed it at the industrial fair in Hannover, they were unable to meet the resulting order, as all the members were heavily involved in research and were reluctant to make time for series production.

The idea of developing their own product again became more concrete when Reiner and Eberhard, cooperating on the same project, had the idea of setting up a producers' *Genossenschaft* together with other collectives. They wanted to start producing windmills, and perhaps other products, en mass. The other half of the collective was not involved in this planning and remained rather skeptical. Reiner and Eberhard maintained that work in the collective would only remain stimulating if it was constantly progressing and expanding. To enter into production and create larger collective structures would mean a new challenge and a step forward for the whole movement. After months of discussion, the *Genossenschaft* was officially founded and two other collectives, *Südwind* (producing vanes for the windmills) and *Cosonanz* (another electronics collective), joined in.

However, enthusiasm for the *Genossenschaft* started to fade when it became clear that the prototype of the large windmill, which was the only one to stand a chance in the market, needed another two years' work before it would be ready to go into production. Other products, such as a measuring instrument, were already being produced by *Wuseltronick* itself, albeit with difficulty. To keep the *Genossenschaft* alive, it was decided to apply for research grants. In fact, only a few members of *Wuseltronick* were interested in spending their time in actual production, and even Reiner and Eberhard, the initiators of the idea, preferred research. The utopian idea of freely associating collectives joining together to produce a complicated order was far from realisation. *Wuseltronick* collectivists were not only afraid that the entry into production and the direct confrontation with the market might radically alter their structure of organisation but also that they would become the managers for the whole *Genossenschaft*, as it was they who had initiated the idea and developed most of the products.

At a meeting of the *Genossenschaft* in the summer of 1984, the other collectives complained that *Wuseltronick* was losing interest, that members no longer attended meetings, and that they were withholding information. For members of other collectives, the success of the cooperative was almost a question of survival, as they lacked orders and other financial means, whereas *Wuseltronick* would be able to survive on its own resources and in cooperation with business enterprises.

In the last years, the situation has completely reversed. *Wuseltronick* is now producing and marketing a wide range of products through the *Genossenschaft*. Over 60 percent of their turnover now comes from the production and/or marketing of wind-measuring instruments, telemetry systems, control systems, and so on. Wind energy systems are produced and marketed by *Südwind*, but outside the *Genossenschaft*. All members of *Wuseltronick* and *Cosonanz* have also become associates of the *Genossenschaft*, while only two of the thirteen members of *Südwind* have joined in. As they had predicted, *Wuseltronick* collectivists became the managers of the whole *Genossenschaft*. All four members of the board of directors belong to *Wuseltronick*.

The Problem of Working Together

A relatively low degree of cooperation and flexibility is required from the workers in collectives in the sense that they do not have to adapt their work pace to colleagues sharing their tasks. They normally work alone on an order they themselves took on and interact only loosely with their fellow members. Therefore, all the more stressful are the times when members are suddenly

obliged to adapt to one another and when a high degree of personal cooperation is suddenly necessary. Members going on holiday and handing over
"their" order to a colleague, the acceptance of larger orders that require the
close cooperation of several members — such situations reverse the ordinary
structure of the organisation and suddenly demand a relatively high degree of
adaptability.

During my fieldwork with *Oktoberdruck*, tremendous tensions arose in
the repro-mounting department because Udo had gone on holidays leaving
his colleague Herbie a complicated order to complete without sufficient ex-
planation. The order comprised a large collection of articles offering practical advice for an "alternative" lifestyle, illustrated with numerous drawings
and photographs, which had to be enlarged, screened, and mounted on the
correct pages. The drawings and photographs were numbered, but no page
number was given; sometimes the corresponding number was missed off the
page, and not infrequently it had been cut off by accident. On top of this, the
sequence of the numbers did not correspond to that of the almost three hundred pages. Herbie became frantic trying to sort all this out. He cursed the
"alternative" customers, accusing them of being too lazy or inexperienced to
mark the photographs with the proper page numbers, and even composed a
hymn of praise to bourgeois customers. The publishers of *STATTbuch*
claimed they were innocent — they had explained everything fully to Udo —
and in turn criticised the sloppiness of the printing collective. Finally, however, they agreed to stay till ten one night to reorganise the drawings and photographs while Herbie went home at five.

Nevertheless, the book, *energisch leben* (Live Energetically), still required more time than originally estimated, and Herbie did not hesitate in
charging part of the time spent sorting out the muddle to *STATTbuch*. The
rest was time lost for the repro section, where first Herbie and later also his
colleagues had to work unpaid overtime.

Herbie had the unpleasant task of dealing with the impatient customer,
who blamed him for his colleague's mistakes. This role is assumed in an ordinary enterprise by the boss, who would have dealt with the customer and dis-
ciplined the worker responsible. In the collective, everybody must assume
the role of boss and put right any damage done. While in an ordinary enterprise the workers would be paid for overtime worked, even if it was to compensate for the negligence of one of their colleagues, in *Oktoberdruck* the
whole section had to work unpaid overtime in order to maintain the same level of income, as each section kept its own accounts and incomes depended on

the monthly balance. If the order had been delivered too late, they would have had to pay the penalty. Udo himself was unaffected as his holiday was unpaid and did not therefore depend on the results of the collective's endeavours in his absence.

In those larger collectives, which have established a certain formal division of labour, the critical point in the organisation is when one section takes over the tasks from another. The printing section of *Oktoberdruck*, for instance, can only use its machinery efficiently if the repro-montage section has the printing plates ready on time. In 1983, when the two sections still calculated their incomes independently, tensions were high if a printer was slack and consequently earned less because of the inefficiency of his colleagues in the repro-montage section. Both sections had to rely, in turn, on the information given by the office in order to carry out the order correctly. The introduction of a single basis for the calculation of income alleviated some of the tensions but also created new ones – for instance, when large and expensive mistakes made by the printing section had to be taken on board by the whole collective.

Within the sections, as well as in collectives without a formal division of labour, the members' mutual interdependence becomes most obvious in the common use of machinery and tools. A smooth beginning to the working day for an *Oktoberdruck* printer, for instance, depends on the care with which his or her colleague on the previous shift has cleaned the print drums. As nobody is employed solely to maintain the machinery, the printers depend on their colleagues. Donald, one of the older printers, complained that the young newcomers with whom he was working tried to dodge this unpleasant task. In *KoMet*, members complained repeatedly that they had to remove kilos of scobs before they were able to use a machine. Although maintenance schedules were worked out, they were rarely effective for longer than a few days. Similarly, in the *FahrradBüro*, the amount of stress suffered by collective members during a busy day in the shop depended to a large extent on how carefully their colleagues had priced up the goods and ordered the merchandise. After a series of conflicts about repairs that had been accepted by members who then did not have time to do them, members only did the repairs they themselves had accepted.

Collectivists tend to regard responsibility and discipline as ambiguous values, and, not infrequently, they seem to congratulate themselves for not respecting them. Almost every collectivist I interviewed about his work situation mentioned the chaos and disorder as one of the most serious difficulties in collective production. But at the same time, they talked about "the creative chaos" that makes collective work so much more interesting.

Most members of *KoMet* defended their casual attitude. Fritz, for instance, was convinced they would only be able to achieve a higher level of discipline by introducing a system of supervision and control, which he rejected. According to him, collectivists must be free to decide to create chaos, if they wish, and earn less. Gisela hated the lack of order and cleanliness, but she did not regard the lack of discipline as a complete disadvantage:

> Discipline has always been maintained through fear, so I clearly cannot advocate it. ... We don't want to be as quick as a worker in an ordinary enterprise (*Normalbetrieb*) because then the work would not be fun any more. (Gisela, *KoMet*, 9.8.1984)

Even Noppe, who would have liked to introduce elaborate work schedules, admitted that the chaos had its positive side, since it stimulated the imagination as well as individual problem-solving. However, he was convinced that collective responsibility can only be achieved if people learn to respect the common planning. He was certain that formal plans were necessary when members did not voluntarily assume the common responsibilities.

As the sloppiness and inaccuracy of colleagues become more obvious in work situations with an intensive division of labour, those members tend to cooperate who have a good personal relationship. Both *Oktoberdruck* and *KoMet* sometimes accepted large orders that would occupy one worker for weeks or months and could only be completed rapidly and efficiently if several members cooperated. For example, *KoMet* accepted the production of a small series of 110-lathed parts for its most important customer, *Mirotec*. Three members cooperated on this order: Günther milled the side flat, while Fritz milled the openings, and Gisela drilled the holes using a drill-jig. As soon as Günther had finished the first step, he made the dips into the holes Gisela had drilled. As the drilling of the holes took longest, Günther had to adjust his work pace to that of Gisela. While she was boring the holes, the drill head broke twice; and when Günther, and later Fritz, tried to show her how to do the job properly, they only succeeded in breaking two more drill heads, leaving only one more. In the end, they decided to try immobilizing the drill-jig to reduce the vibration, and this was successful. The drilling proceeding without further problems. In an ordinary enterprise, such a problem would have been solved by the foreman or master; the other workers would not have been allowed to interrupt their own work, and as a result waste materials, and they would not have been permitted to find their own solution to the problem.

The organisation of work depends on personal factors in a way different to that in an ordinary business enterprise, where how and when workers cooperate is dictated by a superior. In a business enterprise, each worker in theory has his or her clearly delimited field of activity and is supposed to work hand in glove with his or her colleagues. In a piece rate system, such as Haraszti (1976) describes in Hungary and Burawoy (1970) in the United States, the worker who is eager to "make out," to exceed the quota, is to a large extent dependent on good relations with the auxiliary workers paid on a time basis, such as the scheduling staff giving out the piecework, crib attendants handing out tools, setup men preparing the machines, and so on (Burawoy 1979:53-55). Bad personal relations lead inevitably to delays in the execution of a job and to a reduction in income. In a collective this formal division of tasks does not exist: the *KoMet* toolmakers have no piece rates, they fetch their tools themselves and set up their own machine for production. Informally, however, they are to a large extent dependent on the direct support of their colleagues. They need their advice when filling a difficult order, their help when searching for a tool, and their cooperation in lifting heavy pieces of metal. This support, however, is neither automatic nor self-evident but depends on personal sympathies. While collectivists do not directly lose part of their income, they might lose their temper if their colleagues do not cooperate. As in principle all members are expected to be able to do every task, their work domains overlap, responsibility is not clearly delimited, and good informal communication is necessary if the enterprise is to run smoothly.

The cooperation in collectives is based on what Fox (1974:71) calls high-trust relations. It involves the principle that one person does another a favour in the general expectation of some future return, the exact nature of which is not stipulated in advance. This long-term reciprocity engenders feelings of personal obligation and gratitude. However, contrary to business firms, which can switch from a regime of high trust to one of close supervision enforced through an organisational hierarchy, in a collective the organisation of work is dependent on spontaneous consensus.

Gisela was in her sixth month of pregnancy when she needed the help of her old workmate and opponent, Noppe, to complete an order on which she had already worked for 75 hours in the course of that particular week. She hesitated for a long time before asking him, because their relationship had been strained before her boyfriend, Fritz, left the group. When asked, Noppe immediately postponed completing his own work and put in two days exclusively on Gisela's. Their friendly cooperation was a sign of their improving personal relationship.

Transmitting Knowledge

The training of newcomers, and their introduction into the specific requirements of collective production, is a constantly repeated task, since the turnover of members is high. Even experienced newcomers well trained in the production process in a business enterprise must get used to the extensive autonomy, the self-management, and the direct contact with customers.

It might be supposed that only the efficient and smooth introduction of new members can guarantee the continuity of the enterprise and establish a relative equality of status between members. The reality is quite the opposite, with the new member being "thrown in at the deep end," having to find his or her own way through the chaos of collective organisation.

"Newcomers have to find out by themselves" seems to be the pedagogic strategy of the *KoMet* collective; "if they don't know, they can always ask." A high degree of initiative is expected from beginners. Most collectives let the newcomer try working in the group for one or two months, and only if he or she has proved themselves sufficiently autonomous will he or she then start the probationary period. This lasts from six months to a year, after which he or she becomes a full associate. Members of longer standing describe their first months in the collective as very demanding. They felt left alone with a burden of responsibilities weighing on their shoulders.

> Newcomers have to make their way through all the same problems as everyone else. Every newcomer should experience a saw blade bursting because nobody has explained how to avoid this. (Noppe, *KoMet*, 8.8.1984)

Noppe was in favour of more systematic training for beginners, but his opinion came up against the resistance of most of his colleagues, especially his adversary Fritz. The latter preferred to assign inexperienced members difficult tasks so that they would acquire skills more rapidly as well as learn to find their own solutions to the problems that arose. This method of "alterna

KoMet member Friedel explaining the grinder to the newcomer Otto (photo by author).

tive learning" could take an extreme form as in the case of Otto, who, having been away from this type of work for three years, wanted to start his new job by drilling holes in a steel plate with precision tolerance of one-hundredth of a millimeter. He tried to do this task for days and had to start all over again several times.

Generally, an experienced member tends to work with an inexperienced one, but he does not actually instruct him. The newcomer must discover and formulate the difficulties that he finds, then ask his experienced colleagues specific questions. For example, Gisela manufactured her first complicated machine tool in cooperation with Wolfgang. He had accepted the order, knew the customer, and had drawn the design. For every production step, Gisela had to get the exact details from Wolfgang. The information he would give her was not of a descriptive kind — such as, "You have to drill a hole of 0.51 mm diameter at 6.5 mm distance from the edge of the tool" — but involved posing a technical problem: "This hole has to be adapted to this kind of screw, which joins the upper part of the tool to the base." Gisela then had to calculate for herself the specifications of the hole by making small sketches.

The *Oktoberdruck* collective also wants its newcomers to find their own methods and rhythm of work. However, leaving them entirely alone with unknown tasks and unfamiliar machinery is not only motivated by the wish to create highly autonomous workers but also to a certain extent by the listlessness of the experienced members. When Ingrid and Klaus started to work in the repro-montage section, they had to find out for themselves how the large repro-camera worked. Their colleague Herbie, tired of introducing yet more newcomers to its functioning, only showed them the bare minimum but, nevertheless, still criticised their poor performance. Klaus soon felt so uncomfortable that he announced after a couple of weeks that he intended to leave the collective. The others then persuaded him to stay and promised to help him.

The methods members of *Oktoberdruck* use to introduce new members are reminiscent to some extent of the teaching methods of anti-authoritarian schools. The new members are confronted with problems arising out of their work, which they must solve to continue production. They are not given ready-made solutions from the outset. On the other hand, pressure of work and flux in membership is such that there is also not enough time and energy left to engage in extensive formal training.

The difficulty is that beginners in collectives are certainly less productive than beginners in an ordinary enterprise. They often have no work experience at all when they start, and the capabilities they acquired during their traineeship are insufficient for independent and profitable production. Beginners in ordinary enterprises are not more skilled, but the skills they possess are used in a way that is more profitable for the enterprise. In a machine shop operated on a piece rate basis, such as Burawoy describes it, newcomers are trained by experienced workers who, however, often show marked reluctance to introduce the youngsters to the complicated setup and to tricks to "make out," to make more money. Hostility between trainer and trainee may be particularly pronounced when the newcomer poses some threat to the incumbent (Burawoy 1979:102).

Examining the job satisfaction and expectations of young toolmakers in ordinary industry, Lappe found that the first job of a trained toolmaker tends to demand fewer skills than he or she learned during apprenticeship (Lappe 1984:30). Although the job of toolmaker is one of the most skilled in the metal industry, after their traineeship beginners acquire further skills only very slowly. They are put on simple jobs that they can perform efficiently with the skills they already have, usually only rising up the hierarchy of qualifications by attending special training courses. Beginners without further work experience are often at risk of dequalification, as they have to accept transitory jobs beneath their level of qualification, paid at piece rate. They usually keep such temporary jobs until they eventually find a job in the profession they have learned (Lappe 1984:65-66). For some of them, these difficulties in getting started in their professional career may enhance the attraction of poorly paid but skilled work in collectives like *KoMet*. In fact, two of *Ko-Met*'s new members had come from as far afield as West Germany because they had read an article about the collective. Although toolmaking is still one of the most skilled jobs in the metal industry, it is threatened by rationalisation. The actual making of tools has to some extent been replaced by the assembling of devices (Lappe 1984:29), and recently, CNC and CNB machines have been introduced, which delegate the intelligent part of toolmaking to the technician who programs the production computer. Skilled toolmakers, though, have great interest, according to Lappe (1984:31-32), in integral activities and generally invest considerable effort in acquiring further qualifications.

In collectives, the training of members is essential and depends on the assumption that everyone is willing to increase his or her qualifications, acquire new skills, and retain the value of those already possessed. Collectivists, however, who overestimate their own capabilities can pose even greater problems to the smooth running of the enterprise than those incapable of working independently. *KoMet*, for instance, was confronted with the problem of the overwhelming self-confidence of their new member Otto. He accepted, and even asked permission to carry out orders that he could not complete. The tasks he attempted had either to be redone entirely or to be fixed up by other members, who became increasingly reluctant to entrust him with orders. At the same time, they had to accept the internal contradiction of wanting to encourage his independence and of limiting the damage he did. After six months, another newcomer, Thomas, who had arrived with Otto, was integrated as an associate. But Otto decided to continue on probationary terms, thereby avoiding a group decision against his integration, and ultimately left the collective.

Although in theory all members should work independently, the differences in skill mean that the experienced members become the centre of production activities. Their advice is asked constantly; they must explain how the machines work and are even asked to pass judgement on the work of their less experienced colleagues before it is sent out. The level of efficiency of the collective as a whole, and even the range of products it can make, depends on its most skilled members. For instance, since Wolfgang left *KoMet* in December 1984, the collective can no longer offer to produce the complicated hydraulic tools that were his speciality.

As the division of labour in collective enterprises is far less pronounced, the qualifications each member has to acquire are much broader, but gaining skill in the depth necessary to carry out specialised tasks becomes more difficult. Members wishing to acquire further skills not infrequently must work longer hours and learn by experimenting with new fields of production, in the course of which they become trailblazers attracting interested customers.

To achieve the ideal of abolishing the division of labour, newcomers are thrown in at the deep end without preparation and are expected to adapt quickly, learning to be completely interchangeable with any other member. However, there are some difficulties with the realisation of this ideal. Firstly newcomers starting work without instructions on a complicated job are not productive. Moreover, as long as they have not acquired an equally high level of skill as the experienced members, an informal division of labour necessarily exists between skilled and unskilled, or semiskilled members. However, this informal division of labour is difficult to overcome as the skills each member obtains are largely dependent on his or her personal commitment. The systematic training of new members, and of those less qualified, has not been able to be undertaken to date, due to the high pressure of work and lack of organisation. Some members have even lost some of their specialised skills in the course of obtaining broader ones. Noppe, for instance, claimed that he had been a far better die-maker *(Schnittbauer)* before he joined *KoMet*, but, on the other hand, he has obtained a considerable number of additional skills ranging from design to administration. In fact, as soon as a member acquires the entire range of skills needed in the enterprise and becomes able to replace any of his or her colleagues, he or she becomes of singular importance for the collective and is not interchangeable with any newcomer from outside.

The Limits of Collectivity: Sexual Division of Labour

The constant feuds around tidying up at length become unbearable, and in the end it is always a woman who puts things back in order. In the office, for instance, one day I clear away the stuff on the table and the next day somebody covers it with rubbish again. Then I have the choice between tidying up or working in the midst of rubbish. Ultimately I always do tidy up, but I am angry with myself. I don't want to resort to brutal methods like flinging the stuff in a corner. I really don't want to. (Ulrike, *FahrradBüro*, Nov. 1983)

The tasks of tidying up, cleaning, cooking, and washing up are considered in the dominant western culture, though not in the alternative counterculture, as part of the female domain. In the early days, collectivists regarded it as self-evident that such a division of labour would never occur in their enterprise and that men and women would share out their tasks equally. Since then, the sexual division of labour has become one of the most heatedly debated issues at alternative meetings and congresses. As in so many progressive communes and communal households, these daily services to the community remain a problematic chapter in collective life. As they still bear the stigma of inferior and unproductive work, they are considered undesirable tasks. With the formal abolition of the sexual division of labour, the different values accorded to certain tasks were not removed (Flieger 1984:221). It is not self-evident but rather a sign of particularly harmonious relationships between members if these tasks are accomplished without problem.

A lack of motivation characterised the increasingly chaotic organisation of work in the *FahrradBüro* when a serious conflict opposed male and female members. At the meeting, the women, in particular Veronika, a radical feminist and a lesbian, called attention for the first time to the sexual division of labour in the collective and to the fact that the women were bearing the brunt of the most unpleasant tasks, such as cleaning up, putting things back in order, and pricing wares. They were fed up with battling against the chaos that their colleagues Hans and Bernhard tended to ignore. Hans claimed that he himself suffered because of the chaos, but his solution did not lie in a daily effort to keep things in order. He wanted to restructure the entire organisation according to the principles of modern management, involving the introduction of an electronic till to record all the types of merchandise sold and to evaluate the sales performance of each member. Significantly, he did not participate in the general cleaning up which took place after the meeting.

The sexual division of labour exists to some degree in all the collectives I analysed. In conformity with their "traditional" social role, men tend to ignore dirt and disorder and attribute only minor importance to tasks like cooking. When I interviewed the members of *KoMet* for the first time in October 1982, when it was an all-male collective, they complained about the lack of care with which food was prepared at lunchtime. Everybody seemed to consider the production of tools the task to be given absolute priority but suffered from eating canned food. Two years later, I interviewed one of the first women to work in *KoMet*, who explained that an equal division of labour for cooking, sweeping up, and cleaning the toilets did not exist. The "qualified men" dodged these tasks, pretending they had something more important to do, while the women did the cleaning because they could not stand the dirt. During the period of my fieldwork, the collective employed a woman on a temporary basis to do the cookin and wash the members' work clothes. The discussions about undesirable tasks ceased because the female role was taken on by a female outsider.

Women who work in the collectives I analysed generally want to break from the traditional female role and become familiar with the male domain of technical work. They therefore become printers, metalworkers, and mechanics, professions that are still largely reserved for men in the labour market. As one of the female members of the *Handwerker Genossenschaft Mannheim* explained:

> I want to acquire the capability to do the tasks that previously men did for me. I want to learn a technical skill, represent myself to official bodies, finance my own living, and I want to cook and tidy up together with men. (Flieger 1984:221)

Very conscious of the discrimination women suffer if they try to take on typically male jobs, most of the time women in collectives are not prepared to accept the reintroduction of the old sexual division of labour into the alternative enterprises. Because of their experiences as female apprentices in business enterprises, where they often did not receive an appropriate training, they were frequently less qualified than their male colleagues when they entered the collective, but nevertheless were determined to become equally skilled.

Andrea, the only woman printer with *Oktoberdruck*, was a typical example of a woman who had tried to cope with a male job:

> After my apprenticeship in Dortmund, I could not get a job in the firm where I trained. I would not have wanted it anyway, because the master had pestered me unbelievably during my apprenticeship, and did not give me a proper training. He wanted to prove to me that printing was not the right profession for me as a woman. I then found a job in Hamburg. I was dismissed after three months because I was unable to print, and because we had a quarrel. Then I was without work for five months, and I started to doubt my own abilities. I had been rejected by numerous printing shops either just because I was a wo-

man or because I was not good enough. I finally responded to an advertisement by *Oktoberdruck* in *die tageszeitung*. They were willing to accept me,
even though I told them I was a poor printer. (Andrea, *Oktoberdruck*,
27.9.83)

During the months that I spent with *Oktoberdruck* in the summer of 1983,
Andrea worked very hard to improve her skills and performance, at the same
time criticising her male colleagues for their sloppy work. They in turn accused her of being arrogant and aggressive and saw her as responsible for the
rising tensions in the printing section. She attributed this joint attack from her
male colleagues to the conflict between male and female roles, because it
arose after she had shifted from being an inexperienced and helpless female
to a skilled printer. "I think men have difficulties getting along with a self-
confident woman. Formerly, I often used to stand crying at the machine, and
then they could take me in their arms to comfort me." The fear of being
pushed into the role of scapegoat for the whole printing section, together with
a serious allergy to the chemicals used for washing the print cylinders, led
her to look for another job outside.

Andrea's colleague Marita, working in the office in a typically female
job, told a similar story. She resented the fact that she was excluded from the
technical knowledge by her male colleagues. She claimed that they explained details to her in such a way that she could not understand, although
she would understand perfectly when Andrea explained. She was convinced
that the men were taking personal problems onto a technical level where she
could no longer argue with them.

If there is a complaint about a printing order and I want to argue with the printer because he did a sloppy job, he tells me the machine has broken down. Then
I can only reply, 'That's because you did not look after it properly,' but I can't
refute him. I would only be capable of doing so if I had sufficient insight into
production itself. (Marita, *Oktoberdruck*, 13.7.1983)

As a consequence Marita insisted on the opportunity of changing to a job in
one of the production sections.

The systematic refusal of the female members to be content with the less
skilled work and to take over the typically female tasks may have contributed
to the fact that for some of these tasks the collectives have started to employ
temporary helpers from outside. In spite of Marita's protests (see Chapter

6), *Oktoberdruck* repeatedly employed female labour to do the cooking and cleaning; the construction engineers' office, *Baubüro*, employed a cleaning woman twice a week. The principle that the monotonous and disagreeable tasks should also be shared out equally among members is gradually weakening, especially in the larger collectives. The justification for this is always given as being the enormous pressure of work, making it impossible to spend sufficient time on cooking and cleaning. However, a proper fulfillment of these services makes work in the collective much more agreeable and improves personal relationships. Some collectivists, therefore, regard it as a special service they can do for the "collectivity" if they employ somebody to do the cooking. Others, mainly women like Marita, criticise this as the old exploitation of women reintroduced silently through the back door.

Conclusion

The ideal that underlay the effort not to divide the production process was that each member should become able to keep control over the manufacturing of his product from beginning to end. Collectivists were to plan, produce, sell, discuss, and administer equally, making foremen and technicians superfluous and cooperating without constraints and overriding authority. In practice, however, the individualistic work-style, which resulted from members working very much on their own, proved problematic. The organisation of production, particularly, showed weak points where members had to work together and share tasks. Cooperation was cheerful and satisfying as long as personal relations were harmonious but became tiresome and stressful when enmity developed between members who had to work together. Individual likes and dislikes, convictions and doubts, had a strong impact on an organisation of work that was not coordinated by a superior and made it more vulnerable than that of a business enterprise.

It was assumed that each member would be equally committed to the enterprise and that differences in skill and experience could be compensated for. In practice, however, a division between skilled and inexperienced members continued to exist as the fluctuation in membership remained high and newcomers were left to train themselves. The unpleasant tasks were not voluntarily shared by all, and female members had to fight hard to make their male colleagues participate in the cooking and cleaning.

While collective work is more stimulating and challenging than jobs in hierarchically organised business enterprises, because one collectivist is responsible for all the different stages in the producion process, this organisation of complex work is inherently less efficient than the divided work executed by several different wage-labourers in a business enterprise.

Marx, and before him Adam Smith (1981:112), observed in the nineteenth century the advantage in efficiency for manufacturers with clearly divided work-tasks as compared to craftshops practising simple cooperation. Marx wrote about the worker carrying out all the steps in making a product:

> It is obvious that this direct dependence of the operations, and therefore of the workers, one upon the other, makes it incumbent upon each individual to expend no more than the amount of time necessary for his particular function. Thus the continuity, uniformity, regularity, orderliness and above all intensity of the work became very different in such a manufacturing process from what they are in independent craftmanship or even simple cooperation. (Marx 1930 I:363)

The collectives, practising simple cooperation, are at an economic disadvantage in relation to any business enterprise with a more specialised allocation of tasks. Most alternative enterprises I analysed have only been able to survive in the market because they produce complicated or crafted products, which cannot yet be manufactured more efficiently in industrial production or which are not produced en mass. Many of their business competitors are also small enterprises in which the division of labour is not as pronounced as in industry.

Also, in future competition the development of new technologies allowing for decentralised production may be more decisive than a high level of division of labour. The micro-electronic "revolution" has brought about a new vision for the future of work in industrial society, where fewer workers will produce in less time highly "intelligent" products in a self-determined way. (Gorz 1990:23)

8

Work-Time and Social Boundaries

When, in the spring of 1984, the West German steel and printing workers went on strike to fight for a 35-hour week, such jokes circulated among members of collectives as: "We have had a 35-hour week for a long time – only our hour has ninety minutes!" or "We call for a reduction of the work week – to 48 hours!" The jokes expressed what everybody felt acutely every day: that workers in collectives worked far longer hours for far lower pay than their counterparts in business industry.

When the industrial workers began their action for a shorter work week, the collectivists in the printing enterprises discussed the possibility of coming out on a solidarity strike but rapidly abandoned the idea since they realised they would be striking against themselves. It became obvious to them that collectivists and wage-labourers had different priorities of interest, not only because collectivists were at the same time the owners of their enterprises and a strike would damage them in their interests as owners but also because they wanted to conceive of their work-time in a different way to that of the industrial worker.

"In a society where labour power is purchased and sold, working time becomes sharply and antagonistically divided from non-working time, and the worker places an extraordinary value upon his 'free' time, while on-the-job time is regarded as lost or wasted," wrote Braverman in the 1970s (1974:278). This, however, was not the only reason why the workers strove for a reduction in the work week. For the wage-labourer, a 35-hour week with full wage-adjustment meant a reduction of the capitalist owner's profit margin and the hope that, for the moment, fewer workers would be made redundant following automatisation. In a collective, the hours worked per week could only be reduced if the members were willing to forego some of their immediate spendings and invest in labour-saving devices or if they were willing and able to speed up their work pace in order to maintain the same level of profitability. Greater efficiency and a higher work performance, though, could become contradictory to one of the key principles of collective work: to maintain a rhythm of work that is not substantially different from the rhythm of life outside work.

As E. P. Thompson (1967:94) pointed out, a different pattern of values separates time at work from time outside work in industrial societies. Whereas linked to work are values such as impersonality, rationality, punctuality, deference to authority, and respect for property rights, outside work values include love for the family, expression of aesthetic capacities, and similar ideas. However, in capitalist society "leisure" increasingly becomes a problem, as men become incapable of "losing the restless urgency" to "consume time purposely" and of filling "the interstices of their days with enriched, more leisurely, personal and social relations" (Thompson 1967:95).

For the collectivists, however, the problem posed itself in the opposite way. Members can experiment with this different approach to work-time inside their collectives while renouncing larger incomes. Having enriched their work-time with personal relations and by leaving room for creativity, the pressures of the "social system" then bear upon them in the time outside work, when they must see that their children go to school on time, must respect appointments with doctors, administrators, and acquaintances who follow the dominant pattern of time. As we saw in the discussion on investments in collectives, outside material pressures and values influence the choices of collectivists and have consequences for their work-effort and use of time.

A Different Rhythm at Work

Timed labour is closely related to the introduction of wage-labour, as Thompson (1967:61-69) pointed out. At first, farmhands were paid roughly according to the number of "bushels per day" they harvested, but with the advent of the Industrial Revolution, labour had to be more precisely synchronized, and clocks and watches began to appear in workshops. With the introduction of the Taylorist division of labour, a structure was imparted to all labour processes "that at its extremes polarizes those whose time is infinitely valuable and those whose time is worth almost nothing" (Braverman

1974:83).

The introduction of wage-labour allowed the employer to determine how the labour-time purchased was to be spent and to exclude increasingly from work-time all social activities. Thompson (1967:81) quotes a factory owner at the beginning of the industrial era concerning the workers at the Crowley Iron Works:

> This service must be calculated 'after all deductions for being at taverns, ale-houses, coffee houses, breakfast, dinner, playing, sleeping, smoaking, singing, reading of news history, quarelling, contention, disputes or anything foreign to my business, any way loytering.'

A task-oriented notation of time was prevalent in the preindustrial era, as Thompson (1967:60) explains. He writes:"A community in which task-orientation is common appears to show least demarcation between "work" and "life." Social intercourse and labour intermingled — the working-day lengthens or contracts according to the task. The task-oriented attitude of traditional craftsmen is a positive model for members of collectives and their supporters. They like to see their enterprises as standing in the same tradition.

"Work in a sociable atmosphere, which in accomplishing economically necessary tasks, also fulfils specific social obligations, is in some languages distinguished from work that has no specific social dimension" (Wallman 1979:11). In collectives, all time should be spent "sociably." Work-time should in principle not be different from time spent at home, in political groups or with friends, and strong personal relationships should be equally possible. Listening to another member's personal problem, for example, should be as important — if not more so — as finishing a piece of work on time. Interrupting work to participate in political action is regarded as part of the identity of the collective. The individual member should feel well at his or her work, take a break whenever he or she is tired, and have a coffee whenever he or she feels like it. Emotional problems and the stresses of love are considered perfectly legitimate reasons for not working well.

Time as a nondivided entity that belongs to the working individual is part of a fund of ideas prevalent in the alternative movements of the last twenty years. Since the student movements of the 1960s, this has been closely linked to criticism of "performance-oriented society." Together with Marcuse, the students criticised the dividedness of life, especially for the working population (Marcuse 1970:62f.). They maintained that the wage-labourer was rewarded for the work effort he offered the capitalist by leisure time, in which he was expected to buy himself pleasure through the consumption of goods that enhanced his social status. He thereby reaffirmed the capitalist system of commodity production and his own dependence on wage-labour.

The movements of the 1960s, supported mainly by intellectuals, centred their political actions on consumption and education. They criticised the "savage" accumulation of status symbols such as second cars, colour televisions, and photographic equipment, denouncing this as a means of deflecting the critical energy of the population. Anti-authoritarian kindergardens and "free schools" were founded in order to give the coming generation the chance to learn values different from those of performance and competition.

The collectives stand in the cultural tradition of these movements but contribute to their initiatives the aspect of wanting to change the use of time in production itself. Collectivists want to leave room in the production time for "relaxation," "inspiration," and "self-management." They reject the idea that increase in productivity should be a value in itself. Almost no watches are worn in collectives, lunch is hardly ever at exactly the same time each day, clocks that are wrong are left so for weeks, people arrive late or not at all. They work in the evenings and arrange appointments with their customers outside ordinary working hours.

As a reversal of the logic of a capitalist enterprise, different levels of efficiency are played down in an alternative enterprise. In 1984 in *KoMet*, for instance, every member kept track of the hours he or she spent in the collective in a book of working-hours, in which not only the hours spent in actual production were entered but also those spent in organisation, maintenance, cooking, and recreation. Everyone kept his own book and made sure he did not work more or less than 45 hours per week on average. Working-hour books were never left lying open or exchanged in order to avoid one person calculating another's individual work-effort. Nevertheless, informally everybody knew perfectly well who the most productive members were, but this knowledge was glossed over and rarely talked about.

Some members even feel guilty if they have a more obviously assiduous work-style than their colleagues. Veronika of the *FahrradBüro* felt that she was being unfair to expect from her fellow members the same conscientious work-style as she herself had. At work, she hardly ever gave herself a break for coffee or to read one of the professional magazines her colleagues enjoyed, but she did not want to make them feel guilty about her.

Everybody has a different concept of work, a different rhythm. I am for example very rigid and I hardly allow myself to sit down.... I am always conscious of the work still to be done, and then I do it. I don't think this is very good because it often makes me short tempered with the others who don't react in that way. (Veronika, *FahrradBüro*, 19.12.1983)

Observing collectivists in their work, it struck me that they worked in a relaxed way even when there was a good deal to do. The *KoMet* members claimed sometimes that they were overwhelmed by pressure of work but then, during the day, hardly anybody was actually working. Only toward late evening did the group fall into intense activity, which sometimes continued all through the weekend. In *Oktoberdruck*, the beginning of the summer off-peak season seemed to affect the members' rhythm of work in a similar way. They hung around during the day, drinking coffee and gossiping, often realising too late in the evening that the work they had to do would take more time than they had expected. Despite a low order inflow, they then stayed on until late at night.

A similar work pattern was found by Thompson among seventeenth and eighteenth century craftsmen "who were in control of their own lives." "The work pattern was one of alternate bouts of intense labour and idleness... The temptation to lie in an extra hour in the morning, pushed work into the evening, candlelit hours" (Thompson 1967:73).

During the 1983 summer off-peak season, which lasted from mid-June to mid-August, the printing presses of *Oktoberdruck* sometimes stood idle all day, but the members still came into the collective although they could have stayed at home. Some of them came in the mornings to have breakfast with their colleagues, others sat around for some hours to talk about politics or personal matters. Swimming parties were organised at one of the Berlin lakes, they had barbecues in the courtyard or ice cream sitting in the sun at the open entrance to the printroom. It was only after a couple of weeks of relaxation that they started to busy themselves with the maintenance work, which they had neglected during the year, and began to worry about the results they were going to have at the end of the month. Some of the printers, who calculated their income by the hour, started to stay around in order to take a greater share of the collective income at the end of the month. But in any case, the average hourly wage was low, as it depended on the collective output. Other members considered taking temporary jobs to make ends meet.

Although in times of low work pressure the collectivists seem to enjoy each others' company, this pleasure is offset by the expectation of low results. Especially in collectives like *Oktoberdruck*, where income is directly dependent on result, a prolonged period without work causes tensions, and after a while a relaxed rhythm of work is no longer felt to be a privilege.

The rhythm of work members are free to choose in ordinary times depends to a large extent on their type of activity and the machines they use. Collectives with a short span of orders, a formal division of labour, or those active in the service sector, tend to respect more rigid working hours, whereas those with long-term orders that can be executed by one or two people are more flexible.

The bicycle collective *FahrradBüro* had to adapt its working hours to ordinary shop opening times and to seasonal fluctuations. In summer, members worked, without a break at lunchtime, from 9.30 a.m. to 6.30 p.m., and in winter from 10 a.m. to 1 p.m. and from 2 p.m. to 6 p.m.

In production collectives, the rhythm of work is influenced by the type of machinery in use. The speed and capacity of *Oktoberdruck*'s large printing presses determine the printers' and repro-monteurs' rhythm of work to a large extent. The need to coordinate work between these two interdependent sections requires that the working time is structured fairly rigidly. The workers in the montage sections cannot keep their colleagues in the printing section waiting, and the printers themselves must work in shifts to utilise the large *Miller* press to its optimum.

Donald, the *Miller* printer, maintained in 1984 that his rhythm of work was entirely determined by the machine. Although generally he enjoyed this, he was sometimes overwhelmed by operating the large press entirely on his own, a task that would have been shared in his previous job. When he was fitting the sheets to the machine, he had to make several manipulations at a time and run back and forth around the machine checking the sheet, changing the colour flow, setting the distances, and making sure the sheets did not stick to one another. During the printing process, he was so absorbed in the running of the machine that he no longer realised what was happening around him. He hated it then if somebody distracted him or asked him a question.

Having a coffee or going to the toilet also became impossible. In 1988, the number of printers was increased to seven, and the *Miller* press was run by two people, which reduced the production stress considerably.

Donald's colleagues in the repro-montage section have a more independent pace of work. They can do some work in advance, as we saw Ingrid do (in Chapter 7). They can work on Sundays and take days off during the week.

The only restriction they have is to pass the printing plates over to the printers on time. The repro-photography and montage is still basically a handicraft, independent of machinery. The printing press, on the contrary, was conceived for the production of series in a business enterprise and imposes this same rhythm on the worker in the collective. The work of the printer is the only example of mechanical series production I came across in a collective.

In other collectives highly equipped with machinery, such as *KoMet*, this was used for the production of specialised, one-off parts. These machines are tools in the hands of the workers and do not dictate the pace. In 1984, the skilled toolmakers of *KoMet* worked about 45 hours per week, five more than their skilled counterparts in business and industry. Toolmakers are among the privileged workers in the metal industry, as they are generally paid by the hour, not at piece rate (Lappe 1984:34). Their average net salary was, in 1984 DM 2,400, almost double the income of a collectivist.

Members of *KoMet* greatly appreciated their completely flexible working hours. Some worked on their orders from nine to six, others from eleven to nine o'clock. Some preferred to work on Sundays and then have a weekday free. The independent and irregular rhythm of work, though, was not viewed favourably by all members. Noppe, for instance, regarded it as crucial for the smooth functioning of the enterprise that everybody start work at the same time and respect similar working hours. He would have preferred to have everybody present at the same time in order to exchange information more directly and coordinate the work tasks more efficiently. Wolfgang, a member fiercely opposed to any regulation of the working time, admitted nevertheless that a continuous presence in the collective was necessary to keep track of the organisational running of the enterprise and, therefore, rejected the idea of working part-time.

The engineers of *Wuseltronick*, who invented new technologies without having direct pressure from customers, had the most flexible working hours. Very intense peaks of work on weekends and all night alternated with a more leisurely rhythm at other times. *Wuseltronick* members maintained that their work was similar to that of academics and that their most "productive" periods might be when they were out walking in the Grunewald Forest and suddenly had a brilliant idea for solving a technical problem. When the collective began the production of control and measuring instruments, their rhythm of work became somewhat more regular.

For *KoMet* and *Wuseltronick*, producing highly specialised single parts, an intensive work rhythm was not alone responsible for their economic success; their attraction for customers lay rather in their creative ideas and high degrees of flexibility.

The motivation collectivists find in their work seems to be an important element in determining whether they consider work as divided from the rest of their lives or not. Collectivists who believe they are doing something useful — or at least skillfull — maintain that they identify so strongly with their work that they cannot stop thinking about it, even in their leisure time. As Andrea told me:

> With *Oktoberdruck* I take care of so many more things about the place, like the organisation and the economic side. This is a pleasure for me, because it makes me think. But it is also the reason why work with *Oktoberdruck* is so stressful. I am constantly thinking about it, and my friends are getting fed up with me talking so much about it. (Andrea, *Oktoberdruck*, 27.9.1983)

Collective work, because it is meaningful and satisfying, has a tendency to swamp members and invade their leisure time. Members who identify very strongly with the collective and who do not have demanding external obligations allow this to happen. They spend their evenings in political discussions with other collectivists, write for the collectives' newspaper, and organise national meetings. But those who do not identify so intensely start to reclaim more leisure time to realise a wider range of interests.

Conflicting Demands of Private and Collective Spheres

In the early years of many collectives, the ideal of abolishing the separation between work and leisure also included the idea that times of work and of nonwork should be spent with the same people and that the workplace should be close to the habitation. The model for this was the traditional Berlin *Kiez*-culture, with its close intertwining of small workshops and living quarters.

In the founding period of many collectives, there was no strict division between work and leisure. The effort to build up the new enterprise with a minimum of original capital required such an extensive input of labour that no time was left for leisure activities. Every collective can tell stories about the founding members who used to spend all night working, ate and slept in the collective, and did not even take out any money. Most founding members remember this early period as very pleasurable and exciting. A strong feeling of solidarity inspired the group, as members voluntarily submitted their private lives to the building up of the enterprise. Relationships with people outside the group were either neglected or integrated into the common effort. Fascinated by this new experience, friends and lovers of the early members helped renovate the workshops and not infrequently participated in meetings.

The first contradictions appeared when the enterprise started to become economically viable, and the members began to relax. Private and individual interests reappeared. Friends, lovers, and communal households (*Wohngemeinschaften*) ceased to be understanding and put pressure on members to resume their obligations toward them. Some members began to realise that the collective alone did not fulfill all their emotional and intellectual desires. A differentiation began to emerge between those who continued to identify completely with the collective and those who wanted to reclaim a private sphere. As Fritz of *KoMet* described it:

> We were not able to realise the aim of becoming a circle of friends who undertook a lot of things together outside work and who lived together. The group was simply too heterogenous. After the phase of stabilization, everybody retreated into his own circle of friends. This exploded a lot of illusions about *KoMet*, as in the beginning some people had had the strong desire to create a functioning group for "living and working." As this idea was only shared by a few, the first tensions arose relatively quickly, after the first six months or a year. (Fritz, *KoMet*, 13.4.1984)

Numerous collectives were founded on the initiative of a small group of close friends who perhaps participated in similar political activities, lived in the same housing community, or had previously worked for the same employer. Many members of collectives lived together in changing constellations, though often only for a limited period. The closest group I encountered was the bicycle collective *Räderwerk*. The founding group of eleven people consisted of six friends and their five girlfriends, seven of whom shared a house and had come from the same part of West Germany. Two and a half years after the foundation, in August 1984, the composition of the group had scarcely changed.

Abandoning the ideal of living and working together is particularly painful for collectives with closed structures. The three founding members of *Wuseltronick*, for instance, had started their enterprise in their joint apartment and had lived for years in the midst of electronic equipment. Their close community of friends only expanded when the enterprise became too big and had to be moved out into a separate work-space. New members joined and with them came new links with the outside, which had to be integrated. The group's self-image required that these relationships be brought in and assumed by the whole group. A weekly social night was instituted where members could meet informally, along with their friends and girlfriends. But this not altogether relaxed event did not meet with general approval. Some of the members' lovers boycotted it deliberately, insisting on more time and privacy for their love relationships.

The problem was debated in great detail. The group even invited a psychologist to analyse it with them, but he was unable to help as the group 'elders' continued to uphold the conviction that they must strive for the closest possible unity between life and work. The "monastery model," as this concept of a collective later came to be called, shows common characteristics with the total institutions described by Goffman. He points to a kind of "institutional incest taboo" functioning to prevent dyads withdrawing from the total institution (Goffman 1961:59).

Included in the goal of integrating the persons closest to their members was that of making financial provision for dependent family and for different consumption requirements by the principle of income according to need. From 1977 to 1984, members took what money they needed or wanted from the collective money chest, but, as their domestic situations were similar, the amounts taken did not differ greatly. The situation changed in the autumn of 1983 when the bookkeeper, Michael, married a Hungarian immigrant, Maria, and had to keep her while she was unemployed. Even before he married, Michael had been the member with the highest consumption requirements. A list of members' expenses in 1983 shows that Michael took out DM 2,500 per month, which included DM 861 rent for his apartment, while members like Julius and Reiner did not spend more than DM 1,000. Despite the collective's claim to integrate members' closest relations, Julius, who had been living with his girlfriend for years, introduced separate household accounts so that it could not be said to his detriment that his girlfriend was profiting from the collective resources.

The other members' feelings were against Michael at the meeting in February 1984, when the issue of supporting Maria was discussed. His colleagues resented heavily the fact that without asking them he had borrowed DM 7,000 from the collective money chest before going off to Hungary. Several colleagues expressed their unease and lack of confidence in Michael but tried to dissociate this from the needs of Maria, who took part in the meeting. Matze, who claimed not to feel responsible for the needs of his colleagues' family members, was reminded by the others that he and the other founders had been maintained partly by their girlfriends during the first difficult years of the collective and that they could now repay part of this by supporting Maria. Some members, however, feared that the enterprise's financial situation would be difficult in the coming year and that an additional effort would be required from all of them to support her. A discussion arose as to whether the money should be made available as a gift or a loan, until Maria herself intervened, insisting on a loan. When the final decision was made, nine of the ten members expressed themselves in favour of supporting Maria, though four of them with the reservation that the income according to need and want policy must be thoroughly reconsidered.

The "monastery model" finally collapsed when one of the founders, Hansi, became involved in an intense love-relationship and was expecting a child. Hansi started to shift priorities drastically from the collective to his small family. He refused to work in the evenings or on weekends, as he wanted to take on part of the responsibilities of childcare. His colleagues discussed for weeks whether, and to what extent, he should be allowed to have a private sphere outside the collective. But as the group grew bigger during this period, it became increasingly unrealisable to create a total community sharing all aspects of its life. Enormous tensions arose when Hansi purchased a house in West Germany for his young family. He had to pay the mortgage with money from the collective chest but refused his colleagues' request to make the house part of the collective property. This private appropriation made it impossible to continue the system of income according to want. As Julius put it, "Hansi's house broke the heart of many members of *Wuseltronick.*"

When Hansi left, followed shortly by another highly skilled new member — both for the same reason that they needed more time and money to care for their children — the collective decided to abandon the "monastery model" for good. Shortly afterwards, the principle of income according to need was abolished and a unitary payment of DM 1,400, which made an allowance for family obligations, was substituted.

Parenthood was also the prime cause of unanticipated tension in the Cambridge (USA) law collective studied by Sager. Suddenly, parents had less time for work and needed more money. They had a new focal point in their lives, which became more important than their group. Their emotions were caught up in an experience not shared by all, and as a result more effort was demanded of those who did not have children (Sager 1979:144). Talmon noted a similar pattern in the kibbutz. She writes: "In the new kibbutz, new families are the source of centrifugal tendencies. They are competing foci of intense emotional involvement" (Talmon 1965:3).

Whereas in the beginning most members of collectives lead a somewhat similar lifestyle and spend the money they earn mainly on their own immediate needs, tensions arise when some start to enter into a different phase of their life-cycle: they begin to think about having children and, consequently, take on increased family responsibilities. These members are willing to put in a greater work-effort in order to increase the returns of the enterprise and thereby earn a higher income. They want to adjust their work-effort to the higher consumption demands of their families.

Chayanov (1966:76) analysed a similar economic behaviour among Russian peasants on farms using family labour. In these Russian peasant farms, as in a Berlin collective, members can decide on the amount of work-effort they will expend. At the beginning of the century, the Russian peasant farmer sold his produce on the market but depended on the labour power of family members. There were considerable fluctuations in the level of labour input according to the consumption needs of the family. As the pressure of demands increased, for instance when the family consisted of young parents with small children, the farmer would deploy greater energy and accept a rate of self-exploitation he would have otherwise refused (Chayanov 1966:81). However, "there comes a moment at a certain level of rising labour income when the drudgery of the marginal labour expenditure will equal the subjective evaluation of the marginal utility of the sum obtained by this labour" (Chayanov 1966:81), and the peasant will cease to increase his effort.

Contrary to the Russian family, where all the consumers were also potential workers and shared the same interest in consumption, the working members of collectives experience unequal pressures. Their dependents are outside the group and put pressure only on that one particular member. Members at different stages of their life-cycle have different needs and are therefore unequally disposed to work hard. For a young member with comparatively low consumption needs, the moment comes relatively early when he will no longer consider an increase in returns worth the additional work-effort. An average amount of work is enough to maintain a satisfactory standard of living for the majority of members and still allow them to work at a relaxed pace. Conflicts inevitably arise when the members with higher needs try to speed up their fellow members' pace of work; their own solitary effort for greater efficiency is lost in the general go-slow and does not noticeably increase the overall unitary rate of pay.

In spring 1981, eighteen months after the founding of *KoMet*, Hans-Christian, one of the most active founding members, became dissatisfied with the income he drew. He wanted to work fewer hours and earn more and became totally unwilling to use his labour power to help the collective as a whole achieve a better result. As the father of two children, he had higher consumption needs than his fellow members and no comprehension of their relaxed attitude toward work. As his efforts to speed up his colleagues' pace of work were disregarded and attributed to his "chief-like" attitude toward the enterprise, he claimed payment according to performance. When the others refused, he proposed to work at his usual pace but then leave work when his task was finished and lie in the sun while the others were still "hanging around in the sticky workshop." This attitude brought the conflict to such a head that he was asked to leave.

Hans-Christian, who had always disagreed with the mixing of leisure and work, accused his fellow members of putting too much leisure into their working time, wasting time cooking and gossiping. He said of his colleagues, "They consider each hour spent in the collective equally valuable because it is an hour of their life, regardless of how much they produce in it." As the conflict appeared insoluble and the two different sides irreconcilable, the outcome was that the two parties found themselves facing an arbitration committee composed of members of other collectives.

This committee decided that *KoMet* could dismiss Hans-Christian provided they paid him DM 12,000 to found a new collective. He did in fact set up a new enterprise a year later, but with a structure that determined exactly the share each individual member had in the overall results. Each member calculated his result independently, taking in the profits for himself but, from this, paying his share of the monthly maintenance costs. This organisational structure later became an alternative for *KoMet* collectivists who had grown tired of the "chaotic work situation" and low pay there.

In collectives, the extent to which parenthood is felt to be a problem seems to depend to a large extent on the lifestyle of the parents. Of the eleven members and ex-members with children in the four collectives I studied closely, the five who had left because they were unable to reconcile childcare with collective work all lived in nuclear families. Two of the remaining fathers, who lived in communal households, considered work in collectives more advantageous for childcare because of the more flexible working hours. Some of the mothers held a similar view. They emphasized, however, that they had only been able to cope with both child and work because they lived in communal households, shared all the tasks equally with the father, and had the advantage of the dense network of alternative playgroups in Berlin.

The fact of having dependent family members does not always weigh so heavily as in the case, of Hans-Christian and Michael, who are their families' breadwinners. Most of the other collectivists who have children share the cost of childraising with the other parent, who has his or her independent income. For them, childcare is not a financial problem but often rather a problem of lack of free time, because members with children are still expected to put in a substantial amount of work whenever required. Jürgen, working in the *Oktoberdruck* office, seems to be the one with fewest problems in combining childcare and work. Since Lisa was born ten years ago, he has cared for her every other day, alternating the childcare with her mother, with whom he is no longer living. The organisation of his working hours allows him to leave work every other day at three to fetch Lisa from school and to work until seven or eight the next day to make up the time, when Lisa's mother is caring for her.

None of the older collectivists would now continue to maintain that members should spend all parts of their lives together. The concept of collective use of time has become more subtle since the early days. Instead of claiming that the same persons should be together during work and leisure time, now collectivists say that they want the same types of relationship with their workmates as with their friends, acquaintances, and family outside the collective.

For some of them, though, this does not necessarily make for leisure and relaxation. Friedel, a *KoMet* member, feels his life is being divided between his family of two children, the squatters' house where they live, and the collective. He feels overwhelmed by the personal commitment demanded of him from all sides. The sporadic bursts of work with *KoMet* and the nightlong discussions with his fellow squatters drain his energies. When his housemates were negotiating in the spring of 1984 to prevent the evacuation of the squat, Friedel used to arrive at work at lunchtime, having been discussing the future of the squatter' community until dawn. When personal conflicts arose between his colleagues at work, he tried to remain aloof, for as he said, "if I made all these personal difficulties my problems, I would have so many of them, where I live and where I work, that I couldn't endure them. I have adopted an 'I don't give a shit' attitude."

Although members with strong external obligations may enjoy the more relaxed rhythm of work, they feel the need to increase the profitability of the enterprise to raise their incomes and limit the hours worked. If these needs are not fulfilled, it is unlikely they will stay long, torn as they are between their obligations inside and outside the collective. Fluctuation, however, seriously damages both the economic viability of the enterprise and the personal bonds holding the collective together. In particular, those collectives that have existed for a number of years have to account for the fact that the living situation of their members has changed.

Labour Power Is Not for Sale

As the external interests of their members make themselves more and more acutely felt, the tendency in most collectives is to make an effort to reduce the working hours. But this is only possible if greater attention is devoted to work-effort and efficiency.

> The larger personal free-play, which you normally have in collectives, is limited in the *FahrradBüro* by the shop opening hours. Nevertheless, some get the feeling that they work more than others. Ulrike S. thinks she is slaving away while Bernhard sits lazily in the office all day. Bernhard maintains that Ulrike S. is only thinking about her holidays and how she can put together her days off as conveniently as possible. Everybody watches everybody else, but nobody can actually prove who works more and who works less. (Veronika, *FahrradBüro*, 19.12.1983)

Thus did Veronika, a member of the *FahrradBüro*, describe rather bluntly the tensions that arose between her colleagues over their respective commitments to work. Ulrike, an almost frantically active member, became impatient with her slower colleague Bernhard, who had already spent over four years in collective work. Bernhard, who in 1983 was still full of strong moral principles, despised Ulrike for her eagerness to take weekends off instead of dedicating her life fully to the collective.

Tensions of this kind arise in all collectives at certain points. Members compare among themselves the amount of work everybody does. But as their political convictions are at odds with the "capitalist" performance principle, they do not necessarily express this openly.

By abolishing wage-labour in their enterprises, the collectivists also reversed the assessment of work-time as all kinds of labour — skilled or unskilled — is paid at a similar rate. The categories that apply for controlling and measuring labour-time are purposely blurred: the collectivists generally do not assess how many hours each member works, and, if they do count the hours spent in the enterprise, no attempt is made to find out how much has been produced by each person in that time. Time spent drinking coffee is not always distinguished from time spent in production, and gossip with a customer is hardly differentiated from serious business talk.

Income according to want is the most radical way of breaking with the logic of capitalist labour. It means the conscious blurring of the link between personal expenditure and work performance. Similarly to *Wuseltronick*, *KoMet* also set out with an income-according-to-want system, which was maintained for eighteen months. In a self-portrayal from 1980, the members explained this principle:

> The problem: satisfaction cannot be measured in numbers or money. It is obvious everybody's idea of a fair income is different. The practice: each takes as much out of the money-chest as he thinks is right. Everybody has to decide for himself how much he needs, whether this is feasible for the collective and whether the money taken out stands in an adequate relation to that of the others. There are sometimes frictions because of unequal withdrawals. But then the arguments are not about the amount of money, but about the use that is made of it. Everybody is ready to discuss his own way of living with the other *KoMet* members and also to question it. Up to now this system has worked well. We know, however, that this system can only be practised in small groups on the basis of mutual trust. (Self-portrayal of *KoMet* from 1980)

This system was abolished in 1981 because Hans-Christian claimed a higher income than his colleagues, not only on the grounds of his greater personal needs but also because he thought he worked more efficiently.

Unitary income is prevalent in Berlin collectives although sometimes with modifications, as working hours have started to be valued differently. In the café collective *die Straßenbahn* the night hours are paid more highly. The newspaper *die tageszeitung* developed an elaborate system of payment to account for the fact that some working hours involve more tiring and monotonous jobs. In 1990, all members earned the same income of DM 1,500 net plus DM 400 for each child, but the members working at the screen in the typesetting and layout section only worked six hours a day, while those working in administration worked seven hours and those editing spent between eight and twelve hours daily at work. This system was meant to alleviate the monotonous tasks and give those members doing them more opportunities to participate in other activities connected with the newspaper. But the different work-sections have become clearly divided and are no longer able to integrate layerout workers and typesetters into other sections. So these members tend to go home after their four hours' work and have developed something like a job mentality, as their contact with the larger concerns of the paper is very limited.

Unitary pay, spread out equally among the members regardless of performance and often also of hours spent, responds to a sense of justice, which assumes that each member will automatically give his best for the enterprise. It carries the risk, though, that members lose sight of the enterprise's financial situation. Even worse for the morale of the group is that it may make members suspect each other of laziness, and some may begin to resent the poor time-keeping or irregular hours of their colleagues as a personal injustice. As Ireland and Law (1982) observed, this mechanism seems to be generalised in labour-managed enterprises where the residual is shared independently of effort. The additional effort of one member must be shared between all the others and, therefore, is hardly worthwhile for the individual personally. As a result, workers start to take note of one another's work-effort and to work less if the efforts are too uneven. As a consequence, the average performance may even be reduced (Ireland and Law 1982:63). The major internal problem labour-managed enterprises encounter, if they want to increase their efficiency, when they combine their members' individual work-performances into a collective effort. The greater the number of workers, the smaller the incentive for individual additional effort (Ireland and Law 1982:63).

In 1984, *KoMet* members became increasingly concerned about their low productivity, but they still shied away from control of individual work-performance, as they remembered the tremendous tension that arose as a result of the only attempt, made in 1982, to attribute turnovers to individual members. It then became obvious that some members were making DM 8,000 to DM 12,000 turnover per month, while others made only DM 800 to DM 4,000, which on average was about half the turnover of an ordinary toolmaking enterprise, as Fritz maintained (Fritz, *KoMet*, 13.8.1984). He believed that the actual levels of performance were almost the same in 1984 as three years earlier and that it would create rifts between those at the top and those at the bottom to make public the results.

The members themselves often have difficulty in evaluating their own work-performance. They estimate the production time roughly in advance but are incapable of discovering why a job took longer than planned. Hanne, a *KoMet* member, described her difficulties:

> At the beginning of my time with *KoMet* I would have liked to calculate an order together with a colleague and then assess the time needed for each work-step to find out why it took me longer than I had initially expected. Was there a day when I had worked sluggishly? Was it because I had not realised that I would need special tools for the order, for which I then had to search for ages? Was it because I lacked routine in the movements or because I wasn't operating the machine fast enough to make it turn at its optimal speed? However, nobody ever found the time to test this out with me on two or three orders, so I never found out in which direction I ought to change. (Hanne, *KoMet*, 8.8.1984)

Hanne found neither help nor support among her fellow members in her search for a more efficient work-style. The other members scrupulously avoided comparing testing or assessing the work efficiency of one another, and they refused to have the actual time spent in production recorded. Fritz, for instance, was convinced that overall results and individual productivity could not be estimated without introducing a system of control and of time measurement, in the style of Taylor.

> It's all a matter of a lack of self-discipline, and this you can only compensate for if you introduce a system of control, and we don't intend to do that. If you want to muddle along, then you'll just do it. This will make itself felt as less money for the whole enterprise.... You can't tell anybody how many breaks he is supposed to take, nor that he should work more efficiently. You can only say in general that it is necessary to work efficiently. As long as you don't want piece rates and payment according to performance, you can't say anything because everything is all very subjective. (Fritz, *KoMet*, 13.8.1984)

In the following years, the tensions over low incomes and fluctuation in membership increased. The collective experimented until May 1986 with a closer monitoring of the labour process. Productive and unproductive hours were written down separately, and breaks were no longer counted as paid working time, the latter in fact being reduced to 35 hours per week. As the overall results of the enterprise did not improve, a proportion of the members proposed in 1986 to introduce payment conditional on the returns of the orders on which the various groups of members cooperated (*auftragsabhängiger Gruppenlohn*). They wanted to relate group performance to income and time worked. Their concept did not convince the other members, who rejected this scheme as a form of payment according to performance and also because they were afraid of competition between the work-groups within the collective. The group of would-be reformers eventually split with the collective in 1988 and set up a firm in which each member worked on his or her own account or cooperated with some of the other members as desired. They were convinced that work performance would improve as each member had to bear the consequences of his or her individual sloppiness; or, as Gisela put it, "I admit that it makes a difference whether one works for oneself or for the idealistic idea of the collective."

A form of payment according to return had already been initiated in 1981 by Constantin, one of the founders of *Oktoberdruck*. He was at that time not only the formal owner of all the machines the collective possessed but was also paying back debts, which dated from the financial collapse of the enterprise in 1978. He felt in 1981 that he was the only member acutely aware of the enterprise's financial situation and accused his fellow members of developing the mentality of wage-labourers, receiving their pay at the end of the month without caring too greatly about the returns the firm was making. To remedy their indifference, he wanted to incite them to calculate their individual results and receive an income according to individual performance. He saw the collective as "independent craftsmen grouped together", who were sharing tools, customers, and machinery without being dependent upon a capitalist owner and who were receiving the "real value" of their work.

The other members were fiercely opposed to the monitoring of individual performance. Although they agreed to the calculation of income based on the monthly returns, they insisted on assessing the returns collectively. They decided that each section should establish its returns independently and pay its members accordingly. Each section was treated, for the purposes of the accounts, like a separate enterprise. The printing section, with a higher average turnover, had on its own to raise the money for the maintenance of and repayments on the printing presses. Each printer had to behave like a small entrepreneur, laying aside money in the good months to cover the costs in the bad ones or for a holiday. The members of the printing section paid themselves by the hour, whereas those in the repromontage section calculated their incomes per working day, putting aside a certain sum to pay for the fixed costs of the whole section at once. The system was intended to improve members' efficiency because their good or bad performance as a section directly affected their salaries, but it also intensified the jealousies and tensions between the sections. In September 1983 the print and repromontage sections reunited their calculation of results in order to avoid these problems.

Today, the members of each section are paid by the hour according to a rate that is fixed each month. The hours are counted globally without reference to the particular orders members have been working on. Each member notes down the fixed time-units and the material spent on an order. For instance, mounting an eight-page mounting foil without photographs or drawings is written down as taking fifteen minutes, even if it actually took the repro-monteur twenty minutes to do that particular one. Every work-step has its predetermined price and only if unforeseen difficulties arise that are not the collectivist's fault may the price quoted to the customer be raised. As income is linked to collective performance, each serious mistake or misprint is felt acutely in the monthly payments. The enterprise is largely protected from bankruptcy by this system, but the members individually are not.

Oktoberdruck's system of income was widely discussed in the "Alternative Scene" but was hardly ever imitated, not least because the other collectives did not have the same fixed work-steps as *Oktoberdruck*. In the course of these debates it was pointed out that the nonassessment of individual levels of performance was one of the basic characteristics of a collective enterprise. Enterprises that were jointly owned but paid their members according to individual performance started to be called "communal workshops" (*Gemeinschaftswerkstätten*) to distinguish them from "real collectives."

The carpenters' workshop in Kreuzberg, *Holzmanufaktur*, was such an enterprise when I visited it in November 1982. It was explained to me that the members took on orders alone or as a group, executed them, and were then paid for them. In the quotation the customer received before the order was executed, the estimated number of hours' work was set down, the price being fixed at DM 40 per hour. A craftsman who worked more efficiently than estimated in the quotation was therefore able to achieve a higher hourly rate, but if he made mistakes and took longer, his average hourly rate decreased. From the fixed hourly wage, DM 4 were deducted for maintenance of the machinery and craftshop. Each worker had to pay his own insurance from his wage. This form of payment favoured an individualistic work-style but did not meet with the approval of those members who would have preferred to receive the same income and cooperate more closely.

The refusal to measure time and work efficiency is not characteristic of cooperative forms of production as such. In the nineteenth century writings on *Genossenschaften*, a higher work performance and a more efficient use of working time were described as strong points of cooperatives (Oppenheimer 1822:54). Compared to the wage-labourers in nineteenth century industry who were using sabotage and go-slow strikes to limit the exhaustion of their labour power, cooperative workers were much more willing to work harder and more efficiently as they no longer felt exploited by a capitalist.

Workers in the Klek factory in Yugoslavia, for instance, claimed income according to piece-rates, arguing that "only people who work should get paid" (Comisso 1979:170). The blue-collar workers believed that all work, including office work, should be monitored to increase the firm's income. The skilled, part-time, women workers at the Fakenham cooperative also favoured piece rates because this would allow them to earn more in less time and have enough time for their children (Wajcman 1983:119).

Contemporary theoreticians of cooperative work-forms, such as Velasquez, advocate the precise evaluation of members' different work performances as a means of avoiding conflict: "Only if it were possible to determine unequivocally the figure of productivity for the individual contributors, then this could be the basis for evaluating the different work-performances and it would eliminate conflicts about payments" (Velasquez 1975:57).

Conclusion

Between 1982 and 1988, discussions about efficiency and profitability increased in frequency. Members began to admit that professionalisation was a necessary condition for greater stability. Labour-saving devices that they had observed in their previous employment in business industry were introduced to reduce the time wasted in searching for tools and materials. They became concerned with estimating the level of efficiency of their work, with the aim of finding a means to reduce the working hours.

The initial "pure" model of a community living and working together has been modified to meet the external obligations and interests developed by members. "Efficiency" became an issue again when members with strong external obligations threatened to leave. Once the time spent in the collective was no longer regarded by all as equally pleasurable, and outside commit- ments had created differences in priorities and loyalties, equal pay for different performance became a latent point of conflict. This brought about the tacit monitoring of productivity and occasional outbursts of anger about others' "laziness." Since the most dynamic and hard-working members could not claim higher status or income than their less efficient colleagues, this sometimes resulted in bitterness and frustration. Although the collectives still refrain from pinpointing individual differences in performance, some have started to introduce hourly pay or have tried to agree on more regular working hours.

Work in a collective still proceeds at a much more relaxed pace than in a business enterprise, as "no boss stands behind you with a watch in his hand." Collectivists have reacquired some of the "art of living" that Thompson (1967) saw lost as a consequence of the Industrial Revolution. He wrote: "Men might have to relearn some of the arts of living lost in the industrial revolution... how to break down once more the barriers between work and life" (Thompson 1967:95). To uphold this achievement, however, it is insufficient to change the style of work in collectives alone. The level of technology in contemporary society would allow for a more relaxed pace of work if the work load was equally distributed. Instead, however, useless occupations become paid services and leisure time and income continue to be distributed unequally (Gorz 1990:23). The collectivists who attempt to create different structures inside work cannot escape from the pressures and constraints of this society they live in.

9

Conclusion

How political convictions of collectivists influence their social and economic practice and how ideas about society emerge and are transformed in concrete life situations has been the underlying theme of this book. Seen in a historical perspective, the foundation of collectives at the end of the 1970s was a consequence of a reassessment of the viability of political movements after 1968 in the light of internal fragmentation, excessive authoritarianism, and massive political repression. When the dream of a powerful, revolutionary Marxist party vanished, founders of collectives turned to realising their ideal of an anti-authoritarian, socialist model of production on a small scale. The intentions they started out with were threefold:

— they strove for the self-realisation of the individual at work allowing for self-determination, development of skills, and an individual rhythm of work;

— they wanted to create a collective organisation of work based on the principles of consensus, material equality, and collective property;

— they wanted to have an impact on society at large — by realising a direct interaction between producers and consumers and the production and promoting of ecological products — and be a model for overall social change.

Berlin collectives have tried to practice radical democracy at the point of production in a sphere of life where capitalist society lacks direct democracy. Collectivists believe in an egalitarian community of work based on the principle of spontaneity.

Over the last ten years, these hopes and ideas have been confronted with the reality of the working day, the need to organise, produce, and sell. The day-to-day experience showed the limits of the adaptability of the individual to the collective context, the complexities of collective organisation, and the absorbing character of capitalist society.

Having analysed the intricacies of collective practice, we can now ask what has remained to this day of the initial ideals? What did collective experience bring forth for the people who engaged in it? Are they disappointed, or do they still consider it worth the effort? What was the larger social impact of the collective experiment, and what is its perspective for the future?

In the initial euphoric phase that caused a boom in the foundation of collectives for a couple of years, members invested all their physical and emotional energy, and large parts of their private lives, into the enterprise and committed themselves voluntarily to a tremendous work-effort. Founders of collectives were workaholics and engaged passionately in collective work. Their overmotivation was only reduced to proper proportions when some members started to work less, to withdraw increasingly into private life, or even to leave the collective.

The two most frequent and, at the same time, opposite reasons for leaving were disillusioned idealism and unfulfilled material needs. Highly motivated members left disappointed because the collectives had not been able to function on an entirely egalitarian basis. They found their "political energies" bound up in the daily work of the enterprise and decided that they could be used more effectively outside. Other idealistically motivated members went into the "inner emigration" disappointed about rising personal tensions and conflicts among their fellow members. They withdrew from political activities, started therapies, or discovered a new body consciousness.

Other members became dissatisfied with the risk-aversion and low performance of their fellow members because their individual needs and wants had changed when they entered into a phase of their life that involved increased family obligations. Working in an alternative way, but earning little, was not attractive any more. No longer were they willing, however, to work for a boss in a business enterprise, either. They chose to practice a self-determined style of work in individualistic structures of production where they did not have to share the fruits of their efforts. They tended to split off from the collective, sometimes with part of the capital, to work on their own account in a loosely associating team. They were able to profit hereby from the entrepreneurial skills acquired in the collective. In Berlin, their example became attractive for small entrepreneurs who set up firms with an "alternative" touch, like bicycle shops, travel agencies, etc., that had never been collectives.

Remaining members started to reflect on the causes of fluctuation of membership. While the time spent in the collective was considered by most leaving members as a valuable experience and an important phase in their lives, the collective enterprise itself suffered more than any ordinary firm from fluctuating membership, as its organisational structure was based on strong personal relations. In a still ongoing process of self-reflection, collectives attempted to adapt their structures to the changing needs of the members. Responsibilities were delegated (e. g., for cooking, and dealing with customers) and tasks were clearly divided (e. g., office work). More emphasis was put on the monitoring of group performance, rentability, and continuous order inflow. Perpetually, however, collectives continued to encounter three basic organisational problems:

– They were confronted with the emergence of informal leaders and the need to reduce the complexity of the structures of self-management. They experienced what sociological theory had long been pointing out (Sofer 1972): assuming responsibilities and making decisions can become a burden, especially if important issues are at stake and risks are involved.

– Different levels of performance that were paid equally led to tensions and to the covert observation of fellow members' job performances.

– External obligations requiring time and money were in contradiction with personal involvements and financial investments in the collective enterprise. This contradiction, which also arises in family businesses, is infinitely sharper in collectives where capital is "neutralized" and members cannot own private shares in the collective.

In spite of their structural problems, the way collectives organised their work provoked debates that go far beyond their economic impact. Collectives received considerable media coverage, and not only in left-wing and alternative newspapers. Liberal printed media such as the news magazine *Der Spiegel* and the weekly newspaper *DIE ZEIT* (Dec. 1981, April – May 1984) published whole series about the alternative economy, describing it with a mixture of admiration and compassion. The established economic journals *Die Wirtschaftswoche* (22.2.1985, 27.9.1985) and *Das Handelsblatt* (27-28.6.1985) analysed that the strong points of alternative enterprises were their capacities to "integrate its members with all their thinking, feeling and will. " In these journals, management consultants maintained that they had learned from collectives that material incentives have to be complemented with an intangible participation, touching the feelings of the staff.

Established trade unions, on the contrary, rejected almost entirely alternative ideas about production. They have criticised the fact that the material conditions of collective work fell far behind the achievements for which wage-labourers had fought for decades (collective wage agreements, overtime agreements, labour conventions, etc.). They did not consider the emancipatory aspect important enough to compensate for these disadvantages. The youth organisations of the trade unions started, nevertheless, to enter into a dialogue with the collectives.

To sum up, the social and cultural transformations of society to which the collective experiments have contributed are basically on three levels.

First, for the ecology movement collectives served as a concrete example for a more ecological way of producing. Intellectuals fascinated by ecological production and a self-determined style of work carried the debate into wider circles of industry and politics, and adolescents, considering for themselves a future job in a collective, brought it into their parents' homes. Not least, the fact that German industry took the lead in the international market in the domain of environmental technology has to do with public debate about ecologically sound products and alternative ways of producing. In the 1970s, massive popular protest against nuclear power stations went hand in hand with proposals for exploiting alternative sources of energy, such as wind, sun, and tides. Equipment was first developed by small alternative enterprises and, only at a later stage, was included into the research programmes of the big energy-producing combines. Tougher laws following massive popular protest against the ongoing pollution of water, air, and soil obliged German industry to introduce sophisticated air filters and sewage plants. Industry also started to respond to environmentally conscious consumer organisations advocating ecologically sound products. Items originally available only in small alternative shops, such as phosphate-free soaps, toilet paper made of recycled paper, vegetables without chemicals grown by ecological farmers, and wholegrain bread baked by small collective bakeries, were soon to be bought in major supermarkets.

The "ecology economy," however, as conceived by *Die Grünen* and the *Alternative Liste*, goes beyond the mere reparation of industrial pollution. From their marginal political position the ecologists also raised unpopular issues asking for major changes in the consumption habits dear to the German citizen, such as the limitation on individual transportation and the prohibition of excessive packaging material. As a countercurrent to the current political and economic trend — with 16 million East Germans discovering the pleasures of consumption and the West Germany economy booming at the expense of the collapsing East German one — they still claim that the Germans should grow less and produce differently if they want to have any chance to preserve the remains of their natural environment.

Second, collectives — especially in the big cities — integrated individuals into the production process who would have otherwise stayed outside, such as unemployed academics or proletarianised students. Collective enterprises absorbed their critical intellectual potential in a creative way. Since November 1989, their entrepeneurial experiences have become relevant for workers and academics in East Germany who, having lost their jobs in industry or academia, are obliged to create their own jobs and find flexible responses to unemployment. The alternative advisory office *STATTwerke*, in cooperation with the Senate of Berlin, has started to advise them on how to start a cooperative business.

Third, it sharpened the awareness of a new generation of apprentices and students of a self-determined style of work. This awareness may result in powerful demands for a new culture of work. The idea that one should determine one's own work pace, conceive and produce a product from beginning to end, and have a say in the organisation of the work shows striking similarities with the most recent theories of modern management (*Handelsblatt* 20.12.1988:3). The global economy and industrial organisation is changing in a way that enhances the value of creativity and devalues "mere" efficiency. Due to the international division of labour between industrial countries (exporting know-how and high-tech products) and "developing" countries (providing cheap labour and raw materials), the leading capitalist enterprises are beginning to consider the brains of their most imaginative collaborators as their most valuable capital. To keep their "brain trust" from leaving, modern managers had to learn to let workers choose their own style of work, to take initiatives, and assume responsibilities.

This change validates some of the principles explored by alternative collectivists and brings their ideas from the margin into the "mainstream" of economic activity. The originally "revolutionary" values are thus becoming marketable. At the same time, the elite of collective enterprises is starting to do well in the freshly affirmed, dominant system of competitive high-tech capitalism. Although their ideas about collective work may still be inspired by the ideal of sharing, in economic practice weak and dependent individuals, who were originally protected by the collective, now hardly stand a chance. The tougher selection criteria inhibit their admission, and the tendency of efficient members eventually to leave an inefficient collective seals the destiny of those alternative enterprises that have refused to adapt to their competitive environment.

Appendix

Questions to Collective Enterprises

1) *Legal Form:*
   a) Does the enterprise belong legally to a company of limited liability (*GmbH*), an association, a partnership (*GbR*), or to a cooperative (*Genossenschaft*)?
   b) Has the legal form changed over time?
   c) Are all co-workers also co-owners? Is there a probatory period after which they must become associates?
   d) Are there silent partners? If yes, how much capital do they have in the enterprise? In what kinds of decisions concerning the enterprise are they allowed to participate? What would they receive if the enterprise was liquidated?
   e) Is the legal form of the enterprise going to be changed?

2) *Economic Situation:*
   a) What is the value of the enterprise? How large are the shares of the associates? Are there debts and mortgages? How was the enterprise financed initially and how has it made further investments since its foundation?
   b) Turnover: What is the average monthly turnover? Over the year, to what extent do monthly turnovers fluctuate? Did the enterprise make a profit or a loss in the past year, or was the balance equilibrated?
   c) Investments: What kinds of investments have been made? Value of these investments? Points in time? Are you planning new investments at the moment?
   d) Market: For what kind of customers are you producing? Has your circle of customers changed considerably over time? Would your customers be able to obtain the same goods more cheaply from a capitalist enterprise? If yes, why do they buy them from a collective enterprise? How strongly does competition make itself felt? Competition with other collectives? Competition with business enterprises? What are the perspectives for the future?

3) *Internal Structure:*

a) Personnel: For how long has the enterprise existed? How many of the founders still work in the collective? How many members do you have today? What are their qualifications? Average age? Ages of oldest and youngest members? Has the sex ratio changed over time? How is it today? How many members are married? Have children? How many members live in a communal household (*Wohngemeinschaft*)? For how many years did each member stay?

b) Recruitment and Dismissal: What is the procedure to become a member of the collective? Is it difficult to find new members? Was it formerly easier or more difficult to find qualified new members? Or was qualification not an important criteria then? Have members ever been excluded from the collective? If yes, why? What is the most important reason for people leaving? Do you train apprentices?

4) *Development of Wages:*

a) Level and Form of Wage Payments: What is the average wage at the moment? Does it cover social contributions? What form of wage payment have you chosen? According to the result of the enterprise? Unitary pay? According to want? Other? How has the form and level of wage payment changed over time? Were these changes related to developments in the labour market? How is the working time regulated? Do you also work "on the side"? Do some individual members do so? Does the collective as a whole? How regularly are wages paid?

b) "Short time work": Do you often have to work short time? How do you deal with peaks of orders? Do you work overtime?

5) *Organisation of Work:*

a) Machines: What machines did you already have at the foundation and what have you bought since then? Have the new machines caused changes in the organisation of work? Did the types of products change after you bought the new machines?

b) Division of Labour: How are work-tasks divided — in production, in marketing? Are the tasks rotated? Are the books kept by a specialist? Is he/she the managing partner?

c) Decision making: How do you plan production and marketing? How often does the collective meet? What are the functions of this meeting? Does the managing partner have special authority in decision-making processes?

Questions to Individual Members

1) *Workplace:*
   a) For how many years have you worked here?
   b) Which tasks do you do? Have they changed over time?
   c) What is your (average) monthly income?
   d) Were you trained for this job?
   e) Do you share your workplace with others? Do they change frequently?

2) *Personal Situation:*
   a) How old are you? Male/female?
   b) What is your housing situation?
   c) Do you have any commitments? Are you married? Do you have to care for children (on your own)?
   d) Do you have to sustain yourself exclusively from income from the collective?

3) *Antecedents:*
   a) What kind of training did you receive (school, apprenticeship, university)?
   b) Where did you work previously? For how long? Doing what? What was your income? Why did you leave?
   c) Have you ever been out of work for long?
   d) When did you come to Berlin? Where did you live previously?
   e) Did you previously work in another collective?
   f) How did you get your job here? Why did you take it?

4) *Perspectives:*
   a) What are the advantages and disadvantages of working in a collective?
   b) What about your work here would you like to change?
   c) To what causes would you attribute (any) difficulties?
   d) For how long are you planning to work in this collective? If you change your job, will you choose to work in another collective?
   e) If you could change your job now, what kind of work would you like to do?
   f) What capabilities do people need to have in order to be able to work in a collective?

Bibliography

Abrams, P. and McCulloch, A.
  1976, *Communes, Sociology and Society*. Cambridge: Cambridge University Press.
Bahro, R.
  1977, *Die Alternative*. Köln: *Europäische Verlagsanstalt*.
Barlett, W. and Uvalic, M.
  1985, *Bibliography on Labour-Managed Firms and Employee Participation*. Florence: draft version for presentation to the 4th conference of the International Association for the Economics of Self-Management, Liege.
Barth, F.
  1959, *Political Leadership Among the Swat Pathan*. London: Athlone Press.
Bartning, C.
  1982, "Lohnarbeit und Kollektiv" IN: *STATTbuch 2*. Berlin: STATTbuch Verlag.
Bartsch, F.-J. and Rulff, D.
  u.p., *Der Alternativsektor — Produktion zwischen Utopie und Notwendigkeit: Das Beispiel Berlin*. 38 pages mimeo.
Becker, H.S.
  1960, "Notes on the Concept of Commitment" IN: *American Journal of Sociology* 66.
Bensele, F., Heinze, R. G. and Klohne, A. (eds.)
  1982, *Zukunft der Arbeit*. Hamburg: VSA.
Berger, J. and Kostede, N.
  1981, "Wie autonom ist der autonome Sektor?" IN: *Aesthetik und Kommunikation* 43: May.
Bergmann, K.
  1984, "Vernetzung, Verbände und Zusammenarbeit" IN: *Hick-Hack* 0.

Beynon, H. and Blackburn, R.M.
   1972, *Perceptions of Work.*Cambridge: Cambridge University Press.
Beynon, H. and Nichols, T.
   1977, *Living with Capitalism.* London: Routledge and Kegan Paul.
Bischoff, J.
   1976, *Die Klassenstruktur der BRD.* Berlin: VSA.
Blau, P.
   1964, *Exchange and Power in Social Life.* New York: Wiley and Sons.
Bloch, E.
   1982, *Das Prinzip Hoffnung* (3 volumes). Frankfurt: Suhrkamp Verlag
Bloch, M.
   1971, "Decision-making Councils Among the Merina" IN: Richards, A.
      and Kuper, A., *Councils in Action.* Cambridge: Cambridge Uni-
      versity Press.
   1973 "The Long Term and the Short Term: the Economy and Political
      Significance of the Morality of Kinship" IN:Goody, J.R. *The Cha-*
      racter of Kinship. Cambridge: Cambridge University Press.
Braverman, H.
   1974, *Labour and Monopoly Capital.* New York: Monthly Review Press.
Brown, J.
   u.d., *How to Start a Workers' Cooperative. Leeds: Beechwood College*
      Publication.
Bücher, K.
   1909, Arbeit und Rhythmus. Leipzig: B.G. Teubner.
Burawoy, M.
   1979, *Manufacturing Consent.* Chicago: Chicago University Press.
   1984a, *The Contours of Production Politics.* Berlin: Publication Series of
      the International Institute for Comparative Social Research.
   1984b, "Karl Marx and the Satanic Mills: Factory Politics under Early
      Capitalism in England, the United States and Russia" IN: *Ameri-*
      can Journal of Sociology vol. 90 n. 2.
   1985, *The Politics of Production.* London: Verso (New Left Books).
Buurman, M., Jensen, O., Lischke, G., Rock, F.
   1990, *Untersuchungen über Finanzierungsprobleme bei sozial-innovati-*
      ven Betrieben unter besonderer Berücksichtigung des Förderin-
      strumentariums für kleine und mittlere Unternehmen in Berlin.
      Berlin: im Auftrag der Senatsverwaltung für Wirtschaft.

Callenbach, E.
 1978, *Ökotopia*. Berlin: Ökotopia Verlag.
Cartier, M. (ed.)
 1984, *Le travail et ses représentations* Paris: *éditions des archives contemporaines*.
Chayanov, A. V.
 1966, *The Theory of Peasant Economy*. Homewood, Ill.: The American Economic Association (1. ed. 1924).
Child, J. and Partridge, B.
 1982, *Lost Managers*. Cambridge: Cambridge University Press.
Claussen, D.
 1981, "Im Universum der totalen Verdinglichung" IN: Claussen, D (ed.) *Spuren der Befreiung — Herbert Marcuse*. Darmstadt: *Luchterhand*.
Cockerton, P., Gilmour-White, T., Pearce, J. and Whyatt, A.
 1980, *Workers' Cooperatives — A Handbook*. Aberdeen: Aberdeen People's Press.
Cohn-Bendit, G. and Cohn-Bendit, D.
 1968, *Der linke Radikalismus*. Reinbek: Rowohlt.
Colletti, L.
 1974, "Marxism as Sociology," "Marxism: Science or Revolution" IN: *From Rousseau to Lenin*. New York: Monthly Review Press.
Comisso, E. T.
 1979, *Workers' Control under Plan and Market*. New Haven: Yale University Press.
Coser, L. A.
 1967, "Greedy Organisations" IN: *Archives européennes de sociologie* 8,2 p.196-215.
Cressey, P. and MacInnes, J.
 1980, "Voting for Ford: Industrial Democracy and the Control of Labour" IN: *Capital and Class*. Vol 11.
Crozier, M. and Friedberg, E.
 1984, "Selbstverwaltung ist ein Problem und keine Lösung" IN: Flieger, B. *Produktivgenossenschaften*. München: *AG Spak*.
Démerin, P.
 1975, *Communautés pour le socialisme*. Paris: *Maspero*.

Eger, T. and Weise, P.
 1978, "Einzel- und gesamtwirtschaftliche Aspekte des Investitionsverhaltens arbeiterselbstverwalteter Unternehmen" IN: *Partizipation in Betrieb und Gesellschaft*. Frankfurt: *Campus Verlag*.
Elwert, G.
 1983, "Aufbruch und Krise. Überlegungen zur Dynamik sozialer Bewegungen" IN: Hanisch R. (ed.) *Soziale Bewegungen in Entwicklungsländern*. Baden-Baden: *Nomos*.
Fabian, F. (ed.)
 1972, *Arbeiter übernehmen ihren Betrieb*. Reinbek: *Rowohlt*.
Fel, E., Hofer, T.
 1972, *Bäuerliche Denkweise in Wirtschaft und Haushalt*. Göttingen: *Verlag Otto Schwarz & Co.*
Flieger, B. (ed.)
 1984, *Produktivgenossenschaften oder der Hindernislauf zur Selbstverwaltung*. München: *AG Spak*.
Fortes, M.
 1971, "Introduction" IN: Goody, J. R. (ed), *The Developmental Cycle of the Domestic Group*. Cambridge: Cambridge University Press.
Fox, A.
 1974, *Beyond Contract: Work, Power and Trust Relations*. London: Faber and Faber ltd.
Friedman, Y.
 1977, *Machbare Utopien*. Frankfurt: *Fischer Verlag*.
Friedmann, G.
 1955, "Quelques aspects et effets récents de l'éclatement des tâches industrielles" IN: Meyerson, I., Vernant, J.P., Soboul, A. (eds.) *Le travail, les métiers, l'emploi*. Paris: *PUF*.
Gizycki, H. and Habicht, H. (eds.)
 1978, *Oasen der Freiheit*. Frankfurt: *Fischer TB*.
Goffman, E.
 1962, *Asylums*. Chicago: Aldine Publishers.
 1969, *The Presentation of Self in Everyday Life*. London: Penguin.
Goody, J. R.
 1962, *Death, Property and the Ancestors*. London: Tavistock.
Gordon, D. M.
 1976, "Kapitalistische Effizienz und sozialistische Effizienz" IN: *Monthly Review*. Sept 1976 n.3 special issue p. 21-41.

Gorz, A.
  1980, *Adieux au prolétariat* Paris: *éd. Galilée*.
  1990, "Pourquoi la société salariale a besoin de nouveaux valets" IN: *Le monde diplomatique.* juin (22-23).

Gouldner, A. W.
  1971, *The Coming Crisis of Western Sociology.* London: Heinemann.

Gramsci, A.
  1975, *Quaderni del Carcere* (4 volumes) Torino: *Giulio Einaudi.*

Gui, B.
  1981, "Investment Decisions in a Worker Managed Firm" IN: *Economic Analysis and Workers Management* Vol XV.

Gunn, C. E.
  1980, "Plywood Cooperatives of the Pacific Northwest: Lessons for Workers' Self-Management in the United States" IN: *Economic Analysis and Workers' Self-Management* XIX 3 p.393-416.

Gunther, H.
  1982, "Utopie nach der Revolution" IN: Vokamp W. (ed.) *Utopie-forschung.* vol.3, Stuttgart: *J.B. Metzlersche Verlagsbuchhandlung.*

Gutzmer, M.
  1981, *Entstehungsbedingungen und Entwicklungsperspektiven des Produktionssektors innerhalb der Alternativbewegung.* Berlin: unpublished diploma dissertation at the *Otto Suhr Institut, Freie Universität Berlin.*

Haraszti, M.
  1976, *Salaire aux pieces.* Paris: *Seuil.*

Heinrich, M.
  1981, *Legitimationsprobleme der Mitbestimmung.* Stuttgart: *Haupt Verlag.*

Herbst, P. G.
  1976, "Non-hierarchical Forms of Organisation" IN: *Acta Sociologica.* Vol. 19.

Hirschman A. O.
  1970, *Exit, Voice and Loyality.* Cambridge MA: Harvard University Press.

Hollstein, W.
  1981, *Die Gegengesellschaft.* Reinbek: *Rowohlt*

Holy, L.
1979, "Nuer Politics" IN: *Queen's University Papers.* vol.4.
Huber, J.
1979a, *Anders Arbeiten — Anders Wirtschaften.* Frankfurt: *Fischer Taschenbuch Verlag.*
1979b, "Wohin galoppiert die schwarz-rote Sau auf grünem Grund" IN: *Netzwerk Rundbrief.* No. 6, September.
1980, *Wer soll das alles ändern.* Berlin: *Rotbuch Verlag.*
Huber, J., Härlin, B., Werner, K.H., and Dannert, R.
1979, "Rettungsaktivitäten für Oktoberdruck" IN: *Netzwerk Rundbrief* Nr.6, September.
Humphrey, C.
1983, *Karl Marx Collective.* Cambridge: Cambridge University Press.
Illich, I.
1975, *Selbstbegrenzung.* Reinbek: *Rowohlt.*
Ireland, N.J. and Law, P.
1982, *The Economics of Labour Managed Enterprises.* London: Croom Helm.
Israelsen, L.D.
1980, "Collectives, Communes and Incentives" IN: *Journal of Comparative Economics.* Vol 4, No 2, June.
Jarchow, K. and Klugmann, N.
1980, *Heumarkt.* Berlin: *Rotbuch Verlag.*
Jungk, R. and Müllert, N.R. (eds.)
1980, *Alternatives Leben.* Baden-Baden: *Signal Verlag.*
Kanter, R.M.
1972, *Commitment and Community.* Cambridge, Mass: Harvard University Press.
Kofler, L.
1983, *Zur Kritik der "Alternativen" Kongress Zukunft der Arbeit 1982 in Bielefeld, Materialienband.* Hamburg: *VSA*
Korczak, D.
1979, *Neue Formen des Zusammenlebens.* Frankfurt: *Fischer TB.*
Kraushaar, W.(ed.)
1978, *Autonomie oder Ghetto? Kontroversen um die Alternativbewegung.* Frankfurt: *Verlag Neue Kritik.*

Kück, M.

1985, *Neue Finanzierungsstrategien für selbstverwaltete Betriebe*. PhD-thesis, *Freie Universität*, Berlin mimeo (published 1985 Frankfurt: *Campus Verlag*).

1984, "Bank für Freaks" IN: *die tageszeitung* 15.5.84.

1982, "Ein Plädoyer für die Vernetzung" IN: *Netzwerk Rundbrief*. No 17, June.

Kuper, A.

1971a, "The Kalagari Lekgota" IN: Richards, A. and Kuper, A., *Councils in Action*. Cambridge: Cambridge University Press.

1971b, "Council Structure and Decision-making" IN: Richards, A. and Kuper, A., *Councils in Action*. Cambridge: Cambridge University Press.

The Labour Party

1980, *Workers' Cooperatives*. London: Labour Party Publications.

Lammers, C.

1989, "Competence and Organizational Democracy: Concluding Reflections" IN: Szell, G., *The State, Trade Unions and Self-Management*. Berlin: *de Gruyter*.

Lappe, L.

1984, *Die Einfügung des jungen Facharbeiters in den Produktionsprozess*. Berlin: *Max Planck Institut für Bildungsforschung*.

Leach, E.

1977, *Custom, Law and Terrorist Violence*. Edinburgh: Edinburgh University Press.

Lockett, M.

1978, *Fakenham Enterprises*. Milton Keynes: The Open University Monograph Series, No 1.

Louis, R.

1983, *Labour Cooperatives Retrospect and Prospects*. Geneva: International Labour Organisation.

Luhmann, N.

1969, "Komplexität und Demokratie" IN: *Politische Vierteljahresschrift* 10 p. 314-325.

Makowski, M.

1984, "Mehr Anarchie wagen" IN: *STATTbuch 3*. Berlin: STATTbuch Verlag.

1984, "Finanzierung" IN: *Hick-Hack*. 0, May.

Mandel, E.
1975, "Self-management – Dangers and Possibilities" IN: *International-al*. Vol. 2, No 3.

Marcuse, H.
1968, *One Dimensional Man*. London: Routledge and Kegan Paul.
1970, "The End of Utopia" IN: *Five Lectures*. London: Penguin Press.

Marx, K.
1930, *Capital*. London: J. M. Dent & Sons Limited.

Matzner, E.
u. d., *Zur Entwicklung des autonomen Sektors. Diskussionspapier des Wissenschaftszentrums Berlin*.

Meixner, H., Robke, T. and Causemann, B.
1979, "Vom Netzwerk zum Netzzwerg?" IN: *Links* July/August.

Melman, S.
1985, "Decision-making Democracy and Kibbutz" IN: *Kibbutz Studies*. June.

Nahoun, P.
1972, *Allemagne antiauthoritaire*. Paris: *éd du Cercle et de la Tête de Feuilles*.

Nick, O.
1984, "An Examination of Organisational Commitment in Six Workers' Cooperatives in Scotland" IN: *Human Relations*. vol. 37 n. 1 p. 29-46.

Nitsche, R. (ed.)
1982, *Hauserkämpfe*. Berlin: *Transit*.

Nutzinger, H. G.
1975, "Investment and Financing in a Labour-managed Firm and its Social Implications" IN: *Economic Analysis and Workers' Management*. vol. IX n. 1-2. p. 181-201.

Oppenheimer, F.
1922, *Siedlungsgenossenschaften*. Jena: *G. Fischer* (1. ed. 1896).

Parsons, T. and Bales, R. F.
1956, *Family, Socialisation and Interaction Process*. London: Routledge and Kegan Paul.

Pasic, N., Grozdanic, S. and Radevic, M.
1982, *Workers Management in Yugoslavia*. Geneva: International Labour Office.

Pelly, D.
1980, *Co-operation or Co-option?* Milton Keynes: Caits.
u.d., *Workers Co-operatives — 'New Wave' on an Old Beach.* Mimeo.
Peters, E.L.
1972, "The Control of Moral Ambiguity" IN: Gluckman, M. *Allocation of Responsibility.* Manchester: Manchester University Press.
Petrin, T. and Humphries, J.
1980, "Women in the Self-Managed Economy of Yugoslavia" IN: *Economic Analysis and Workers' Self-Management* 1, XIV P:69-91.
Pospisil, L.
1971, *Anthropology of Law.* New York: Harper and Row.
Radcliffe-Brown, A.R.
1952, *Structure and Function in Primitive Society.* Glencoe, Ill: Free Press.
Ribeill, G.
1980, "Travailleurs salariés, producteurs et/ou consommateurs" IN: Duclos D. (ed.) *De l'usine on peut voir la vi(ll)e.* Arcueil: *échanges sciences sociales.*
Rigby, A.
1974, *Alternative Realities: A Study of Communes and Their Members.* London: Routledge and Kegan Paul.
Rose, D., Saunders, P., Newby, H. and Bell, C.
1976, "Ideologies of Property: A Case Study" IN: *Sociological Review.* Vol 24, No 4, November.
Ruiz Quintanilla, S.A. and Weber, W.
1985, "Arbeitsorientierungen von Beschäftigten in Alternativbetrieben" IN: *Psychologie und Praxis — Zeitschrift für Organisationspsychologie.*
Sager, A.P.
1979, "Radical Law: Three Collectives in Cambridge" IN: Case, J. and Taylor, R.C.R. (eds.) *Co-ops, Communes and Collectives.* New York: Pantheon Press.
Sahlins, M.
1972, *Stone Age Economics.* London: Tavistock Publishers.
Schwendter, R.
1979, "Ja, Schnecke besteige nur den Futschi" IN: Huber, J. (ed.) *Anders arbeiten anders wirtschaften.* Frankfurt: *Fischer TB.*

Seibel, H.D. and Damachi, U.G.
  1982, *Self-Management in Yugoslavia and in the Developing World.*
      London: Macmillan Press.
Smith, A.
  1981, *The Wealth of Nations.* Harmondsworth: Penguin Books.
Sofer, C.
  1972, *Organisations in Theory and Practice.* New York: Basic Books.
Sohn-Rethel, A.
  1970, *Geistige und körperliche Arbeit.* Frankfurt: *Suhrkamp AG SPAK.*
  1976, *Materialien zur Alternativen Ökonomie.* Berlin: *AG SPAK.*
  1978, *Zur Alternativen Ökonomie III.*, Berlin: *AG SPAK.*
Spittler, G.
  1989, *Vorindustrielle Arbeitswelt. Beitrag auf der Tagung der Sektion
      Entwicklungssoziologie und Sozialanthropologie der Deutschen
      Gesellschaft für Soziologie am 1.12 1989 in Thurnau.* Mimeo.
Statistisches Bundesamt (ed.)
  1984, *Statistisches Jahrbuch 1984.* Bonn: *Verlag Kohlhammer.*
STATTbuch 2 Arbeitsgruppe
  1982, *STATTbuch 2.* Berlin: *STATTbuch Verlag.*
STATTbuch 3 Arbeitsgruppe
  1984, *STATTbuch 3.* Berlin: *STATTbuch Verlag.*
Talmon, Y.
  1972, *Family and Community in the Kibbutz.* Cambridge, Mass: Har-
      vard University Press.
  1965, *The Family in a Revolutionary and Collectivist Society.* UNESCO
      Conference on Human Rights, Oxford, Nov.
Talmon-Garber, Y.
  1955, "Differentiation in Collective Settlements" IN: *Scripta Hierosoly-
      mitana.* Vol III, Studies in Social Science.
Taylor, R.C.R., and Case, J.
  1979, *Co-ops, Communes and Collectives: Experiments in Social
      Change in 1960's and 1970's.* New York: Pantheon Press.
Teufel, F.R.
  1982, "Die geheimen Geschäftsführer" IN: Teufel, F. and Langhans, R.,
      (eds.) *Klau Mich.* Berlin: *Rixdorfer Verlagsanstalt.*

Thaler, J.
   1984, "Eine andere Technologie produzieren, Alternativökonomie, Macht und Technologie" IN: *Sympathy for the Devil. Internationaler Kongreß,* April 1984. Berlin: *Wechselwirkung, ASTA-TU.*
Thompson, E.P.
   1967, "Time, Work Discipline and Industrial Capitalism" IN: *Past and Present.* No 38.
Thornley, J.
   u.d., *The Product Dilemma for Workers' Co-operatives.* Milton Keynes: Cooperatives Research, Occasional Paper No 1.
Tynan, E.
   u.d., *Unit 58.* Milton Keynes: Cooperatives Research, Case Study No 1.
Unter Geiern
   1982, *Unter Geiern.* Berlin: *Stattbuch Verlag.*
Vanek, J.
   1977, *The Labour Managed Economy.* New York: Cornell University Press.
Velasquez Villegas, R.
   1975, *Zur Funktionsfähigkeit von Produktivgenossenschaften.* Tübingen: *Paul Siebeck Verlag.*
Vernant, J.P.
   1965, *Mythe et pensée chez les Grecs, études de psychologie historique.* Paris : *Maspero.*
Volksmasse, V.
   1982, "Die Konkrete Utopie" IN: *Netzwerk Rundbrief* No 17, June.
Wainwright, H. and Elliott, D.
   1982, *The Lucas Plan.* London: Allison and Busby.
Wajcman, J.
   u.p., *Workers Cooperatives — a Middle-class Ideal?* Mimeo.
   1983, *Women in Control.* Milton Keynes: Open University Press.
Wallmann, S. (ed.)
   1979, *Social Anthropology of Work.* A.S.A. Monogaph No 19, London: Academic Press.
Webb, S. and Potter, B.
   1893, *Die britische Genossenschaftsbewegung.* Leipzig: E Brentano.

Weber, M.

1924, "Zur Psychophysik der industriellen Arbeit" IN: *Gesammelte Aufsätze zur Sociologie und Sozialpolitik*. Tübingen: *Mohr*.

1964, *Social and Economic Organisation*. New York: First Free Press.

Weichler, K.

1983, *Gegendruck*. Reinbek: *Rowohlt*.

Whitehorn, A.

1979, "Alienation and Industrial Society: A Study of Workers' Self-Management" IN: *Canadian Review of Sociology and Anthropology* 16(2).

Witte, L.

1984, "Was ist ein Einbruch in eine Bank..." IN: *die tageszeitung* May 8.

Wuseltronick-Kollektiv

1984, "Was kann Technologie mit Politik zu tun haben?" IN: *Sympathy for the Devil. Internationaler Kongreß*. Berlin: *Wechselwirkung ASTA TU*.

Newspapers and Bulletins Used:

die tageszeitung (TAZ), daily national newspaper issued in Berlin — organised as a collective.

Netzwerkrundbrief, bulletin for the members of *Netzwerk* Berlin

Contraste, previously *Hick-Hack, Wandelsblatt*, national bulletin of collective enterprises, issued in turn by collectives in Berlin, Hamburg, Freiburg and Frankfurt.

Die Viererbande, bulletin of the association of alternative projects in Hessen.

Die Wirtschaftswoche weekly economic newspaper.

Das Handelsblatt weekly economic newspaper.

DIE ZEIT, weekly newspaper.

Der Spiegel, weekly magazine.

Index